ANNUAL EDITIONS

Aging 12/13

Twenty-Fifth Edition

EDITOR

Harold Cox
Indiana State University

Harold Cox, professor of sociology at Indiana State University, has published several articles in the field of gerontology. He is the author of *Later Life: The Realities of Aging* (Prentice Hall, 2006). He is a member of the Gerontological Society of America and the American Sociological Association's Occupation and Professions Section and Youth Aging Section.

ISBN 978-0-07-805120-3
MHID 0-07-805120-7
ISSN 0272-3808 (print)
ISSN 2158-3528 (online)

Managing Editor: *Larry Loeppke*
Developmental Editor II: *Dave Welsh*
Permissions Supervisor: *Shirley Lanners*
Senior Marketing Communications Specialist: *Mary Klein*
Senior Project Manager: *Joyce Watters*
Design Coordinator: *Margarite Reynolds*
Cover Designer: *Studio Montage, St. Louis, Missouri*
Buyer: *Susan K. Culbertson*
Media Project Manager: *Sridevi Palani*

Compositor: Laserwords Private Limited
Cover Image Credits: Design Pics/Don Hammond (inset); Design Pics/Design Pics BRO
(background)

Editors/Academic Advisory Board

Members of the Academic Advisory Board are instrumental in the final selection of articles for each edition of ANNUAL EDITIONS. Their review of articles for content, level, and appropriateness provides critical direction to the editors and staff. We think that you will find their careful consideration well reflected in this volume.

ANNUAL EDITIONS: Aging 12/13
25th Edition

EDITOR

Harold Cox
Indiana State University

ACADEMIC ADVISORY BOARD MEMBERS

Editors/Academic Advisory Board continued

Preface

In publishing ANNUAL EDITIONS we recognize the enormous role played by the magazines, newspapers, and journals of the public press in providing current, first-rate educational information in a broad spectrum of interest areas. Many of these articles are appropriate for students, researchers, and professionals seeking accurate, current material to help bridge the gap between principles and theories and the real world. These articles, however, become more useful for study when those of lasting value are carefully collected, organized, indexed, and reproduced in a low-cost format, which provides easy and permanent access when the material is needed. That is the role played by ANNUAL EDITIONS.

The decline of the crude birth rate in the United States and other industrialized nations, combined with improving food supplies, sanitation, and medical technology, has resulted in an ever-increasing number and percentage of people remaining alive and healthy well into their retirement years. The result is a shifting age composition of the populations in these nations—a population composed of fewer people under age 20 and more people 65 and older.

In 1900, in the United States, approximately 3 million Americans were 65 years old and above, and they comprised 4 percent of the population. In 2000, there were 36 million persons 65 years old and above, and they represented 13 percent of the total population. The most rapid increase in the number of older persons is expected between 2010 and 2030, when the baby boom generation reaches the age of 65. Demographers predict that by 2030 there will be 66 million older persons representing approximately 22 percent of the total population.

The growing number of older people has made many of the problems of aging immediately visible to the average American. These problems have become widespread topics of concern for political leaders, government planners, and average citizens. Moreover, the aging of the population has become perceived as a phenomenon of the United States and the industrialized countries of Western Europe—it is also occurring in the underdeveloped countries of the world as well. An increasing percentage of the world's population is now defined as aged.

Today, almost all middle-aged people expect to live to retirement age and beyond. Both the middle-aged and the elderly have pushed for solutions to the problems confronting older Americans. Everyone seems to agree that granting the elderly a secure and comfortable status is desirable. Voluntary associations, communities, and state and federal governments have committed themselves to improving the lives of older persons. Many programs for senior citizens, both public and private, have emerged in the last 50 years.

The change in the age composition of the population has not gone unnoticed by the media or the academic community. The number of articles appearing in the popular press and professional journals has increased dramatically over the last several years. While scientists have been concerned with the aging process for some time, in the last three decades there has been an expanding volume of research and writing on this subject. This growing interest has resulted in this twenty-fifth edition of *Annual Editions: Aging 12/13*.

This volume is representative of the field of gerontology in that it is interdisciplinary in its approach, including articles from the biological sciences, medicine, nursing, psychology, sociology, and social work. The articles are taken from the popular press, government publications, and scientific journals. They represent a wide cross section of authors, perspectives, and issues related to the aging process. They were chosen because they address the most relevant and current problems in the field of aging and present a variety of divergent views on the appropriate solutions to these problems. The topics covered include demographic trends, the aging process, longevity, social attitudes toward old age, problems and potentials of aging, retirement, death, living environments in later life, and social policies, programs, and services for older Americans.

The articles are organized into an anthology that is useful for both the student and the teacher. Two new learning features have been added to this edition to aid students in their study and expand critical thinking about each article topic. Located at the beginning of each unit, *Learning Outcomes* outline the key concepts that students should focus on as they are reading the material. *Critical Thinking* questions, located at the end of each article, allow students to test their understanding of the key concepts. A *Topic Guide* assists students in finding other articles on a given subject within this edition, while a list of recommended *Internet References* guides them to the best sources of additional information on a topic. The goal of *Annual Editions: Aging 12/13* is to choose articles that are pertinent, well written, and helpful to those concerned with the field of gerontology. Comments, suggestions, or constructive criticism are welcome to help improve future editions of this book. Any anthology can be improved. This one will continue to be improved—annually.

Harold Cox

Harold Cox
Editor

The Annual Editions Series

VOLUMES AVAILABLE

Adolescent Psychology

Aging

American Foreign Policy

American Government

Anthropology

Archaeology

Assessment and Evaluation

Business Ethics

Child Growth and Development

Comparative Politics

Criminal Justice

Developing World

Drugs, Society, and Behavior

Dying, Death, and Bereavement

Early Childhood Education

Economics

Educating Children with Exceptionalities

Education

Educational Psychology

Entrepreneurship

Environment

The Family

Gender

Geography

Global Issues

Health

Homeland Security

Human Development

Human Resources

Human Sexualities

International Business

Management

Marketing

Mass Media

Microbiology

Multicultural Education

Nursing

Nutrition

Physical Anthropology

Psychology

Race and Ethnic Relations

Social Problems

Sociology

State and Local Government

Sustainability

Technologies, Social Media, and Society

United States History, Volume 1

United States History, Volume 2

Urban Society

Violence and Terrorism

Western Civilization, Volume 1

World History, Volume 1

World History, Volume 2

World Politics

Contents

UNIT 1
The Phenomenon of Aging

The concepts in bold italics are developed in the article. For further expansion, please refer to the Topic Guide.

UNIT 2
The Quality of Later Life

UNIT 3
Societal Attitudes toward Old Age

The concepts in bold italics are developed in the article. For further expansion, please refer to the Topic Guide.

UNIT 4
Problems and Potentials of Aging

UNIT 5
Retirement: American Dream or Dilemma?

The concepts in bold italics are developed in the article. For further expansion, please refer to the Topic Guide.

UNIT 6
The Experience of Dying

The concepts in bold italics are developed in the article. For further expansion, please refer to the Topic Guide.

UNIT 7
Living Environment in Later Life

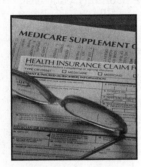

UNIT 8
Social Policies, Programs, and Services for Older Americans

The concepts in bold italics are developed in the article. For further expansion, please refer to the Topic Guide.

The concepts in bold italics are developed in the article. For further expansion, please refer to the Topic Guide.

Correlation Guide

The *Annual Editions* series provides students with convenient, inexpensive access to current, carefully selected articles from the public press. **Annual Editions: Aging 12/13** is an easy-to-use reader that presents articles on important topics such as *living longer, retirement, health care, dying,* and many more. For more information on *Annual Editions* and other *McGraw-Hill Contemporary Learning Series* titles, visit www.mhhe.com/cls.

This convenient guide matches the units in **Annual Editions: Aging 12/13** with the corresponding chapters in two of our best-selling McGraw-Hill Aging textbooks by Quadagno and Ferrini/Ferrini.

Annual Editions: Aging 12/13	Aging and the Life Course: An Introduction to Social Gerontology, 5/e by Quadagno	Health in the later Years, 5/e by Ferrini/Ferrini
Unit 1: The Phenomenon of Aging	**Chapter 1:** The Field of Social Gerontology **Chapter 2:** Life Course Transitions **Chapter 3:** Theories of Aging	**Chapter 1:** Our Nation's Elders: The Facts **Chapter 2:** Biologic Aging: Theories and Longevity **Chapter 3:** The Body and Its Age Changes
Unit 2: The Quality of Later Life	**Chapter 6:** Biological Perspectives on Aging	**Chapter 2:** Biologic Aging: Theories and Longevity **Chapter 3:** The Body and Its Age Changes **Chapter 9:** Physical Activity **Chapter 11:** Sexuality
Unit 3: Societal Attitudes toward Old Age	**Chapter 7:** Psychological Perspectives on Aging	**Chapter 1:** Our Nation's Elders: The Facts
Unit 4: Problems and Potentials of Aging	**Chapter 6:** Biological Perspectives on Aging **Chapter 7:** Psychological Perspectives on Aging **Chapter 8:** Family Relationships and Social Support Systems **Chapter 11:** Health and Health Care **Chapter 12:** Caring for the Frail Elderly	**Chapter 2:** Biologic Aging: Theories and Longevity **Chapter 3:** The Body and Its Age Changes **Chapter 4:** Chronic Illnesses: The Major Killers **Chapter 5:** Other Chronic Diseases and Conditions **Chapter 6:** Acute Illness and Accidents **Chapter 7:** Mental Health and Mental Disorders **Chapter 8:** Medication Use **Chapter 9:** Physical Activity **Chapter 11:** Sexuality
Unit 5: Retirement: American Dream or Dilemma?	**Chapter 10:** Work and Retirement **Chapter 14:** The Economics of Aging	
Unit 6: The Experience of Dying	**Chapter 13:** Death, Dying, and Bereavement	**Chapter 15:** Dying, Death, and Grief
Unit 7: Living Environment in Later Life	**Chapter 8:** Family Relationships and Social Support Systems **Chapter 9:** Living Arrangements **Chapter 12:** Caring for the Frail Elderly **Chapter 15:** Poverty and Inequality	**Chapter 13:** Medical Care **Chapter 14:** Long-Term Care
Unit 8: Social Policies, Programs, and Services for Older Americans	**Chapter 4:** Demography of Aging **Chapter 5:** Old Age and the Welfare State **Chapter 11:** Health and Health Care **Chapter 14:** The Economics of Aging **Chapter 15:** Poverty and Inequality **Chapter 16:** The Politics of Aging	

Topic Guide

This topic guide suggests how the selections in this book relate to the subjects covered in your course. You may want to use the topics listed on these pages to search the Web more easily.

On the following pages a number of websites have been gathered specifically for this book. They are arranged to reflect the units of this Annual Editions reader. You can link to these sites by going to www.mhhe.com/cls

All the articles that relate to each topic are listed below the bold-faced term.

Internet References

The following Internet sites have been selected to support the articles found in this reader. These sites were available at the time of publication. However, because websites often change their structure and content, the information listed may no longer be available. We invite you to visit www.mhhe.com/cls for easy access to these sites.

Annual Editions: Aging 12/13

General Sources

Alliance for Aging Research
www.agingresearch.org

The nation's leading nonprofit organization dedicated to improving the health and independence of Americans as they age through public and private funding of medical research and geriatric education.

ElderCare Online
www.ec-online.net

This site provides numerous links to eldercare resources. Information on health, living, aging, finance, and social issues can be found here.

FirstGov
www.firstgov.gov

Whatever you want or need from the U.S. government, it's here on FirstGov.gov. You'll find a rich treasure of online information, services, and resources.

UNIT 1: The Phenomenon of Aging

The Aging Research Centre
www.arclab.org

The Aging Research Centre is dedicated to providing a service that allows researchers to find information that is related to the study of the aging process.

Centenarians
www.hcoa.org/centenarians/centenarians.htm

There are approximately 70,000 centenarians in the United States. This site provides resources and information for and about centenarians.

National Center for Health Statistics
www.cdc.gov/nchs/agingact.htm

NCHS is the federal government's principal vital and health statistics agency. NCHS is a part of the Centers for Disease Control and Prevention, U.S. Department of Health and Human Services.

UNIT 2: The Quality of Later Life

Aging with Dignity
www.agingwithdignity.org

The nonprofit Aging with Dignity was established to provide people with the practical information, advice, and legal tools needed to help their loved ones get proper care.

The Gerontological Society of America
www.geron.org

The Gerontological Society of America promotes the scientific study of aging, and it fosters growth and diffusion of knowledge relating to problems of aging and of the sciences contributing to their understanding.

The National Council on the Aging
www.ncoa.org

The National Council on the Aging, Inc., is a center of leadership and nationwide expertise in the issues of aging. This private, nonprofit association is committed to enhancing the field of aging through leadership, service, education, and advocacy.

UNIT 3: Societal Attitudes toward Old Age

Adult Development and Aging: Division 20 of the American Psychological Association
www.iog.wayne.edu/APADIV20/APADIV20.HTM

This group is dedicated to studying the psychology of adult development and aging.

American Society on Aging
www.asaging.org/index.cfm

The American Society on Aging is the largest and most dynamic network of professionals in the field of aging.

Canadian Psychological Association
www.cpa.ca

This is the contents page of the Canadian Psychological Association. Material on aging and human development can be found at this site.

UNIT 4: Problems and Potentials of Aging

AARP Health Information
www.aarp.org/bulletin

Information on a BMI calculator, the USDA food pyramid, healthy recipes, and health-related articles can be found at this site.

Alzheimer's Association
www.alz.org

The Alzheimer's Association is dedicated to researching the prevention, cures, and treatments of Alzheimer's disease and related disorders and providing support and assistance to afflicted patients and their families.

A.P.T.A. Section on Geriatrics
http://geriatricspt.org

This is a component of the American Physical Therapy Association. At this site, information regarding consumer and health information for older adults can be found.

Caregiver's Handbook
www.acsu.buffalo.edu/~drstall/hndbk0.html

This site is an online handbook for caregivers. Topics include nutrition, medical aspects of caregiving, and liabilities of caregiving.

Caregiver Survival Resources
www.caregiver.com

Information on books, and seminars and information for caregivers can be found at this site.

Internet References

International Food Information Council
www.ific.org

At this site, you can find information regarding nutritional needs for aging adults. The site focuses on information for educators and students, publications, and nutritional information.

University of California at Irvine: Institute for Brain Aging and Dementia
www.alz.uci.edu

The Institute for Brain Aging and Dementia is dedicated to the study of Alzheimer's and the causes of mental disabilities for the elderly.

UNIT 5: Retirement: American Dream or Dilemma?

American Association of Retired People
www.aarp.org

The AARP is the nation's leading organization for people 50 and older. AARP serves their needs through information, education, advocacy, and community service.

Health and Retirement Study (HRS)
www.umich.edu/~hrswww

The University of Michigan Health and Retirement Study surveys more than 22,000 Americans over the age of 50 every two years. Supported by the National Institute on Aging, the study paints an emerging portrait of an aging America: physical and mental health, insurance coverage, financial status, family support systems, labor market status, and retirement planning.

UNIT 6: The Experience of Dying

Agency for Health Care Policy and Research
www.ahcpr.gov

Information on the dying process in the context of U.S. health policy is provided here, along with a search mechanism. The agency is part of the Department of Health and Human Services.

Growth House, Inc.
www.growthhouse.org

This award-winning website is an international gateway to resources for life-threatening illness and end-of-life care.

Hospice Foundation of America
www.HospiceFoundation.org

On this page, you can learn about hospice care, how to select a hospice, and how to find a hospice near you.

UNIT 7: Living Environment in Later Life

American Association of Homes and Services for the Aging
www.aahsa.org

The American Association of Homes and Services for the Aging represents a not-for-profit organization dedicated to providing high quality health care, housing, and services to the nation's elderly.

Center for Demographic Studies
http://cds.duke.edu

The Center for Demographic Studies is located in the heart of the Duke campus. The primary focus of its research is long-term care for elderly populations, specifically those 65 years of age and older.

Guide to Retirement Living Online
www.retirement-living.com

An online version of a free publication, this site provides information about nursing homes, continuous care communities, independent living, home health care, and adult day care centers.

The United States Department of Housing and Urban Development
www.hud.gov

News regarding housing for aging adults can be found at this site sponsored by the U.S. federal government.

UNIT 8: Social Policies, Programs, and Services for Older Americans

Administration on Aging
www.aoa.dhhs.gov

This site, housed on the Department of Health and Human Services website, provides information for older persons and their families. There is also information for educators and students regarding the elderly.

American Federation for Aging Research
www.afar.org

Since 1981, the American Federation for Aging Research (AFAR) has helped scientists begin and further careers in aging research and geriatric medicine.

American Geriatrics Society
www.americangeriatrics.org

This organization addresses the needs of our rapidly aging population. At this site, you can find information on health care and other social issues facing the elderly.

Community Transportation Association of America
www.ctaa.org

CTAA is a nonprofit organization dedicated to mobility for all people, regardless of wealth, disability, age, or accessibility.

Consumer Reports State Inspection Surveys
www.ConsumerReports.org

To learn how to get state inspection surveys and to contact the ombudsman's office, click on "Personal Finance," then select "Assisted Living."

Medicare Consumer Information from the Health Care Finance Association
http://cms.hhs.gov/default.asp?fromhcfadotgov_true

This site is devoted to explaining Medicare and Medicaid costs to consumers.

National Institutes of Health
www.nih.gov

Information on health issues can be found at this government site. There is quite a bit of information relating to health issues and the aging population in the United States.

The United States Senate: Special Committee on Aging
www.senate.gov/~aging

This committee, chaired by Senator Gordon Smith of Oregon, deals with the issues surrounding the elderly in America. At this site, you can download committee hearing information, news, and committee publications.

UNIT 1

The Phenomenon of Aging

Unit Selections

Learning Outcomes

After reading this Unit, you will be able to:

• Describe the age composition of the American population.

• Identify what makes the age composition of the current American population different from previous generations.

• Enumerate the factors that when programmed into human cells contribute to the aging process.

• List the steps a person could take to slow the aging process.

• Identify the foods you can eat to increase the antioxidants in the human body.

• Describe the effect of caloric restriction on the body's free radicals.

• Report the diseases that are less likely to be experienced by persons living in the earth's few blue zones.

• Identify the factors in the daily lives of Ikarians that reduce the stress in their lives.

• Identify the health problems that may increase if one consumes a high fat and high protein diet.

• List the risk of various diseases that are associated with being obese.

• Identify the life expectancy in the United States for all persons regardless of sex in 2009.

• List the life expectancy of men and women in the United States in 2009.

Student Website

www.mhhe.com/cls

Internet References

The Aging Research Centre
    www.arclab.org
Centenarians
    www.hcoa.org/centenarians/centenarians.htm
National Center for Health Statistics
    www.cdc.gov/nchs/agingact.htm

The process of aging is complex and includes biological, psychological, sociological, and behavioral changes. Biologically, the body gradually loses the ability to renew itself. Various body functions begin to slow down, and the vital senses become less acute. Psychologically, aging persons experience changing sensory processes; perception, motor skills, problem-solving ability, and drives and emotions are frequently altered. Sociologically, they must cope with the changing roles and definitions of self that society imposes on the individual. For instance, the role expectations and the status of grandparents is different from those of parents, and the roles of the retired are quite different from those of the employed. Being defined as "old" may be desirable or undesirable, depending on the particular culture and its values. Behaviorally, aging individuals may move more slowly and with less dexterity. Because they are assuming new roles and are viewed differently by others, their attitudes about themselves, their emotions, and, ultimately, their behavior can be expected to change.

Those studying the process of aging often use developmental theories of the life cycle—a sequence of predictable phases that begins with birth and ends with death—to explain individuals' behavior at various stages of their lives. An individual's age, therefore, is important because it provides clues about his or her behavior at a particular phase of the life cycle—be it childhood, adolescence, adulthood, middle age, or old age. There is, however, the greatest variation in terms of health and human development among older people than among any other age group.

While every 3-year-old child can be predicted to have certain developmental experiences, there is a wide variation in the behavior of 65-year-old people. By age 65, we find that some people are in good health, employed, and performing important work tasks. Others of this cohort are retired but in good health or are retired and in poor health. Still others have died prior to the age of 65. The articles in this section are written from biological, psychological, and sociological perspectives. These disciplines attempt to explain the effects of aging and the resulting choices in lifestyle, as well as the wider, cultural implications of an older population. In the article "Elderly Americans," Christine L. Himes delineates the increases in life expectancy and the aging of the American population that has occurred during the last century. In "You Can Stop 'Normal' Aging," Henry Lodge gives a number of suggestions on what could be done to slow the aging process. In "Living Longer: Diet and Exercise," the authors discuss how the research findings in the areas of diet and exercise, if followed, could increase the individual's life expectancy by a number of years. In "More Good Years," Dan Buettner points out the 13 factors he believes contribute to persons living longer

© Hill Street Studios/Blend Images LLC

lives in the blue zones. Thomas Perls and Margery Hutter Silver conducted a study at Harvard Medical School of long-living individuals. Following their research, they came up with a quiz that included dietary and lifestyle choices, as well as family histories to help an individual determine what his or her probability is of living to a very old age. In "Long Live . . . Us" the author points out how much life expectancy has increased in the United States by 2009 as well as the difference in men's and women's life expectancy.

Elderly Americans

CHRISTINE L. HIMES

The United States is in the midst of a profound demographic change: the rapid aging of its population. The 2000 Census counted nearly 35 million people in the United States 65 years of age or older, about one of every eight Americans. By 2030, demographers estimate that one in five Americans will be age 65 or older, which is nearly four times the proportion of elderly 100 years earlier, in 1930. The effects of this older age profile will reverberate throughout the American economy and society in the next 50 years. Preparing for these changes involves more than the study of demographic trends; it also requires an understanding of the growing diversity within the older population.

The lives and well-being of older Americans attract increasing attention as the elderly share of the U.S. population rises: One-fifth will be 65 or older in 2030.

The aging of the U.S. population in the next 20 years is being propelled by one of the most powerful demographic forces in the United States in the last century: the "baby boom" cohort, born between 1946 and 1964. This group of 76 million children grabbed media attention as it moved toward adulthood—changing school systems, colleges, and the workplace. And, this same group of people will change the profile and expectations of old age in the United States over the next 30 years as it moves past age 65. The potential effects of the baby boom on the systems of old-age assistance already are being evaluated. This cohort's consumption patterns, demand for leisure, and use of health care, for example, will leave an indelible mark on U.S. society in the 21st century. Understanding their characteristics as they near older ages will help us anticipate baby-boomers' future needs and their effects on the population.

Until the last 50 years, most gains in life expectancy came as the result of improved child mortality. The survival of larger proportions of infants and children to adulthood radically increased average life expectancy in the United States and many other countries over the past century. Now, gains are coming at the end of life as greater proportions of 65-year-olds are living until age 85, and more 85-year-olds are living into their 90s. These changes raise a multitude of questions: How will these years of added life be spent? Will increased longevity lead to a greater role for the elderly in our society? What are the limits of life expectancy?

Increasing life expectancy, especially accompanied by low fertility, changes the structure of families. Families are becoming more "vertical," with fewer members in each generation, but more generations alive at any one time. Historically, families have played a prominent role in the lives of elderly people. Is this likely to change?

As much as any stage of the life course, old age is a time of growth, diversity, and change. Elderly Americans are among the wealthiest and among the poorest in our nation. They come from a variety of racial and ethnic backgrounds. Some are employed full-time, while others require full-time care. While general health has improved, many elderly suffer from poor health.

The older population in the 21st century will come to later life with different experiences than did older Americans in the last century—more women will have been divorced, more will have worked in the labor force, more will be childless. How will these experiences shape their later years?

The answers to these questions are complex. In some cases, we are confident in our predictions of the future. But for many aspects of life for the elderly, we are entering new territory. This report explores the characteristics of the current older population and speculates how older Americans may differ in the future. It also looks at the impact of aging on the U.S. society and economy.

Increasing Numbers

The United States has seen its elderly population—defined as those age 65 or older—grow more than tenfold during the 20th century. There were just over 3 million Americans age 65 or older in 1900, and nearly 35 million in 2000.

At the dawn of the 20th century, three demographic trends—high fertility, declining infant and child mortality, and high rates of international immigration—were acting in concert in the United States and were keeping the population young. The age distribution of the U.S. population was heavily skewed toward younger ages in 1900, as illustrated by the broad base of the population age-sex pyramid for that year in Figure 1. The pyramid, which shows the proportion of each age and sex group in the population, also reveals that the elderly made up a tiny share of the U.S. population in 1900. Only 4 percent of Americans were age 65 of older, while more than one-half (54 percent) were under age 25.

But adult health improved and fertility fell during the first half of the century. The inflow of international immigrants slowed considerably after 1920. These trends caused an aging of the U.S. population, but they were interrupted after World War II by the baby boom. In the post-war years, Americans were marrying and starting families at younger ages and in greater percentages than they had during the Great Depression. The surge in births between 1946 and 1964 resulted from a decline in childlessness (more women had at least one child) combined with larger family sizes (more women had three or more children). The sustained increase in birth rates during their 19-year period fueled a rapid increase in the child population. By 1970, these

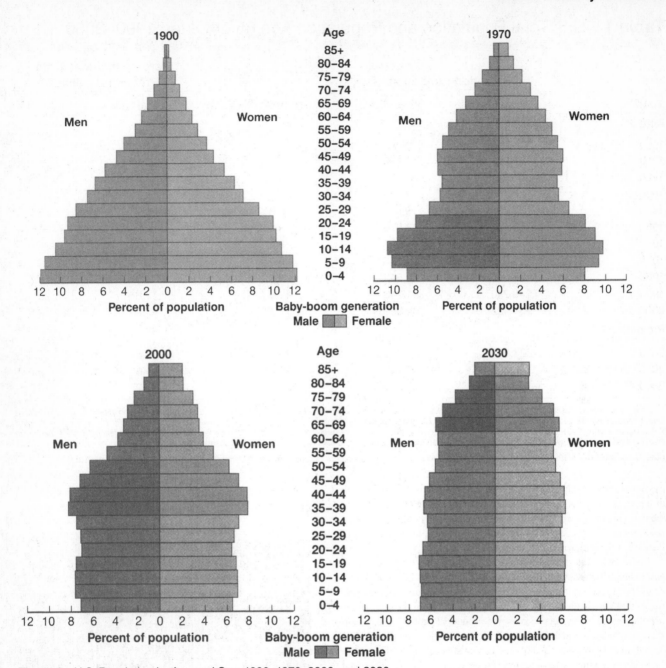

Figure 1 U.S. Population by Age and Sex, 1900, 1970, 2000, and 2030.

Sources: U.S. Census Bureau Publications: *Historical Statistics of the United States: Colonial Times to 1970* (1975); *Census 2000 Summary File* (SFI) (http://factfinder.census.gov, accessed Sept. 5, 2001); and "Population Projections of the United States by Age, Sex, Race, Hispanic Origin, and Nativity: 1999 to 2100" (www.census.gov/population/projections/nation/summary/np-t4-a.txt, accessed Sept. 25, 2001).

Note. U.S. population in 1900 does not include Alaska or Hawaii. The baby-boom generation includes persons born between 1946 and 1964.

baby boomers had moved into their teen and young adult years, creating a bulge in that year's age-sex pyramid shown in Figure 1.

The baby boom was followed by a precipitous decline in fertility: the "baby bust." Young American women reaching adulthood in the late 1960s and 1970s were slower to marry and start families than their older counterparts, and they had fewer children when they did start families. U.S. fertility sank to an all-time low. The average age of the population started to climb as the large baby boom generation moved into adulthood, and was replaced by the much smaller baby-bust cohort. By 2000, the baby-boom bulge had moved up to the middle adult ages. The population's age structure at younger and older ages became more evenly distributed as fluctuations in fertility diminished and survival at the oldest ages increased. By 2030, the large baby-boom cohorts will be age 65 and older, and U.S. Census Bureau

projections show that the American population will be relatively evenly distributed across age groups, as Figure 1 shows.

The radical shift in the U.S. population age structure over the last 100 years provides only one part of the story of the U.S. elderly population. Another remarkable aspect is the rapid growth in the number of elderly, and the increasing numbers of Americans at the oldest ages, above ages 85 or 90. The most rapid growth in the 65-or-older age group occurred between the 1920s and the 1950s (see Table 1). During each of these decades, the older population increased by at least 34 percent, reaching 16.6 million in 1960. The percentage increase slowed after 1960, and between 1990 and 2000, the population age 65 or older increased by just 12 percent. Since the growth of the older population largely reflects past patterns of fertility, and U.S. fertility rates plummeted in the 1930s,

3

Table 1 U.S. Total Population and Population Age 65 or Older, 1900–2060

Year	Population (in thousands)		Percent 65+	Percent Increase from Preceding Decade	
	Total	Age 65+		Total	Age 65+
Actual					
1900	75,995	3,080	4.1		
1910	91,972	3,950	4.3	21.0	28.2
1920	105,711	4,933	4.7	14.9	24.9
1930	122,755	6,634	5.4	16.1	34.5
1940	131,669	9,019	6.8	7.2	36.0
1950	150,697	12,270	8.1	14.5	36.0
1960	179,323	16,560	9.2	19.0	35.0
1970	203,212	20,066	9.9	13.4	21.2
1980	226,546	25,549	11.3	11.5	27.3
1990	248,710	31,242	12.6	9.8	22.3
2000	281,422	34,992	12.4	13.2	12.0
Projections					
2020	324,927	53,733	16.5	8.4	35.3
2040	377,350	77,177	20.5	7.5	9.8
2060	432,011	89,840	20.8	7.0	9.6

Sources: U.S. Census Bureau publications: *Historical Statistics of the United States: Colonial Times to 1970* (1975); *1980 Census of Population: General Population Characteristics* (PC80-1-B1); *1990 Census of Populations: General Population Characteristics* (1990-CP1); *Census 2000 Demographic Profile,* (www.census.gov/ Press-Release/www/2001/tables/dp_us_2000.xls, accessed Sept. 19, 2001); and *Population Projections of the United States by Age, Sex, Race, Hispanic Origin, and Nativity: 1999 to 2100* (www.census.gov/population/projections/nation/summary/np-t4-a.txt, accessed Sept. 25, 2001).

Note. Data from 1900 to 1950 exclude Alaska and Hawaii. All data refer to the resident U.S. population.

the first decade of the 21st century will also see relatively slow growth of the elderly population. Fewer people will be turning 65 and entering the ranks of "the elderly." Not until the first of the baby-boom generation reaches age 65 between 2010 and 2020 will we see the same rates of increase as those experienced in the mid-20th century.

In the 1940s and 1950s, the rapid growth at the top of the pyramid was matched by growth in the younger ages—the total U.S. population was growing rapidly, and the general profile was still fairly young. That was not the case in the second half of the 20th century, as the share of the population age 65 or older increased to around 12 percent. The elderly share will increase much faster in the first half of the 21st century. This growth in the percentage age 65 or older constitutes population aging.

Many policymakers and health care providers are more concerned about the sheer size of the aging baby-boom generation than the baby boom's share of the total population. The oldest members of this group will reach age 65 in 2011, and by 2029, the youngest baby boomers will have reached age 65. This large group will continue to move into old age at a time of slow growth among younger age groups. The Census Bureau projects that 54 million Americans will be age 65 or older in 2020; by 2060, the number is projected to approach 90 million. The size of this group, and the general aging of the population, are important in planning for the future. Older Americans increasingly are healthy and active and able to take on new roles. At the same time, increasing numbers of older people will need assistance with housing, health care, and other services.

The Oldest-Old

The older population is also aging as more people are surviving into their 80s and 90s. In the 2000 Census, nearly one-half of Americans age 65 or older were above age 74, compared with less than one-third in 1950; one in eight were age 85 or older in 2000, compared with one in 20 in 1950 (see Figure 2).

Percent of 65+ population

◼ Age 65–74   ◼ Age 75–84   ◼ Age 85+

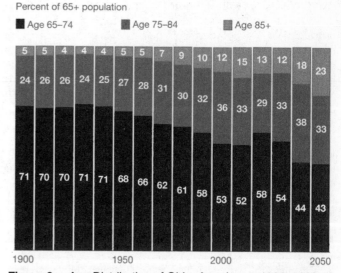

Figure 2 Age Distribution of Older Americans, 1900–2000, and Projection to 2050.

Sources: U.S. Census Bureau publications: *Historical Statistics of the United States: Colonial Times to 1970* (1975); *1980 Census of Population: General Population Characteristics* (PC80-1-B1); *1990 Census of Populations: General Population Characteristics* (1990-CP1); *Census 2000 Demographic Profile,* (www.census .gov/2001/tables/dp_us_2000.xls, accessed Sept. 19, 2001); and "Projections of the Resident Population by Age, Sex, Race, Hispanic Origin, 1990 to 2100" (www .census. gov/population/www/projections/natdet-D1A.html, accessed July 6, 2001).

As the baby boomers enter their late 60s and early 70s around 2020, the U.S. elderly population will be younger: The percentage ages 65 to 74 will rise to 58 percent, as shown in Figure 2. By 2040, however, just 44 percent will be 65 to 74, and 56 percent of all elderly will be age 75 or older.

Those age 85 or older, the "oldest-old," are the fastest growing segment of the elderly population. While those 85 or older made up only about 1.5 percent of the total U.S. population in 2000, they constituted about 12 percent of all elderly. More than 4 million people in the United States were 85 or older in the 2000 Census, and by 2050, a projected 19 million will be age 85 or older. These oldest-old will make up nearly 5 percent of the total population, and more than 20 percent of all elderly Americans. This group is of special interest to planners because those 85 or older are more likely to require health services.

Gender Gap

Women outnumber men at every age among the elderly. In 2000, there were an estimated three women for every two men age 65 or older, and the sex ratio is even more skewed among the oldest-old.

The preponderance of women among the elderly reflects the higher death rates for men than women at every age. There are approximately 105 male babies born for every 100 female babies, but higher male death rates cause the sex ratio to decline as age increases, and around age 35, females outnumber males in the United States. At age 85 and older, the ratio is 41 men per 100 women.[1]

Changes in the leading causes and average ages of death affect a population's sex ratio. In 1900, the average sex ratio for the U.S. total population was 104 men for every 100 women. But during the early 1900s, improvements in health care during and after pregnancy lowered maternal mortality, and a greater proportion of women survived to older ages. Adult male mortality improved much more slowly; death rates for adult men plateaued during the 1960s.

In recent years, however, male mortality improved faster than female mortality, primarily because of a marked decline in deaths from heart disease. The gender gap at the older ages has narrowed, and it is expected to narrow further. The U.S. Census Bureau projects the sex ratio for those age 65 or older to rise to 79 men for every 100 women by 2050. A sex ratio of 62 is anticipated for those age 85 or older.

Most elderly women today will outlive their spouses and face the challenges of later life alone: Older women who are widowed or divorced are less likely than older men to remarry. Older women are more likely than older men to be poor, to live alone, to enter nursing homes, and to depend on people other than their spouses for care. Many of the difficulties of growing older are compounded by past discrimination that disadvantaged women in the workplace and now threatens their economic security.

As the sex differential in mortality diminishes, these differences may lessen, but changes in marriage and work patterns, family structures, and fertility may mean that a greater proportion of older women will not have children or a living spouse. High divorce rates and declining rates of marriage, for instance, mean that many older women will not have spousal benefits available to them through pensions or Social Security.

Ethnic Diversity

The U.S. elderly population is becoming more racially and ethnically diverse, although not as rapidly as is the total U.S. population. In 2000, about 84 percent of the elderly population were non-Hispanic white, compared with 69 percent of the total U.S. population. By 2050, the proportion of elderly who are non-Hispanic white is projected to drop to 64 percent as the growing minority populations move into old age (see Figure 3). Although Hispanics made up only about 5 percent of the elderly population in 2000, 16 percent of the elderly population of 2050 is likely to be Hispanic. Similarly, blacks accounted for 8 percent of the elderly population in 2000, but are expected to make up 12 percent of elderly Americans in 2050.

Percent of population age 65+

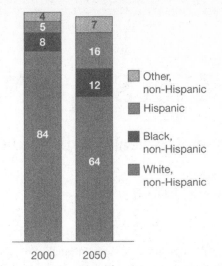

Figure 3   Elderly Americans by Race and Ethnicity, 2000 and 2050.

Sources: U.S. Census Bureau, *Census 2000 Demographic Profile* (2001); and U.S. Census Bureau, "Projections of the Resident Population by Age, Sex, Race and Hispanic Origin, 1999–2100" (www.census.gov/population/www/projections/natdet-D1A.html, accessed Sept. 19, 2001).

Note. The 2000 figures refer to residents who identified with one race. About 2% of Americans identified with more than one race in the 2000 census.

The major racial and ethnic groups are aging at different rates, depending upon fertility, mortality, and immigration among these groups. Immigration has a growing influence on the age structure of racial and ethnic minority groups. Although most immigrants tend to be in their young adult ages, when people are most likely and willing to assume the risks of moving to a new country, U.S. immigration policy also favors the entry of parents and other family members of these young immigrants. The number of immigrants age 65 or older is rapidly increasing as more foreign-born elderly move to the United States from Latin America, Asia, or Africa to join their children.[2] These older immigrants, plus the aging of immigrants who entered as young adults, are altering the ethnic makeup of elderly Americans.

Notes

1. U.S. Census Bureau, *Population Projections of the United States by Age, Sex, Race, Hispanic Origin, and Nativity: 1999 to 2100* (2000), accessed online at: www.census.gov/population/projections/nation/summary/np-t3-a.txt, on Sept. 19, 2001.

2. Janet M. Wilmoth, Gordon F. DeJong, and Christine L. Himes, "Immigrant and Non-Immigrant Living Arrangements in Later Life," *International Journal of Sociology and Social Policy* 17 (1997): 57–82.

Critical Thinking

1. What factors contribute to the increasing life expectancy of the American people?

2. What challenges do aging Americans face?

3. Are older Americans healthier than ever before?

You Can Stop "Normal" Aging

New research reveals surprising facts about our changing bodies.

Dr. Henry S. Lodge

From your body's point of view, "normal" aging isn't normal at all. It's a choice you make by the way you live your life. The other choice is to tell your cells to grow—to build a strong, vibrant body and mind.

Let's have a look at standard American aging. Barbara D. had a baby when she was 34, gave up exercise and gained 50 pounds. Exhausted and depressed, Barbara thought youth, energy and optimism were all in her rearview mirror. Jon M., 55, had fallen even farther down the slippery slope. He was stuck in the corporate world of stress, long hours and doughnuts. At 255 pounds, he had knees that hurt and a back that ached. He developed high blood pressure and eventually diabetes. Life was looking grim.

Most aging is just the dry rot we program into our cells by sedentary living, junk food and stress.

Jon and Barbara weren't getting old; they had let their bodies decay. Most aging is just the dry rot we program into our cells by sedentary living, junk food and stress. Yes, we do have to get old, and ultimately we do have to die. But our bodies are designed to age slowly and remarkably well. Most of what we see and fear is decay, and decay is only one choice. Growth is the other.

After two years of misery, Barbara started exercising and is now in the best shape of her life. She just finished a sprint triathlon and, at 37, feels like she is 20. Jon started eating better and exercising too—slowly at first, but he stuck with it. He has since lost 50 pounds, the pain in his knees and back has disappeared, and his diabetes is gone. Today, Jon is 60 and living his life in the body of a healthy 30-year-old. He will die one day, but he is likely to live like a young man until he gets there.

The hard reality of our biology is that we are built to move. Exercise is the master signaling system that tells our cells to grow instead of fade. When we exercise, that process of growth spreads throughout every cell in our bodies, making us functionally younger. Not a little bit younger—a lot younger. True biological aging is a surprisingly slow and graceful process. You can live out your life in a powerful, healthy body if you are willing to put in the work.

Let's take a step back to see how exercise works at the cellular level. Your body is made up of trillions of cells that live mostly for a few weeks or months, die and are replaced by new cells in an endless cycle. For example, your taste buds live only a few hours, white blood cells live 10 days, and your muscle cells live about three months. Even your bones dissolve and are replaced, over and over again. A few key stem cells in each organ and your brain cells are the only ones that stick around for the duration. All of your other cells are in a constant state of renewal.

You replace about 1% of your cells every day. That means 1% of your body is brand-new today, and you will get another 1% tomorrow. Think of it as getting a whole new body every three months. It's not entirely accurate, but it's pretty close. Viewed that way, you are walking around in a body that is brand-new since Christmas—new lungs, new liver, new muscles, new skin. Look down at your legs and realize that you are going to have new ones by the Fourth of July. Whether that body is functionally younger or older is a choice you make by how you live.

You choose whether those new cells come in stronger or weaker. You choose whether they grow or decay each day from then on. Your cells don't care which choice you make. They just follow the directions you send. Exercise, and your cells get stronger; sit down, and they decay.

This whole system evolved over billions of years out in nature, where all animals face two great cellular challenges: The first is to grow strong, fast and fit in the spring, when food abounds and there are calories to fuel hungry muscles, bones and brains. The second is to decay as fast as possible in the winter, when calories disappear and surviving starvation is the key to life. You would think that food is the controlling signal for this, but it's not. Motion controls your system.

When you don't exercise, your muscles let out a steady trickle of chemicals that tell every cell to decay, day after day after day.

Though we've moved indoors and left that life behind, our cells still think we're living out on the savannah, struggling to stay alive each day. There are no microwaves or supermarkets in nature. If you want to eat, you have to hunt or forage every single day. That movement is a signal that it's time to grow. So, when you exercise, your muscles release specific substances that travel throughout your bloodstream, telling your cells to grow. Sedentary muscles, on the other hand, let out a steady trickle of chemicals that whisper to every cell to decay, day after day after day.

Men like Jon, who go from sedentary to fit, cut their risk of dying from a heart attack by 75% over five years. Women cut their risk by 80%—and heart attacks are the largest single killer of women. Both men and women can double their leg strength with three months of exercise, and most of us can double it again in another three months. This is true whether you're in your 30s or your 90s. It's not a miracle or a mystery. It's your biology, and you're in charge.

The other master signal to our cells—equal and, in some respects, even more important than exercise—is emotion. One of the most fascinating revelations of the last decade is that emotions change our cells through the same molecular pathways as exercise. Anger, stress and loneliness are signals for "starvation" and chronic danger. They "melt" our bodies as surely as sedentary living. Optimism, love and community trigger the process of growth, building our bodies, hearts and minds.

Men who have a heart attack and come home to a family are four times less likely to die of a second heart attack. Women battling heart disease or cancer do better in direct proportion to the number of close friends and relatives they have. Babies in the ICU who are touched more often are more likely to survive. Everywhere you look, you see the role of emotion in our biology. Like exercise, it's a choice.

It's hard to exercise every day. And with our busy lives, it's even harder to find the time and energy to maintain relationships and build communities. But it's worth it when you consider the alternative. Go for a walk or a run, and think about it. Deep in our cells, down at the level of molecular genetics, we are wired to exercise and to care. We're beginning to wake up to that as a nation, but you might not want to wait. You might want to join Barbara, Jon and millions of others and change your life. Start today. Your cells are listening.

Critical Thinking

1. What are the dry rot factors that contribute to the aging of human cells?

2. How does regular exercise by the individual contribute to cell growth?

3. How do our emotions contribute to our health or illnesses over time?

Dr. Henry S. Lodge is on the faculty of Columbia Medical School and is co-author of *Younger Next Year* (Workman).

As seen in *Parade,* March 18, 2007, pp. 6–7; adapted from *Younger Next Year: A Guide to Living Like 50 Until You're 80 and Beyond* (Workman Publishing Co., 2004). Copyright © 2007 by Dr. Henry S. Lodge. All rights reserved. Reprinted by permission of the author and Parade Publications.

Living Longer: Diet and Exercise

Diet

In the search for the fountain of youth, researchers keep coming back to one fact: what you eat has a tremendous impact not only on your health but on your longevity. Here's why every bite you take counts.

DONNA JACKSON NAKAZAWA

It's hard to get through your first cup of morning coffee without reading a headline about food. Eat blueberries! Inhale kale! Such antioxidant-rich foods will clear your arteries and help prevent the buildup of Alzheimer's plaque in your brain. Add in a cup of green tea in the morning and swish down an ounce or two of dark chocolate with a glass of red wine in the evening and you will be nicely tanked up on healthy fuel for the day.

Or will you? Almost every day, it seems, new studies emerge on the antiaging properties of various foods. One day, soy is good; the next, we find out soy's health benefits may have been oversold. To add to the confusion, this year *The Journal of the American Medical Association (JAMA)* published a study that found caloric restriction—eating about 25 percent less than normal—could extend your life.

So which headlines should we believe? And why should we believe them? The answers lie in research that shows exactly how various foods work at the cellular level. In particular, antioxidant-rich fruits and vegetables are emerging as powerful medicine in the fight against cellular aging.

Here's how it works. In the normal process of metabolism, cells produce unstable oxygen molecules—called free radicals—that damage cells. Worse still, the older we get, the more free radicals we produce. Recent studies suggest that the havoc free radicals wreak "plays a central role in virtually every age-related disease, including cardiovascular diseases such as stroke and atherosclerosis, Parkinson's disease, Alzheimer's, and type 2 diabetes," says Mark Mattson, Ph.D., chief of the Laboratory of Neurosciences at the National Institute on Aging at the National Institutes of Health.

It sounds pretty grim, but in this battle there are, thankfully, superheroes. Enter the vibrant world of antioxidants—substances that bind with free radicals and inhibit them from damaging cells. They are abundant in the most colorful fruits and vegetables, including spinach, broccoli, spirulina (blue-green algae), red apples, cranberries, blueberries, cherries, and grapes, as well as in chocolate and red wine. When you hear doctors say that eating five helpings of fruits and vegetables a day is good for you, antioxidants are the main reason. In the past five years an impressive body of research has emerged showing how antioxidants may protect the body and brain against the ravages of aging.

Paula Bickford, Ph.D., a researcher at the University of South Florida Center of Excellence for Aging and Brain Repair, is particularly interested in the role of antioxidants in brain health. The brain is a good place to study the benefits of antioxidants, says Bickford, because it has one of the highest percentages of fats of any organ in the body, and it is in our fats that free radicals inflict much of their damage. As we age, "communications between neurons become damaged, kind of like what happened to the Tin Man in *The Wizard of Oz,*" she explains. "Oxidative damage caused the Tin Man to grow rusty—until Dorothy came along and oiled him." Similarly, antioxidants help to "regrease the lines of communication" in the cells in our brain, says Bickford.

To measure how the communication between cells was affected when groups of rats ate different diets, Bickford and her colleagues placed electrodes in the brains of 20-month-old rats—the equivalent of 60-year-old humans. She then fed one group of rats a diet supplemented with spirulina, another with apples, and a third with cucumbers, which lack the antioxidant qualities of spirulina and apples. Bickford and her colleagues were surprised by the robustness with which "both the spirulina and apple groups demonstrated improved neuron function in the brain, a suppression of inflammatory substances in the brain, and a decrease in oxidative damage." By contrast, there was no improvement in rats fed a diet containing cucumbers. Bickford, who calls the findings "dramatic," reproduced her results in another study, in which rats fed a spinach-rich diet had a reversal in the loss of learning ability that occurs with age.

Most recently, Bickford examined whether eating a diet high in antioxidant-rich spinach and blueberries makes a difference in lab animals suffering from stroke and Parkinson's. "We've seen very positive effects with both of these diseases, as well," she says. "We believe that antioxidants can help people either to delay the onset or to slow the progression of a range of diseases that we tend to get as we age."

Tempting though it may be now to go out and gorge on antioxidant-rich dark chocolate, resist the urge. The hottest discovery in the search to find the fountain of youth through the foods we eat is to—gulp!—eat a lot less of them. A 2006 article in *JAMA* caused a stir by announcing that in both men and women, caloric restriction—as spartan as 890 calories a day—resulted in a decrease in fasting insulin levels and body temperature, two biomarkers of longevity. Why? Because restricting calories also helps to eliminate those nefarious free radicals. Mattson explains: "When you overeat and more energy comes into the cells than you burn off by being active, you are going to have more excess free radicals roaming around." Still, he advises, don't panic over the idea of having to subsist on 890 calories a day. Mattson, who calls such a diet "starvation," believes we can all gain the benefits of healthy eating with a lot less pain.

Richard Miller, M.D., Ph.D., professor of pathology and geriatric medicine at the University of Michigan, agrees. He has spent the last 20 years studying the ways in which dietary and genetic changes can slow the aging process. The research has shown that mice, rats, and monkeys that have undergone severe caloric restriction demonstrate all kinds of mental and physical benefits such as better mental function, less joint disease, and even fewer cases of cataracts. But it's unrealistic to try to replicate that in humans. "To copy what's happening in the lab, a man weighing 200 pounds would have to decrease his caloric intake by 40 percent for life, which would put him at about 120 pounds," Miller explains. "That's just not tenable."

Instead, Mattson and Miller advocate a more moderate approach. According to the Centers for Disease Control and Prevention, the average man in the United States consumes about 2,475 calories a day. That's roughly 500 more, on average, than he really needs. Likewise, the average American woman consumes 1,833 calories, yet probably needs only about 1,600. One way to ratchet down your caloric consumption would be to follow this simple equation: men should aim for about 500 calories at both breakfast and lunch, while women should strive for about 300 at each meal. Both sexes can then shoot for 1,000 calories at dinner.

Bickford, who prefers to think of caloric restriction as caloric selection, underscores the importance of getting as much of your caloric intake as you can not only from antioxidant-rich fruits and vegetables but also from nuts and flaxseed, which are loaded with vitamin E and omega-3 and omega-6 fatty acids. In fact, Bickford takes a page out of her own lab studies and starts

her day with an antioxidant smoothie. You can try it at home by blending together one cup of frozen blueberries with half a tablespoon of spirulina (available in any health food store), half a cup of nonfat plain yogurt, one teaspoon of ground flaxseed, one tablespoon of almond butter or a half-handful of almonds, and a dash of soy milk. Consider what's in that blender as a gas tank full of high-antioxidant fuel for the day.

Of course, one can't help but ask: what's the fun of living to 102 if you're subsisting on spirulina shakes? Not to worry. If you splurge on a stack of pancakes with eggs, bacon, and sausage—packing in 2,000 calories before 10 A.M.—you can always take heart in new data about to emerge from Mattson's lab, which show that periodic fasting—skipping a meal here and there—can also help to eliminate free radicals quite beautifully. "From an evolutionary standpoint we just aren't used to constant access to food," he explains. "Our bodies are used to going days without eating anything. Yet all of a sudden, we are taking in calories all day long."

In other words, we have gone from thousands of years of intermittently restricting our calories and eating a high-antioxidant diet to, in the past century, constantly eating a low-antioxidant diet. And that means more free radicals and more disease. So indulge in the pancakes or the cheese steak, but not both. Then skip a couple of meals and make your next one an all-out antioxidant feast. It may be counter to the don't-skip-meals philosophy our mothers all taught us; yet as it turns out, Mother Nature just might know better.

DONNA JACKSON NAKAZAWA is a health writer whose next book, a medical mystery about what's behind rising rates of autoimmune disease, will be published by Touchstone/Simon & Schuster in 2007.

Exercise

Regular physical activity has been shown to reduce your risk of heart attack, stroke, Alzheimer's, and some cancers. Now we're finding it also may add years to your life. That's powerful medicine indeed.

SUSAN CRANDELL

There are no guarantees in life and even fewer in death. But if you wish to prolong the former and delay the latter, scientists can now pretty much promise that regular exercise will help. "So many of what we thought were symptoms of aging are actually symptoms of disuse," says Pamela Peeke, M.D., a University of Maryland researcher and author of *Body for Life for Women* (Rodale, 2005). "This is a monster statement." It means that your health is not just a throw of the genetic dice but a factor that is largely under your control. "Our bodies are built for obsolescence after 50," Peeke says. "Up to 50 you can get away with not exercising; after that, you start paying the price."

The most dramatic declines due to aging are in muscle strength. "Unless you do resistance exercise—strength training with weights or elastic bands—you lose six pounds of muscle a decade," says Wayne Westcott, Ph.D., the highly respected fitness research director at the South Shore YMCA in Quincy, Massachusetts. That change in body composition not only saps our strength; it also lowers our metabolism and exposes us to greater risk of age-related disease. In fact, the loss of muscle (and accompanying increase in body fat) puts extra strain on the heart, alters sugar metabolism (increasing the risk for diabetes), and can tip the balance of healthy lipids in the blood, leading to heart attack and stroke.

Building muscle is much easier than you might think. Strength training just 20 minutes a day, two or three times a week, for 10 to 12 weeks can rebuild three pounds of muscle and increase your metabolism by 7 percent. Do you really need a boost in metabolism? Yes, if you want to feel more energetic, more alert, more vital and alive. Plus, the added muscle has a halo effect on many systems of the body, reducing blood pressure, improving your ability to use glucose from the blood by 25 percent, increasing bone mass by 1 to 3 percent, and improving gastrointestinal efficiency by 55 percent. "It's like going from a four-cylinder engine to a six," Westcott says.

If that's not enough to get your attention, consider this: a regular exercise program (30 minutes of physical activity at least three days a week) can reduce your risk of dying in the next eight years by 40 percent, improve brain function, cut your risk of Alzheimer's disease by up to 60 percent, and blunt the symptoms of depression. This is powerful medicine, given that 80 percent of the population over 65 suffers from at least one chronic condition, and half have two or more, according to a report from the Census Bureau and the National Institute on Aging.

What is it about physical activity that makes it such a panacea? As scientists learn more about how the aging process works, they're finding that exercise—both aerobic exercise and strength training—has a tremendous impact on every cell in the body, reducing inflammation, increasing blood flow, and even reversing the natural declines in oxygen efficiency and muscle mass that come with aging.

Westcott points to a study his organization conducted at a nursing home in Orange City, Florida. Nineteen men and women with an average age of 89, most of whom used wheelchairs, did just ten minutes of strength training a week. "After 14 weeks almost everybody was out of their wheelchairs," Westcott says. "One woman moved back into independent living." The results were published in *Mature Fitness.*

Another inspiring study, published last spring in the *Journal of the American College of Cardiology,* reported that people in their 60s and 70s who walked or jogged, biked, and stretched for 90 minutes three times a week for six months increased their exercise efficiency—their ability to exercise harder without expending more energy—by a whopping 30 percent. But here's the shocker: a comparison group of people in their 20s and 30s showed an efficiency increase of just 2 percent. The results caught even study author Wayne C. Levy, M.D., an associate professor of cardiology at the University of Washington in Seattle, by surprise. "I hadn't anticipated that the older people would improve more than the group in their 20s and 30s," he says.

The explanation, Levy believes, may involve improvement in the function of the mitochondria—spherical or rod-shaped structures in our cells that take glucose, protein, and fat from the food we eat and turn them into energy. In fact, scientists believe that most of the dramatic benefits we get from exercise can be traced to this improvement in the mitochondria. "Mitochondrial function naturally declines with age," explains Kevin Short, Ph.D., who studies mitochondria and exercise at the Mayo Clinic in Rochester, Minnesota. But exercise, he found, can reverse that decline.

When Short and his colleagues put 65 healthy nonexercisers ranging in age from 21 to 87 on a bicycle training program three days a week, they found that everyone's maximum aerobic capacity had increased by about 10 percent after four months. When they studied thigh-muscle samples, they found out why: the mitochondria were pumping out more adenosine triphosphate (ATP), the fuel muscles use to move.

Now, if mightier mitochondria aren't enough to get you on your exercise bike each morning, this might be: it appears physical activity may also combat oxidative damage (see "Browning apples: oxidation at work"). "During exercise there's a tremendous burst of oxidative agents that are injurious to tissue," says Abraham Aviv, M.D., director of the Center of Human Development and Aging at the University of Medicine and Dentistry of New Jersey.

The theory is that although you take in more oxygen while exercising, regular exercise slows your resting heart rate, thereby decreasing the amount of oxygen you need overall and reducing the rate at which you create harmful free radicals.

Finally, to all these substantial benefits of exercise add one more: Professor Tim Spector, director of the Twins UK registry at St. Thomas' Hospital in London, is conducting experiments to determine whether exercise slows down the rate at which our telomeres shrink. (Telomeres are DNA sequences, located on the ends of chromosomes, that shorten as we age—see "Telomeres: your body's biological clock"). Although the results have not yet been published, preliminary findings suggest that in exercising and sedentary twin pairs, the twin who exercises has much longer telomeres "even when you adjust for differences in weight and smoking," says Spector.

In short, the evidence is clear: daily physical activity can transform your life. And it's never too late to start. "I started strength-training my father when he was 82," recalls Westcott. "He's six feet tall, but he was emaciated by the stress of my mother's death and weighed only 124 pounds. In a year and a half, he added 24 pounds of muscle. At 97, he's stronger than people half his age."

Critical Thinking

1. How do antioxidants affect the free radicals in the human body?

2. What effect do free radicals have on the cells in the human brain?

3. How do antioxidants affect the onset of diseases that people get as they age?

4. What are the health effects of a 30-minute exercise program at least three days a week?

SUSAN CRANDELL is the author of *Thinking About Tomorrow: Reinventing Yourself at Midlife.*

More Good Years

Want to live longer—and healthier? These secrets from a sleepy Greek island could show you the way.

DAN BUETTNER

In 1970 Yiannis Karimalis got a death sentence. Doctors in Pennsylvania diagnosed the Greek immigrant with abdominal cancer and told him he'd be dead within a year. He was not yet 40 years old.

Devastated, Karimalis left his job as a bridge painter and returned to his native island of Ikaria. At least there he could be buried among his relatives, he thought—and for a lot less money than in the United States. Thirty-nine years later, Karimalis is still alive and telling his amazing story to anyone who will listen. And when he returned to the States on a recent visit, he discovered he had outlived all the doctors who had predicted his death.

On Ikaria, a mountainous, 99-square-mile island, residents tell this story to illustrate something they've known all their lives: on average, Ikarians outlive just about everyone else in the world.

For three weeks in April, I led a scientific expedition to Ikaria to investigate the reasons for the islanders' remarkable longevity. It was part of my research into the earth's few Blue Zones: places where an extraordinarily high proportion of natives live past 90. Our team of demographic and medical researchers—funded by AARP and *National Geographic*—found that an amazing one in three Ikarians reaches 90. (According to the U.S. Census Bureau, only one in nine baby boomers will.) What's more, Ikarians suffer 20 percent fewer cases of cancer than do Americans and have about half our rate of heart disease and one-ninth our rate of diabetes. Most astonishing of all: among the islanders over 90 whom the team studied—about one-third of Ikaria's population who are 90 and older—there was virtually no Alzheimer's disease or other dementia. In the United States more than 40 percent of people over 90 suffer some form of this devastating ailment.

How do we explain these numbers? History tells part of the story.

In antiquity Ikaria was known as a health destination, largely for its radio-active hot springs, which were believed to relieve pain and to cure joint problems and skin ailments. But for much of the ensuing two millennia, civilization passed over this wind-beaten, harborless island. To elude marauding pirates, Ikarians moved their villages inland, high up on the rocky slopes. Their isolation led to a unique lifestyle.

Over centuries with no outside influences, island natives developed a distinctive outlook on life, including relentless optimism and a propensity for partying, both of which reduce stress. Ikarians go to bed well after midnight, sleep late, and take daily naps. Based on our interviews, we have reason to believe that most Ikarians over 90 are sexually active.

But what about the Ikarians' culture best explains their long lives? To find out, we let visitors to AARP.org/bluezones direct our team's quest. Our online collaborators voted on what we should research next. One day, for example, we interviewed hundred-year-old Ikarians to discover what they'd eaten for most of their lives. The next day we investigated the chemical composition of herbal teas.

In all, we found 13 likely contributors to Ikarian longevity. The formula below may be the closest you'll get to the fountain of youth:

- **Graze on greens** More than 150 varieties of wild greens grow on Ikaria. Some have more than ten times the level of antioxidants in red wine.
- **Sip herbal teas** Steeping wild mint, chamomile, or other herbs in hot water is a lifelong, daily ritual. Many teas lower blood pressure, which decreases the risk of heart disease and dementia.
- **Throw out your watch** Ikarians don't worry about time. Work gets done when it gets done. This attitude lowers stress, which reduces the risk of everything from arthritis to wrinkles.
- **Nap daily** Ikarian villages are ghost towns during the afternoon siesta, and science shows that a regular 30-minute nap decreases the risk of heart attack.
- **Walk where you're going** Mountainous terrain and a practice of walking for transport mean that every trip out of the house is a mini workout.
- **Phone a friend** With the island's rugged terrain, family and village support have been key to survival. Strong

social connections are proven to lower depression, mortality, and even weight.

- **Drink goat's milk** Most Ikarians over 90 have drunk goat's milk their whole lives. It is rich in a blood-pressure-lowering hormone called tryptophan as well as antibacterial compounds.
- **Maintain a Mediterranean diet** Around the world, people who most faithfully stick to this region's diet—a regimen high in whole grains, fruits, vegetables, olive oil, and fish—outlive people who don't by about six years. The Ikarian version features more potatoes than grains (because they grew better in the mountains) and more meat than fish (because the sea was a day's journey away).
- **Enjoy some Greek honey** The local honey contains antibacterial, anticancer and anti-inflammatory properties. (Unfortunately, the health benefits of Ikarian honey do not extend to American honey, as far as we know.)
- **Open the olive oil** Ikaria's consumption of olive oil is among the world's highest. Residents drizzle antioxidant-rich extra-virgin oil over food after cooking, which preserves healthful properties in the oil that heat destroys.
- **Grow your own garden (or find farmers' markets)** Fruits and vegetables eaten soon after picking are higher in compounds that decrease the risk of cancer and heart disease.

- **Get religion** Ikarians observe Greek Orthodox rituals, and regular attendance at religious services (of any kind) has been linked to longer life spans.
- **Bake bread** The island's sourdough bread is high in complex carbohydrates and may improve glucose metabolism and stave off diabetes.

Do Ikarians possess the true secret to longevity? Well, some combination of their habits is helping them live significantly longer than Americans, who live on average to age 78. We can't guarantee that Ikarian wisdom will help you live to 100. But if Yiannis Karimalis's example is any indicator, it may help you outlive your doctor.

Critical Thinking

1. How much lower is heart disease among the Ikarians in the blue zone than what Americans experience?
2. How much lower is the percent of cancer cases among the Ikarians in comparison to those in America?
3. What percentage of the Ikarian population have lived to 90 years or older?

DAN BUETTNER is the author of *The Blue Zones: Lessons for Living Longer From the People Who've Lived the Longest* (National Geographic, 2008).

Will You Live to Be 100?

THOMAS PERLS, MD AND MARGERY HUTTER SILVER, EdD

After completing a study of 150 centenarians, Harvard Medical School researchers Thomas Perls, M.D., and Margery Hutter Silver, Ed.D., developed a quiz to help you calculate your estimated life expectancy.

Longevity Quiz

Score

1. Do you smoke or chew tobacco, or are you around a lot of secondhand smoke? Yes (−20) No (0)

2. Do you cook your fish, poultry, or meat until it is charred? Yes (−2) No (0)

3. Do you avoid butter, cream, pastries, and other saturated fats as well as fried foods (e.g., French Fries)? Yes (+3) No (−7)

4. Do you minimize meat in your diet, preferably making a point to eat plenty of fruits, vegetables, and bran instead? Yes (+5) No (−4)

5. Do you consume more than two drinks of beer, wine, and/or liquor a day? (A standard drink is one 12-ounce bottle of beer, one wine cooler, one five-ounce glass of wine, or one and a half ounces of 80-proof distilled spirits.) Yes (−10) No (0)

6. Do you drink beer, wine, and/or liquor in moderate amounts (one or two drinks/day)? Yes (+3) No (0)

7. Do air pollution warnings occur where you live? Yes (−4) No (+1)

8. **a.** Do you drink more than 16 ounces of coffee a day? Yes (−3) No (0) **b.** Do you drink tea daily? Yes (+3) No (0)

9. Do you take an aspirin a day? Yes (+4) No (0)

10. Do you floss your teeth every day? Yes (+2) No (−4)

11. Do you have a bowel movement less than once every two days? Yes (−4) No (0)

12. Have you had a stroke or heart attack? Yes (−10) No (0)

13. Do you try to get a sun tan? Yes (−4) No (+3)

14. Are you more than 20 pounds overweight? Yes (−10) No (0)

15. Do you live near enough to other family members (other than your spouse and dependent children) that you can and want to drop by spontaneously? Yes (+5) No (−4)

16. Which statement is applicable to you? **a.** "Stress eats away at me. I can't seem to shake it off." Yes (−7) **b.** "I can shed stress." This might be by praying, exercising, meditating, finding humor in everyday life, or other means. Yes (+7)

17. Did both of your parents either die before age 75 of nonaccidental causes or require daily assistance by the time they reached age 75? Yes (−10) No (0) Don't know (0)

18. Did more than one of the following relatives live to at least age 90 in excellent health: parents, aunts/uncles, grandparents? Yes (+24) No (0) Don't know (0)

19. **a.** Are you a couch potato (do no regular aerobic or resistance exercise)? Yes (−7) **b.** Do you exercise at least three times a week? Yes (+7)

20. Do you take vitamin E (400–800 IU) and selenium (100–200 mcg) every day? Yes (+5) No (−3)

Score

STEP 1: Add the negative and positive scores together. Example: -45 *plus* $+30 = -15$. Divide the preceding score by 5 (-15 divided by $5 = -3$).

STEP 2: Add the negative or positive number to age 84 if you are a man or age 88 if you are a woman (example: $-3 + 88 = 85$) to get your estimated life span.

The Science behind the Quiz

Question 1 Cigarette smoke contains toxins that directly damage DNA, causing cancer and other diseases and accelerating aging.

Question 2 Charring food changes its proteins and amino acids into heterocyclic amines, which are potent mutagens that can alter your DNA.

Questions 3, 4 A high-fat diet, and especially a high-fat, high-protein diet, may increase your risk of cancer of the breast, uterus, prostate, colon, pancreas, and kidney. A diet rich in fruits and vegetables may lower the risk of heart disease and cancer.

Questions 5, 6 Excessive alcohol consumption can damage the liver and other organs, leading to accelerated aging and increased susceptibility to disease. Moderate consumption may lower the risk of heart disease.

Question 7 Certain air pollutants may cause cancer; many also contain oxidants that accelerate aging.

Question 8 Too much coffee predisposes the stomach to ulcers and chronic inflammation, which in turn raise the risk of heart disease. High coffee consumption may also indicate and exacerbate stress. Tea, on the other hand, is noted for its significant antioxidant content.

Question 9 Taking 81 milligrams of aspirin a day (the amount in one baby aspirin) has been shown to decrease the risk of heart disease, possibly because of its anticlotting effects.

Question 10 Research now shows that chronic gum disease can lead to the release of bacteria into the bloodstream, contributing to heart disease.

Question 11 Scientists believe that having at least one bowel movement every 20 hours decreases the incidence of colon cancer.

Question 12 A previous history of stroke and heart attack makes you more susceptible to future attacks.

Question 13 The ultraviolet rays in sunlight directly damage DNA, causing wrinkles and increasing the risk of skin cancer.

Question 14 Being obese increases the risk of various cancers, heart disease, and diabetes. The more overweight you are, the higher your risk of disease and death.

Questions 15, 16 People who do not belong to cohesive families have fewer coping resources and therefore have increased levels of social and psychological stress. Stress is associated with heart disease and some cancers.

Questions 17, 18 Studies show that genetics plays a significant role in the ability to reach extreme old age.

Question 19 Exercise leads to more efficient energy production in the cells and overall, less oxygen radical formation. Oxygen (or free) radicals are highly reactive molecules or atoms that damage cells and DNA, ultimately leading to aging.

Question 20 Vitamin E is a powerful antioxidant and has been shown to retard the progression of Alzheimer's, heart disease, and stroke. Selenium may prevent some types of cancer.

Critical Thinking

1. What stomach problems can be the result of too much coffee consumption?
2. What are the advantages in terms of one's health to being a member of a stable family?
3. What are the health problems associated with smoking?

Adapted from *Living to 100: Lessons in Living to Your Maximum Potential at Any Age* (Basic Books, 1999) by **Thomas Perls, MD**, and **Margery Hutter Silver, EdD**, with **John F. Lauerman**.

Long Live . . . Us

In never-say-die America, life expectancy is longer than ever.

Mark Bennett

Six members of the Class of '74 sit around a restaurant table.

They sip red wine and munch on a trail-mix-style bowl filled with fish oil, flaxseed oil and DHEA gel tabs. A joke about a classmate's spring break photo with her great-grandson's frat brothers on Facebook sparks hysterical laughter. As the chuckles subside, they check their iPhone clocks, realize the abs-crunch marathon fundraiser for the Macrobiotic Diet Consortium starts in an hour, and get busy planning their 85th reunion.

A retro "Dancing with the Stars" theme wins unanimous approval. One guy tweets his mother-in-law about next week's library tax protest, the class president picks up the tab, and they scatter out the door.

Sure, the ages of the folks in that futuristic dinner party would be around 103, but in never-say-die America, life expectancy is longer than ever, according to a report issued this month by the U.S. Centers for Disease Control and Prevention.

A baby born in 2009 will live an average of 78 years and two months. If that kid is a girl, she will likely linger on Earth for 80.6 years, compared to 75.7 for a boy. Back in 1930, a man's life expectancy was 58 and a woman's 62.

The CDC won't say why Americans live longer until the second half of its life expectancy report is released later this year, but the agency has a pretty good guess. Improved medical treatment, vaccinations and anti-smoking campaigns have helped drop the death rate to a record low as deaths from strokes, Alzheimer's, diabetes, heart disease and cancer decreased during the past 12 months.

Plus, our ancestors had no idea that red wine contained antioxidants and resveratol that protect blood vessels and reduce "bad" cholesterol. Or that DHEA supposedly repairs damage to cells in our bodies. Or that fish oil and flaxseed oil fight free radicals, which are cell-damaging molecules, not 1960s fugitives.

So, with almonds stashed in our shirt pockets instead of Marlboros, we've nearly tacked an extra decade onto our lives since 1970, when life expectancy in the U.S. was 70.8 years.

"It does go up every year, little by little," CDC statistician Ken Kochanek said by telephone from Washington, D.C., last week.

Seemingly, this age-defying trend could extend and create bizarre cultural dynamics, not unlike the aforementioned class reunion committee meeting. In Britain, for example, government researchers estimate that by 2014—just a little more than two years from now—the number of Brits ages 65 and older will surpass that of the under-16 population. Think of the implications—there are more people sitting around the UK who look like Keith Richards than fresh-faced kids. Actually, the Stones guitarist (now 67) would be considered a mere pup, if a BBC report is true. That story quoted a *Science* magazine analysis that concluded there is no natural limit to human life. The greeting card companies may be printing a new "Happy 200th" line someday.

Mel Brooks' 2,000-year-old man comes to mind. When asked if he knew Joan of Arc, Mel's character responded, "Know her? I went with her, dummy."

Reality continues to apply, though. Humans are managing to live longer, but not indefinitely. Though 36,000 fewer Americans died in 2009 than the year before, a total of 2.4 million still passed on in '09. The leading causes were, in order, heart disease, malignant neoplasms, chronic lower respiratory diseases, cerebrovascular diseases, accidents, Alzheimer's, diabetes, flu and pneumonia and nephritis. "In general, you have the same problems that have existed for a long time," said Kochanek.

Men show up in those statistics sooner than women, apparently because we do dumb stuff more often, such as smoking and exceeding the speed limit. "Men take more risks, and that affects life expectancy," Kochanek said. Both genders eat less wisely, too, even if we're popping those Omega-3 pills. Americans in the sixtysomething age range are, on average, 10 pounds heavier than folks of a similar vintage a decade earlier, according to FDA statistics cited by *U.S. News & World Report*.

The impact of poor choices in our lifetimes can be tabulated. For those dying to know how much time they've got, Northwestern Mutual Life Insurance Co. provides an online calculator. Just punch in your age, height, weight, then answer 11 other questions about your lifestyle, family history and habits and—voila!—your final number appears. If you want something handy enough to stick onto the front of the fridge, the

U.S. Census Bureau offers a less detailed chart subtitled "Average Number of Years of Life Remaining."

Of course, those are national figures. Averages. They vary by location. According to a nationwide study by the Robert Wood Johnson Foundation of the University of Wisconsin Population Health Institute, Vigo County's mortality rate ranks 69th out of 92 counties in Indiana, which isn't good. The mortality rate is a measure of premature death—the years of potential life lost prior to age 75.

Why do Vigo Countians die so young?

Well, in terms of health behaviors (smoking, binge drinking, car crashes, diet and exercise, STDs and teen birth rates), Vigo County rates an abysmal 80th out of 92 counties. (Apparently, very few of the wine-drinking, fish-oil-eating, fitness-crazed baby boomers described earlier call Vigo County home.) When calculating mortality rates, health behaviors account for nearly one-third of the influencing factors, along with clinical care, socioeconomics and physical environment, the Population Health Institute study said.

Given those real numbers, the secret of long life may not be such a secret after all. Author and psychologist Howard Friedman's new book, *The Longevity Project*, explores the topic. In a *Time* magazine interview this month, he explained that "conscientiousness" was a primary enhancer of life expectancy.

"The most intriguing reason why co[n] live longer is that having a conscientio[us] you into healthier situations and rela[tionships] told *Time*. "In other words, conscientious p[eople] way to happier marriages, better friendships a[nd] work situations. They help create healthy, long-liv[ing] ways for themselves. This is a new way of thinking abo[ut] health."

That should give Keith Richards something to consider every time the Stones play "Time Is On My Side."

Critical Thinking

1. Why is the life expectancy of men lower than the life expectancy of women?

2. What were the leading causes of death in the United States in 2009?

3. How has the weight of persons over 60 changed in the last ten years?

4. Why does Howard Friedman believe that conscientious people live longer?

MARK BENNETT can be reached at (812) 231–4377 or mark.bennett@tribstar.com.

UNIT 2

The Quality of Later Life

Unit Selections

Learning Outcomes

After reading this Unit, you will be able to:

- Describe how resilient people are able to rebound from a crisis or trauma.

- Explain how staying connected helps resilient people survive.

- Explain why life is happier for people in their older years.

- Explain why older people have fewer rows and come up with better solutions to conflict.

- Describe the four attitudinal and personal attributes of a person that contribute to his/her successful aging.

- List the four physical factors that the study listed as contributing to a person's longevity.

- List the six popular myths about longevity that the authors question.

- List the qualifications the authors introduce to the myths to improve their accuracy.

Student Website

www.mhhe.com/cls

Internet References

Aging with Dignity
www.agingwithdignity.org
The Gerontological Society of America
www.geron.org
The National Council on the Aging
www.ncoa.org

Although it is true that one ages from the moment of conception to the moment of death, children are usually considered to be "growing and developing" while adults are often thought of as "aging." Having accepted this assumption, most biologists concerned with the problems of aging focus their attention on what happens to individuals after they reach maturity. Moreover, most of the biological and medical research dealing with the aging process focuses on the later part of the mature adult's life cycle. A commonly used definition of *senescence* is "the changes that occur generally in the postreproductive period and that result in decreased survival capacity on the part of the individual organism" (B. L. Shrehler, *Time, Cells and Aging,* New York: Academic Press, 1977).

As a person ages, physiological changes take place. The skin loses its elasticity, becomes more pigmented, and bruises more easily. Joints stiffen, and the bone structure becomes less firm. Muscles lose their strength. The respiratory system becomes less efficient. The individual's metabolism changes, resulting in different dietary demands. Bowel and bladder movements are more difficult to regulate. Visual acuity diminishes, hearing declines, and the entire system is less able to resist environmental stresses and strains.

Increases in life expectancy have resulted largely from decreased mortality rates among younger people, rather than from increased longevity after age 65. In 1900, the average life expectancy at birth was 47.3 years; in 2000, it was 76.9 years. Thus, in the last century, the average life expectancy rose by 29.6 years. However, those who now live to the age of 65 do not have an appreciably different life expectancy than did their 1900 cohorts. In 1900, 65-year-olds could expect to live approximately 11.9 years longer, while in 2000 they could expect to live approximately 17.9 years longer, an increase of six years. Although more people survive to age 65 today, the chances of being afflicted by one of the major killers of older persons is still about as great for this generation as it was for its grandparents. While medical science has had considerable success in controlling the acute diseases of the young—such as measles, chicken pox, and scarlet fever—it has not been as successful in controlling the chronic conditions of old age, such as heart disease, cancer, and emphysema. Organ transplants, greater knowledge of the immune system, and undiscovered medical technologies will probably increase the life expectancy for the 65-and-over population, resulting in longer life for the next generation.

Although people 65 years of age today are living only slightly longer than 65-year-olds did in 1900, the quality of

© Image Source/Getty Images

their later years has greatly improved. Economically, Social Security and a multitude of private retirement programs have given most older persons a more secure retirement. Physically, many people remain active, mobile, and independent throughout their retirement years. Socially, most older persons are married, involved in community activities, and leading productive lives. While they may experience some chronic ailments, most people 65 or older are able to live in their own homes, direct their own lives, and involve themselves in activities they enjoy.

The articles in this section examine health, psychological, social, and spiritual factors that affect the quality of aging. All of us are faced with the process of aging, and by putting a strong emphasis on health—both mental and physical—a long, satisfying life is much more attainable. In "The Secrets of Resilient People," the author points out that resilient people are seen as those who are capable of navigating through problems and hard times with the minimal amount of frustration and despair. In "The U-bend of Life," the author points out the reasons why older people are happier than young and middle-aged people. Lou Ann Walker gives specific recommendations for what the individual can do to improve his or her chances of aging well in "We Can Control How We Age." Finally, in "The Myths of Living Longer," the author points out six popular beliefs about living longer and attempts to determine their accuracy.

The Secrets of Resilient People

Everyone goes through tough times. Some people just navigate them better.

Beth Howard

"We cried for two solid months." That's how Deborah Robinson describes the painful period in 2002 when her husband, Jim, was diagnosed with early-onset Alzheimer's disease. Just 57 at the time, Jim was soon unable to work or drive, and Deborah became his primary caregiver, while continuing to work for the Disney Corporation in Orlando. Yet she survived the inevitable progression of Jim's disease, and his death in 2007, by reframing the situation in the most positive terms possible.

"I decided that we would rise above it, and it would be our finest hour," says Deborah, 54. She signed up for an Alzheimer's education program, joined a support group of partners of Alzheimer's patients, and asked for help from friends and family members. "It was a time to focus on the limited number of years we had left and make the best of them," she says.

Robinson could be the poster child for resilience, the ability to rebound quickly from a crisis or trauma. Highly resilient people don't fall apart—at least not for long. They call on their inner strength and recruit outside resources to keep moving forward. And they tweak their future expectations to fit their new reality, be it the loss of a loved one, a life-changing diagnosis, or a devastating financial blow. "Resilient people are like trees bending in the wind," says Steven M. Southwick, M.D., professor of psychiatry at Yale University School of Medicine. "They bounce back."

Resilient people are like trees bending in the wind. They bounce back.

Resiliency has become a hot research topic in the wake of such disasters as 9/11, Hurricane Katrina, and the current economic downturn. While there's still much to learn, scientists agree that resilience varies from person to person and has a genetic component—recent studies show that certain genes may protect you against the emotional back draft of trauma. "Some people are naturally more resilient," says Robert Brooks, Ph.D., assistant clinical professor of psychology at Harvard Medical School and coauthor with Sam Goldstein, Ph.D., of *The Power of Resilience*.

Yet, like almost any behavior, resilience can also be learned, says Goldstein, a psychologist at the University of Utah. In fact, research shows that resilient people share some common qualities—ones you can cultivate to master any crisis.

They Stay Connected

Resilient people rely on others to help them survive tough times. After Barbara Smith, 54, of Canton, Georgia, lost her oldest son, Evan, in a motorcycle accident three years ago, she wondered if she could keep going. The turning point came when she joined an online bereavement support group and then launched a subgroup (dailystrength.org/groups/formomsonly) to bring together other women who have lost children. She now spends hours a day on the site and has also organized retreats for group members. "We've saved each other," she says.

Research bears out the importance of connection. In a study of 243 caregivers in British Columbia, Canada, those who reported good social support scored higher on measures of quality of life and well-being, regardless of the burden they carried.

They're Optimistic

Like Deborah Robinson, people who have a sunny outlook do better at managing crises. A University of San Francisco study of caregivers concluded that those who found positive meaning in their caregiving were less likely to become depressed after their loved one died.

But don't fret if you lack a glass-half-full point of view. Experts say negative thinking is just a bad habit, though it may take some work to change your mindset. The first step: Observe the spin you put on your own experiences. When you catch yourself thinking negatively, challenge yourself to frame the situation in more positive terms. For instance, when you open your 401(k) statement, think: "If I change my investment strategy, I'll do better" instead of "I'll never recoup my losses."

They're Spiritual

"Generally people who are active in a religious faith tend to get through difficult times better," says Al Siebert, Ph.D., author of *The Resiliency Advantage*. A Duke University study concluded that people with serious medical conditions who had strong religious convictions and participated in religious activities were

They give Back

"The benefit you derive for yourself is as great as that you give to others," says Goldstein, who cites research showing that people who help others live longer.

New Yorker Renee Weinhouse, 79, would agree. Since surviving stage 4 lymphoma 28 years ago, she's been a regular fixture at Montefiore Medical Center in the Bronx, where she visits cancer patients and now also runs survivor support groups. "Nothing makes me happier than when I give a patient a little hope," says Weinhouse.

They Pick their Battles

"Resilient people tend to focus on things over which they have some influence and not spend time on things they can't control," says Brooks. Wallow in anger or fear, or move on? It's up to you.

Entrepreneur Tim Baumgartner, 59, took the latter route. An independent sales rep in Richmond, Virginia, who sold electronics to Circuit City, he was blind-sided when the company filed for bankruptcy last year. Within months, however, he and his daughter launched an online consumer electronics store. "Whining and complaining about how you find yourself here doesn't help," Baumgartner says. "I've refocused my energy on the start-up."

They Stay Healthy

A good diet and regular physical activity provide crucial buffers against stress. "Exercise literally helps to repair neurons in brain areas that are particularly susceptible to stress," says Southwick. Deborah Robinson made time to practice yoga every day, even when her husband's Alzheimer's required more hands-on care from her. "I realized that if I was going to be good for him, I had to be good to myself," she says.

They Find the Silver Lining

"Resilient people convert misfortune into good luck and gain strength from adversity," says Siebert. They see negative events as an opportunity to better themselves or become better people.

Southwick says the phenomenon is known as post-traumatic growth syndrome. And Barbara Smith seems to have it: "If I hadn't experienced Evan's death, I would not be able to help other mothers get through their grief," she says. "Putting together a place where we could share resources has forced me to set aside my own pain and try to make a difference in the world."

Critical Thinking

1. Why are people who are active in religious faith better able to get through a crisis?
2. How does an exercise program help to reduce stress?
3. How does being optimistic help resilient people?

BETH HOWARD is a writer based in Charlotte, North Carolina.

How Resilient are you?

Rate yourself on each of these statements using a scale from 1 (Do not agree) to 5 (Strongly agree).

_____ **I'm usually upbeat.** I see difficulties as temporary and expect to overcome them. Feelings of anger, loss, and discouragement don't last long.

_____ **I can tolerate high levels of ambiguity and uncertainty about situations.** I'm flexible, and comfortable with my paradoxical traits: optimistic/pessimistic, trusting/cautious, unselfish/selfish, etc.

_____ **I adapt quickly to new developments.** I'm curious. I ask questions.

_____ **I find the humor in rough situations and can laugh at myself.** I feel self-confident.

_____ **I learn valuable lessons from my experiences and from the experiences of others.**

_____ **I'm good at solving problems.** I'm good at making things work well. I'm often asked to lead groups and projects, though I have an independent spirit amid my cooperative way of working with others.

_____ **I'm strong and durable.** I hold up well during tough times.

_____ **I've converted misfortune into good luck and found benefits in bad experiences.**

_____ **Total score**

Scoring

35–40: Highly resilient
30–34: Self-motivated learner
20–29: Somewhat resilient
Less than 20: Poor at handling pressure (but it's never too late to learn).

Note: For a validity check, ask two people who know you well to rate you on these items; see what scores they come up with. Look for discrepancies and discuss them to come up with your true resiliency score.

Adapted from *The Resiliency Advantage* by Al Siebert, Ph.D. Reprinted with permission. Copyright © 2005, Al Siebert, Ph.D.

---

less likely to be waylaid by depression. When these patients did become depressed, the depression lifted sooner than it did for less religious people.

They're Playful

"Resilient people enjoy themselves like children do," Siebert says. "They wonder about things, experiment, and laugh." Take Donna Goldman, 60, of Lincolnshire, Illinois, who was diagnosed with multiple sclerosis in 2001 yet continues to teach preschool. "I let the kids play with my canes—as long as they don't use them as weapons!" she quips. She advertises her attitude on her license plate, which reads: "Get Back Up."

The U-bend of Life

Why, Beyond Middle Age, People Get Happier as They Get Older

THE ECONOMIST

Ask people how they feel about getting older, and they will probably reply in the same vein as Maurice Chevalier: "Old age isn't so bad when you consider the alternative." Stiffening joints, weakening muscles, fading eyesight and the clouding of memory, coupled with the modern world's careless contempt for the old, seem a fearful prospect—better than death, perhaps, but not much. Yet mankind is wrong to dread ageing. Life is not a long slow decline from sunlit uplands towards the valley of death. It is, rather, a U-bend.

When people start out on adult life, they are, on average, pretty cheerful. Things go downhill from youth to middle age until they reach a nadir commonly known as the mid-life crisis. So far, so familiar. The surprising part happens after that. Although as people move towards old age they lose things they treasure—vitality, mental sharpness and looks—they also gain what people spend their lives pursuing: happiness.

This curious finding has emerged from a new branch of economics that seeks a more satisfactory measure than money of human well-being. Conventional economics uses money as a proxy for utility—the dismal way in which the discipline talks about happiness. But some economists, unconvinced that there is a direct relationship between money and well-being, have decided to go to the nub of the matter and measure happiness itself.

These ideas have penetrated the policy arena, starting in Bhutan, where the concept of Gross National Happiness shapes the planning process. All new policies have to have a GNH assessment, similar to the environmental-impact assessment common in other countries. In 2008 France's president, Nicolas Sarkozy, asked two Nobel-prize-winning economists, Amartya Sen and Joseph Stiglitz, to come up with a broader measure of national contentedness than GDP. Then last month, in a touchy-feely gesture not typical of Britain, David Cameron announced that the British government would start collecting figures on well-being.

There are already a lot of data on the subject collected by, for instance, America's General Social Survey, Eurobarometer and

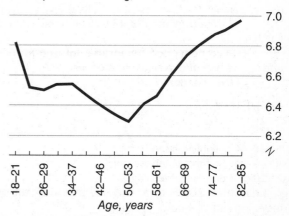

The U-bend
Self-reported well-being, on a scale of 1–10

Age, years

Source: PNAS Paper: "A snapshot of the age distribution of Psychological well-being in the United States" by Arthur Stone

Gallup. Surveys ask two main sorts of question. One concerns people's assessment of their lives, and the other how they feel at any particular time. The first goes along the lines of: thinking about your life as a whole, how do you feel? The second is something like: yesterday, did you feel happy/contented/angry/anxious? The first sort of question is said to measure global well-being, and the second hedonic or emotional well-being. They do not always elicit the same response: having children, for instance, tends to make people feel better about their life as a whole, but also increases the chance that they felt angry or anxious yesterday.

Statisticians trawl through the vast quantities of data these surveys produce rather as miners panning for gold. They are trying to find the answer to the perennial question: what makes people happy?

Four main factors, it seems: gender, personality, external circumstances and age. Women, by and large, are slightly happier than men. But they are also more susceptible to depression: a fifth to a quarter of women experience depression at some point in their lives, compared with around a tenth of men. Which suggests either that women are more likely to experience more extreme emotions, or that a few women are more miserable than men, while most are more cheerful.

Two personality traits shine through the complexity of economists' regression analyses: neuroticism and extroversion. Neurotic people—those who are prone to guilt, anger and anxiety—tend to be unhappy. This is more than a tautological observation about people's mood when asked about their feelings by pollsters or economists. Studies following people over many years have shown that neuroticism is a stable personality trait and a good predictor of levels of happiness. Neurotic people are not just prone to negative feelings: they also tend to have low emotional intelligence, which makes them bad at forming or managing relationships, and that in turn makes them unhappy.

Whereas neuroticism tends to make for gloomy types, extroversion does the opposite. Those who like working in teams and who relish parties tend to be happier than those who shut their office doors in the daytime and hole up at home in the evenings. This personality trait may help explain some cross-cultural differences: a study comparing similar groups of British, Chinese and Japanese people found that the British were, on average, both more extrovert and happier than the Chinese and Japanese.

Then there is the role of circumstance. All sorts of things in people's lives, such as relationships, education, income and health, shape the way they feel. Being married gives people a considerable uplift, but not as big as the gloom that springs from being unemployed. In America, being black used to be associated with lower levels of happiness—though the most recent figures suggest that being black or Hispanic is nowadays associated with greater happiness. People with children in the house are less happy than those without. More educated people are happier, but that effect disappears once income is controlled for. Education, in other words, seems to make people happy because it makes them richer. And richer people are happier than poor ones—though just how much is a source of argument.

The View from Winter

Lastly, there is age. Ask a bunch of 30-year-olds and another of 70-year-olds (as Peter Ubel, of the Sanford School of Public Policy at Duke University, did with two colleagues, Heather Lacey and Dylan Smith, in 2006) which group they think is likely to be happier, and both lots point to the 30-year-olds. Ask them to rate their own well-being, and the 70-year-olds are the happier bunch. The academics quoted lyrics written by Pete Townshend of The Who when he was 20: "Things they do look awful cold / Hope I die before I get old." They pointed out that Mr Townshend, having passed his 60th birthday, was writing a blog that glowed with good humour.

Mr Townshend may have thought of himself as a youthful radical, but this view is ancient and conventional. The "seven ages of man"—the dominant image of the life-course in the 16th and 17th centuries—was almost invariably conceived as a rise in stature and contentedness to middle age, followed by a sharp decline towards the grave. Inverting the rise and fall is a recent idea. "A few of us noticed the U-bend in the early 1990s,"

says Andrew Oswald, professor of economics at Warwick Business School. "We ran a conference about it, but nobody came."

Since then, interest in the U-bend has been growing. Its effect on happiness is significant—about half as much, from the nadir of middle age to the elderly peak, as that of unemployment. It appears all over the world. David Blanchflower, professor of economics at Dartmouth College, and Mr Oswald looked at the figures for 72 countries. The nadir varies among countries—Ukrainians, at the top of the range, are at their most miserable at 62, and Swiss, at the bottom, at 35—but in the great majority of countries people are at their unhappiest in their 40s and early 50s. The global average is 46.

The U-bend shows up in studies not just of global well-being but also of hedonic or emotional well-being. One paper, published this year by Arthur Stone, Joseph Schwartz and Joan Broderick of Stony Brook University, and Angus Deaton of Princeton, breaks well-being down into positive and negative feelings and looks at how the experience of those emotions varies through life. Enjoyment and happiness dip in middle age, then pick up; stress rises during the early 20s, then falls sharply; worry peaks in middle age, and falls sharply thereafter; anger declines throughout life; sadness rises slightly in middle age, and falls thereafter.

Turn the question upside down, and the pattern still appears. When the British Labour Force Survey asks people whether they are depressed, the U-bend becomes an arc, peaking at 46.

Happier, No Matter What

There is always a possibility that variations are the result not of changes during the life-course, but of differences between cohorts. A 70-year-old European may feel different to a 30-year-old not because he is older, but because he grew up during the second world war and was thus formed by different experiences. But the accumulation of data undermines the idea of a cohort effect. Americans and Zimbabweans have not been formed by similar experiences, yet the U-bend appears in both their countries. And if a cohort effect were responsible, the U-bend would not show up consistently in 40 years' worth of data.

Another possible explanation is that unhappy people die early. It is hard to establish whether that is true or not; but, given that death in middle age is fairly rare, it would explain only a little of the phenomenon. Perhaps the U-bend is merely an expression of the effect of external circumstances. After all, common factors affect people at different stages of the life-cycle. People in their 40s, for instance, often have teenage children. Could the misery of the middle-aged be the consequence of sharing space with angry adolescents? And older people tend to be richer. Could their relative contentment be the result of their piles of cash?

The answer, it turns out, is no: control for cash, employment status and children, and the U-bend is still there. So the growing happiness that follows middle-aged misery must be the result not of external circumstances but of internal changes.

People, studies show, behave differently at different ages. Older people have fewer rows and come up with better solutions to conflict. They are better at controlling their emotions, better at accepting misfortune and less prone to anger. In one study, for instance, subjects were asked to listen to recordings of people supposedly saying disparaging things about them. Older and younger people were similarly saddened, but older people less angry and less inclined to pass judgment, taking the view, as one put it, that "you can't please all the people all the time."

There are various theories as to why this might be so. Laura Carstensen, professor of psychology at Stanford University, talks of "the uniquely human ability to recognise our own mortality and monitor our own time horizons." Because the old know they are closer to death, she argues, they grow better at living for the present. They come to focus on things that matter now—such as feelings—and less on long-term goals. "When young people look at older people, they think how terrifying it must be to be nearing the end of your life. But older people know what matters most." For instance, she says, "young people will go to cocktail parties because they might meet somebody who will be useful to them in the future, even though nobody I know actually likes going to cocktail parties."

Death of Ambition, Birth of Acceptance

There are other possible explanations. Maybe the sight of contemporaries keeling over infuses survivors with a determination to make the most of their remaining years. Maybe people come to accept their strengths and weaknesses, give up hoping to become chief executive or have a picture shown in the Royal Academy, and learn to be satisfied as assistant branch manager, with their watercolour on display at the church fete. "Being an old maid", says one of the characters in a story by Edna Ferber, an (unmarried) American novelist, was "like death by drowning—a really delightful sensation when you ceased struggling." Perhaps acceptance of ageing itself is a source of relief. "How pleasant is the day," observed William James, an American philosopher, "when we give up striving to be young—or slender."

Whatever the causes of the U-bend, it has consequences beyond the emotional. Happiness doesn't just make people happy—it also makes them healthier. John Weinman, professor of psychiatry at King's College London, monitored the stress levels of a group of volunteers and then inflicted small wounds on them. The wounds of the least stressed healed twice as fast as those of the most stressed. At Carnegie Mellon University in Pittsburgh, Sheldon Cohen infected people with cold and flu viruses. He found that happier types were less likely to catch the virus, and showed fewer symptoms of illness when they did. So although old people tend to be less healthy than younger ones, their cheerfulness may help counteract their crumbliness.

Happier people are more productive, too. Mr Oswald and two colleagues, Eugenio Proto and Daniel Sgroi, cheered up a bunch of volunteers by showing them a funny film, then set them mental tests and compared their performance to groups that had seen a neutral film, or no film at all. The ones who had seen the funny film performed 12% better. This leads to two conclusions. First, if you are going to volunteer for a study, choose the economists' experiment rather than the psychologists' or psychiatrists'. Second, the cheerfulness of the old should help counteract their loss of productivity through declining cognitive skills—a point worth remembering as the world works out how to deal with an ageing workforce.

The ageing of the rich world is normally seen as a burden on the economy and a problem to be solved. The U-bend argues for a more positive view of the matter. The greyer the world gets, the brighter it becomes—a prospect which should be especially encouraging to *Economist* readers (average age 47).

Critical Thinking

1. How did the stress level in people affect how they responded to wounds and health problems?

2. Why are older people believed to be better at living for the present?

3. What are the human emotions that rise or dip in the middle years?

A Practical Guide to Better Health

We Can Control How We Age

What does it take to age successfully—to maintain both a sound body and mind? A landmark Harvard study has followed individuals from their teens into their 80s.

Lou Ann Walker

How do some people age so successfully? Many of us assume it takes genes or dumb luck. So here's the surprise. Arguably the longest and most comprehensive study of human development ever undertaken is just revealing its final results: *We are very much in control of our own aging.* The secret to a long and happy life, it seems, does not lie as much in our stars as in ourselves.

The Study of Adult Development at Harvard Medical School comprises three projects begun in the 1920s, '30s, and '40s. These careful scientific studies analyze three very different demographic groups: one of Harvard men (the Grant Study), another of inner-city Boston men and the third of gifted California women. In all, 824 men and women have been followed from their teens into their 80s. Over the decades, these people were given psychological tests and asked to evaluate their lives and feelings. They responded to numerous questionnaires, interviews by psychiatrists and physical examinations by doctors.

The study is a medical rarity because it examines the lives of the well, not the sick. "Old age is like a minefield," the study's director, Dr. George E. Vaillant, told PARADE. "If you see footprints leading to the other side, step in them." These results show a clear path that Baby Boomers and Gen X-ers can follow to lead a long, happy life.

The study divides individuals between 60 and 80 years old into two main groups: (1) the "Happy-Well," those who are physically healthy and find life satisfying; and (2) the "Sad-Sick," those with various ailments who do not seem to enjoy life. And it analyzes those who died during the course of the study (the "Prematurely Dead").

It's *Not* in Our Genes . . .

A major finding was that good genes did not account for better aging. Nor did income. Good care obviously is important, said

---

Living with a Full Heart

The Harvard study found these four attributes vital to successful aging:

- Orientation toward the Future. The ability to anticipate, to plan and to hope.
- Gratitude, Forgiveness and Optimism. We need to see the glass as half-full, not half-empty.
- Empathy. The ability to imagine the world as it seems to the other person.
- The Ability to Reach Out. "We should want to do things *with* people, not do things *to* people or ruminate that they do things to us," says Dr. George E. Vaillant. In other words, we need to "leave the screen door unlatched."

Dr. Vaillant, "but the trick is not going to the hospital in the first place."

The study disputes the assumption that with aging comes decay. When 30- and 55-year-old brains are compared, the older one is better developed. Advancing age impairs some motor skills, but maturation can make people sharper at emotional tasks.

. . . but in Ourselves

Many of the study's findings focus on psychological health. As we age, we should try to develop more mature coping styles, Vaillant concluded from the results. "Our defenses are always more mature when we are not hungry, angry, lonely, tired or drunk," he noted.

Seven Keys to Aging Well
What Are the Secrets to a Long, Happy Life?

Dr. George E. Vaillant points out seven major factors that, at 50, predict what life's outcome will be at 80:

1 Not smoking or quitting early: Those who quit the habit before 50 were, at 70, as healthy as those who had never smoked. And heavy smoking was 10 times more prevalent among the Prematurely Dead than among the Happy-Well. "Smoking," said Vaillant, "is probably the most significant factor in terms of health."

Coping with Life's Stresses
Those who learn early how to roll with the punches are much happier in their later years, despite real problems.

2 The ability to take life's ups and downs in stride: If you can make lemonade out of lemons, then you have an adaptive coping style, also known as "mature defenses." Mature defenses don't actually ensure good health at an older age. But a person will suffer less from life's real problems if he or she has the ability to roll with the punches. "Life ain't easy," Vaillant said. "Terrible things happen to everyone. You have to keep your sense of humor, give something of yourself to others, make friends who are younger than you, learn new things and have fun."

An Active Lifestyle
The long-term results of regular exercise are both physical and psychological well-being.

3 Absence of alcohol abuse: "Abusing alcohol destroys both your physical and mental health," Vaillant noted. (He added that a partner's alcoholism can destroy a marriage, which also may have an impact on how one ages.)

4 Healthy weight: Obesity is a risk factor for poor health in later life.

A Strong Marriage
A good marriage contributes to a long and happy life. The study also found that, overall, marriages improved with time—if people were willing to work out the bumps.

5 A solid marriage: This is important for both physical and psychological health. Happy-Well people were six times more likely to be in good marriages than were the Sad-Sick.

6 Physical activity: The study specified that the Happy-Well usually did "some exercise." The benefits of fitness also extended to mental health.

Continuing Education
The more years of school people have, the more they tend to age successfully.

7 Years of education: Vaillant speculated that people to whom "self-care and perseverance" are important are also more likely to continue their educations. These individuals, he surmised, are able to take the long view. "People seek education because they believe it is possible to control the course of their lives," he said. In the study, people with less education also were more likely to be obese. Their physical health at age 65 was close to that of the more-educated group at 75.

People who had four or more of these seven factors at age 50 were one-third less likely to be dead by 80. People who had three or fewer of these factors at 50—even though they were in good physical shape—were three times as likely to die during the following 30 years.

"Taking people inside oneself" emotionally is important, he said, adding, "Popular people can be extraordinarily lonely and depressed. The paradox is that they starve, yet there's plenty of food." He pointed to the example of Marilyn Monroe, who made Arthur Miller and others feel cared for yet was unable to feel that love within herself.

Although developmental psychologists often say that personality is formed by age 5, the study found otherwise. By 70, it's how we nurture ourselves throughout our lifetimes that takes precedence over nature. Interestingly, Vaillant discovered that many people who aged well unconsciously reinterpreted early events in their lives in a more positive light as they grew older. Those who clung to negative events were less happy adults. Forever blaming parents for a rotten childhood seems to impede maturity.

"What goes *right* in childhood predicts the future far better than what goes wrong," he noted. Especially important was a feeling of acceptance.

As one ages, remaining connected to life is crucial—as is learning the rules of a changing world. On the other hand, Vaillant said, "One task of living out the last half of life is excavating and recovering those whom we loved in the first half. The recovery of lost loves becomes an important way in which the past affects the present."

The study's results will be published by Little, Brown in January in a book titled *Aging Well: Surprising Guideposts to a Happier Life from the Landmark Harvard Study of Adult Development.* In addition to facts and figures, the book is filled with life stories of the men and women studied.

Vaillant, who has been called "a big, handsome, humorous psychiatrist," looks a decade younger than his 67 years. He and his wife of 30 years, Caroline, live in Vermont. In addition to his research, he maintains a small clinical practice at Boston's Brigham and Women's Hospital. He calls himself an "oppositional character" who loves "proving other people wrong."

I asked Vaillant what he hopes the results of this study will accomplish. "A heightened appreciation of the positive," he shot back. Then he added: "Worry less about cholesterol and more about gratitude and forgiveness."

Critical Thinking

1. What did Dr. George Vaillant believe was the most significant factor in terms of a person's health?

2. What contribution did a good marriage make to a person's health?

3. What were the seven factors that Dr. Vaillant believed contributed to a person's ability to live to age 80 and beyond?

From *Parade*, September 16, 2001, pp. 4–5. Copyright © 2001 by Lou Ann Walker. Reprinted by permission of the author.

The Myths of Living Longer

At the end of an exhaustive study, it was discovered that many of the mantras you hear (Eat your vegetables! Get married! Relax!) are good for you in lots of ways but don't ensure a longer life.

HOWARD S. FRIEDMAN, PhD AND LESLIE R. MARTIN, PhD

In 1921, two precocious children named Patricia and John were pulled out of their San Francisco classrooms by Lewis Terman, a Stanford University psychologist who was interested in discovering the sources of intellectual leadership.

Eighty years later, both Patricia and John were still alive and in good health—at age 91. What was their secret? As health scientists, we've spent the past 20 years following up with all of Terman's 1,500 subjects—whose lives were tracked for eight decades as they grew up and had kids and grandkids—to discover why some of them thrived well into old age while others did not.

We looked at not only how long each participant lived, but also how they died. We studied a range of other factors—from schools to jobs to personality type—to see which traits predicted longevity. Turns out that some of the things you think you know about longevity simply aren't true.

Myth #1: Marriage Guarantees a Longer Life

That's not necessarily true. Scientific studies show it's not married people who live longer but married men. The bulk of the evidence shows little, if any, advantage for married women. With men, the key risk appears to be divorce, which can disrupt vital ties to family members and friends for years to come. In the Terman study, steadily married men were likely to live to age 70 and beyond, but fewer than a third of the divorced men reached old age. Divorce not only harms men directly but also sets in motion other unhealthy behaviors. Steadily married women in the Terman study lived somewhat longer than women who divorced and then remarried. But women who divorced and never remarried did just fine—in fact, they usually lived long lives.

Myth #2: Taking It Easy Adds Years to Your Life

Relaxation and an early retirement do not ensure long-lasting health.

Terman study subjects with the most career success were the least likely to die young. In fact, on average, the most successful men lived five years longer than the least successful. Ambition, perseverance, impulse control, and high motivation contributed to a resilient work life, and that led to more years overall. Usually, increased responsibility brings more challenges and a heavier workload, but this paradoxically correlates with long-term health.

Findings were especially dramatic among the oldest participants. Continually productive men and women lived much longer than their more laid-back comrades. A sustained work life mattered a great deal more than even their sense of happiness. So think carefully before retiring. Giving up an interesting, demanding job to live in a golf community away from your friends could actually increase the risk to your health.

Myth #3: You Can Worry Yourself to Death

Actually, the opposite is true: Terman's study clearly revealed that the best predictor of longevity in children was conscientiousness—being prudent, well organized, even somewhat obsessive. The same was true later in life. Adults who were thrifty, persistent, detail-oriented, and responsible lived the longest. Patricia, for example, "planned her work in detail" and had "definite purposes." (And dependable doesn't have to mean dull: Many of the most conscientious Terman subjects led exciting lives.)

One of the most obvious explanations is that conscientious people do more to protect their health—for example, wearing seat belts or following doctors' orders—and engage in fewer risky activities, like smoking, drinking to excess, abusing drugs, or driving too fast. They are not necessarily risk-averse, but they tend to be sensible in evaluating how far to push the envelope. Having this trait leads people into happier marriages, better friendships, and healthier work situations. That's right: Conscientious people create long-life pathways for themselves. And you aren't locked into—or out of—this trait. One Terman subject who lived to an old age scored very low in conscientiousness as a youngster. As an adult, he found a job he liked and had a very solid marriage. He became conscientious—and reaped the rewards.

Myth #4: More Degrees Mean More Years

Not so fast. We got some big surprises when we studied the effect of education on life span. During the era when Terman participants were children, it was common for parents to enroll their kids in school early and let them skip grades. But we found that when children entered first grade at age 5, not age 6, they often did not live as long. No single thing explained the higher risk, but because relating to classmates is so important, an early start may have launched some kids down erratic paths.

As for higher education, we found that level of schooling by itself was not a very important predictor of longevity. The-better-educated did tend to be healthier and live a little longer—but much more relevant than how many years of advanced formal education a person received were productivity and persistence in the face of challenges.

Myth #5: Friendly, Outgoing People Thrive

This widely held assumption is flawed. Americans tend to view extroversion as desirable—we worry if our children are shy. But our research indicates that sociable children did not, for the most part, live any longer than their more introverted classmates.

John is a good example: A shy child who tried to avoid playing in large groups, he preferred chess and checkers to tag or charades. He later became a physicist and was healthy into his 90s.

Why doesn't sociability necessarily set one on a path to long life? After all, outgoing children grow up to have better social relations, and that's normally a sign of good health, right? In the study, children like John tended to move into stable jobs, have long-lasting marriages, and work in a responsible manner.

Highly sociable people, in contrast, may be leaders in their businesses because of their enthusiasm and charm—but they're also more likely to go along with social pressures to drink or smoke. A "people person" may often join in the dangers of the moment—and that affects longevity.

Similarly, we often hear that optimism is the secret to a healthy life. But the data suggest that cheerful, optimistic children were actually less likely to live to an old age than their more staid, sober counterparts. Cheerfulness was comparable to high blood pressure and high cholesterol as a risk factor for early death. Happiness and good health often go hand in hand—but that doesn't mean happiness is the direct cause of good health. We found that it is usually some other set of characteristics that makes someone both happier and healthier. And optimism has a serious downside: No-worry folks may underestimate or ignore real threats and thereby fail to take precautions or follow medical advice.

Myth #6: Jocks Outlive Nerds

Regular physical exercise is good for your heart, no question. But if you're athletic when young, then gradually become—and stay—sedentary in your middle years, you lose any longevity benefit. Being active in middle age is the key. And exercise doesn't have to be intense, like running long distances every day, to be effective. John, the shy scientist, loved to ski. Linda, another Terman subject who lived a long life, made time for dancing, tennis, and gardening. The important thing is to find activities that suit you and stick with them over the long haul.

Critical Thinking

1. How does marriage affect longevity of men in comparison to women?

2. How was being retired, as compared to continuing to work and being productive, likely to affect longevity?

3. What personal characteristics did the authors believe lead to happier marriages, better friendships, and healthier work situations?

4. What are the critical factors about exercise and activity that cause them to increase a person's longevity?

UNIT 3

Societal Attitudes toward Old Age

Unit Selections

11. **Society Fears the Aging Process,** Mary Pipher
12. **We Need to Fight Age Bias,** Jack Gross
13. **Friendships, Family Relationships Get Better with Age Thanks to Forgiveness, Stereotypes,** Amy Patterson Neubert
14. **The Under-Reported Impact of Age Discrimination and Its Threat to Business Vitality,** Robert J. Grossman

Learning Outcomes

After reading this Unit, you will be able to:

• Explain why younger adults often avoid spending time around older persons.

• Describe how the media stereotypes the image of older persons.

• Discuss the different decisions that were made by the lower courts and the Supreme Court in the Jack Gross age discrimination in employment case.

• Explain how the Supreme Court's ruling in the Jack Gross case, that age had to be the exclusive factor in the business decision rather than just a motivating factor for age discrimination to have occurred, made it more difficult for demoted older workers to win their cases in court.

• Explain why older adults are inclined to be less confrontational in dealing with others with whom they interact.

• Explain why older adults report better interpersonal relationships than younger age groups.

• Explain how the Age Discrimination in Employment Act passed in 1965 did or did not end the age discrimination policies in the business community for persons from 40 to 65.

• Explain how the Age Discrimination in Employment Act passed in 1965 did or did not end mandatory retirement policies in the business community.

Student Website

www.mhhe.com/cls

Internet References

Adult Development and Aging: Division 20 of the American Psychological Association
www.iog.wayne.edu/APADIV20/APADIV20.HTM
American Society on Aging
www.asaging.org/index.cfm
Canadian Psychological Association
www.cpa.ca

There are a wide range of beliefs regarding the social position and status of the aged in American society today. Some people believe that the best way to understand the problems of the elderly is to regard them as a minority group, faced with difficulties similar to those of other minority groups. Discrimination against older people, like racial discrimination, is believed to be based on a bias against visible physical traits. Because the aging process is viewed negatively, it is natural that the elderly try to appear and act younger. Some spend a tremendous amount of money trying to make themselves look and feel younger.

The theory that old people are a weak minority group is questionable because too many circumstances prove otherwise. The U.S. Congress, for example, favors its senior members and delegates power to them by bestowing considerable prestige. The leadership roles in most religious organizations are held by older persons. Many older Americans are in good health, have comfortable incomes, and are treated with respect by friends and associates.

Perhaps the most realistic way to view the aged is as a status group, like other status groups in society. Every society has some method of "age grading," by which it groups together individuals of roughly similar age. ("Preteens" and "senior citizens" are some of the age-grade labels in American society.) Because it is a labeling process, age grading causes members of the age group, to be perceived, by themselves as well as other, in terms of the connotations of the label. Unfortunately, the tag "old age" often has negative connotations in American society. The readings included in this section illustrate the wide range of stereotypical attitudes toward older Americans. Many of society's typical assumptions about the limitations of old age have been refuted. A major force behind this reassessment of the elderly is that there are so many people living longer and healthier lives, and in consequence, playing more of a role in all aspects of our society. Older people can remain productive members of society for many more years than has been traditionally assumed.

Such standard stereotypes of the elderly as frail, senile, childish, and sexually inactive are topics discussed in this section.

© Jose Luis Pelaez, Inc/Getty Images

Mary Pipher, in "Society Fears the Aging Process," contends that young people often avoid interacting with older persons because it reminds them that someday they too will get old and die. She further argues that the media most often portrays a negative and stereotypical view of the elderly.

In "We Need to Fight Age Bias," Jack Gross was a man who had been demoted from his job to a lower position because of his age and sued the company for age discrimination. The court decisions up through the Supreme Court are presented. In "Friendships, Family Relationships Get Better with Age Thanks to Forgiveness, Stereotypes," the author points out why older people view their interpersonal relationships in more positive terms. Robert J. Grossman, in "The Under-Reported Impact of Age Discrimination and Its Threat to Business Vitality," believes that the legal system is slanted toward the employers who perpetuate many of the negative stereotypes and views of older workers. He sees age discrimination in the workplace as a more serious problem in the future, when labor shortages will make older workers and their skills more critical and in demand.

Society Fears the Aging Process

Americans fear the processes of aging and dying, Mary Pipher contends in the following viewpoint. She claims that younger and healthier adults often avoid spending time around the aging because they want to avoid the issues of mortality and loss of independence. In addition, she contends that negative views of the aging process are portrayed in the media and expressed through the use of pejorative words to describe the elderly. Pipher is a psychologist and author of several books, including *Another Country: Navigating the Emotional Terrain of Our Elders,* the book from which this viewpoint was excerpted.

MARY PIPHER

We segregate the old for many reasons—prejudice, ignorance, a lack of good alternatives, and a youth-worshiping culture without guidelines on how to care for the old. The old are different from us, and that makes us nervous. Xenophobia means fear of people from another country. In America we are xenophobic toward our old people.

How Greeting Cards Reflect Culture

An anthropologist could learn about us by examining our greeting cards. As with all aspects of popular culture, greeting cards both mirror and shape our realities. Cards reflect what we feel about people in different roles, and they also teach us what to feel. I visited my favorite local drugstore and took a look.

There are really two sets of cards that relate to aging. One is the grandparent/grandchild set that is all about connection. Even a very dim-witted anthropologist would sense the love and respect that exist between these two generations in our culture. Young children's cards to their grandparents say, "I wish I could hop on your lap," or, "You're so much fun." Grandparents' cards to children are filled with pride and love.

There is another section of cards on birthdays. These compare human aging to wine aging, or point out compensations. "With age comes wisdom, of course that doesn't make up for what you lose." We joke the most about that which makes us anxious. "Have you picked out your bench at the mall yet?" There are jokes about hearing loss, incontinence, and losing sexual abilities and interest. There are cards on saggy behinds, gray hair, and wrinkles, and cards about preferring chocolate or sleep to sex. "You know you're getting old when someone asks if you're getting enough and you think about sleep."

Fears of Aging and Dying

Poking fun at aging isn't all bad. It's better to laugh than to cry, especially at what cannot be prevented. However, these jokes reflect our fears about aging in a youth-oriented culture. We younger, healthier people sometimes avoid the old to avoid our own fears of aging. If we aren't around dying people, we don't have to think about dying.

We baby boomers have been a futureless generation, raised in the eternal present of TV and advertising. We have allowed ourselves to be persuaded by ads that teach that if we take good care of ourselves, we will stay healthy. Sick people, hospitals, and funerals destroy our illusions of invulnerability. They force us to think of the future.

Carolyn Heilbrun said, "It is only past the meridian of fifty that one can believe that the universal sentence of death applies to oneself." Before that time, if we are healthy, we are likely to be in deep denial about death, to feel as if we have plenty of time, that we have an endless vista ahead. But in hospitals and at funerals, we remember that we all will die in the last act. And we don't necessarily appreciate being reminded.

When I first visited rest homes, I had to force myself to stay. What made me most upset was the thought of myself in a place like that. I didn't want to go there, literally or figuratively. Recently I sat in an eye doctor's office surrounded by old people with white canes. Being in this room gave me intimations of mortality. I thought of Bob Dylan's line: "It's not dark yet, but it's getting there."

We know the old-old will die soon. The more we care and the more involved we are with the old, the more pain we feel at their suffering. Death is easier to bear in the abstract, far away and clinical. It's much harder to watch someone we love fade before our eyes. It's hard to visit an uncle in a rest home and realize he no longer knows who we are or even who he is. It's hard to see a grandmother in pain or drugged up on morphine. Sometimes it's so hard that we stay away from the people who need us the most.

Our culture reinforces our individual fears. To call something old is to insult, as in *old hat* or *old ideas*. To call something young is to compliment, as in *young thinking* or *young acting*. It's considered rude even to ask an old person's age. When we meet an adult we haven't seen in a long time, we compliment her by saying, "You haven't aged at all." The taboos against acknowledging age tell us that aging is shameful.

Many of the people I interviewed were uncomfortable talking about age and were unhappy to be labeled old. They said, "I don't feel old." What they meant was, "I don't act and feel like the person who the stereotypes suggest I am." Also, they were trying to avoid being put in a socially undesirable class. In this country, it is unpleasant to be called old, just as it is unpleasant to be called fat or poor. The old naturally try to avoid being identified with an unappreciated group. . . .

The Elderly Are Treated Poorly

Nothing in our culture guides us in a positive way toward the old. Our media, music, and advertising industries all glorify the young. Stereotypes suggest that older people keep younger people from fun, work, and excitement. They take time (valuable time) and patience (in very short supply in the 1990s). We are very body-oriented, and old bodies fail. We are appearance-oriented, and youthful attractiveness fades. We are not taught that old spirits often shimmer with beauty.

Language is a problem. Old people are referred to in pejorative terms, such as *biddy, codger,* or *geezer,* or with cutesy words, such as *oldster, chronologically challenged,* or *senior citizen.* People describe themselves as "eighty years young." Even *retirement* is an ugly word that implies passivity, uselessness, and withdrawal from the social and working world. Many of the old are offended by ageist stereotypes and jokes. Some internalize these beliefs and feel badly about themselves. They stay with their own kind in order to avoid the harsh appraisals of the young.

Some people do not have good manners with the old. I've seen the elderly bossed around, treated like children or simpletons, and simply ignored. Once in a cafe, I heard a woman order her mother to take a pill and saw the mother wince in embarrassment. My mother-in-law says she sees young people but they don't see her. Her age makes her invisible.

In our culture the old are held to an odd standard. They are admired for not being a bother, for being chronically cheerful. They are expected to be interested in others, bland in their opinions, optimistic, and emotionally generous. But the young certainly don't hold themselves to these standards.

Accidents that old drivers have are blamed on age. After a ninety-year-old friend had his first car accident, he was terrified

that he would lose his license. "If I w[...]
would be perceived as just one of th[...]
"But because I am old, it will be at[...]
course, some old people are bad d[...]
people. To say "He did that because he[...]
as to say, "He did that because he's black" [...]
people burn countertops with hot pans, forget ap[...]
write overdrafts on their checking accounts. But w[...]
do these same things, they experience double jeopardy.[...]
mistakes are not viewed as accidents but rather as loss of fu[...]
tioning. Such mistakes have implications for their freedom.

Media Stereotypes

As in so many other areas, the media hurts rather than helps with our social misunderstandings. George Gerbner reported on the curious absence of media images of people older than sixty-five. Every once in a while a romantic movie plot might involve an older man, but almost never an older woman. In general, the old have been cast as silly, stubborn, and eccentric. He also found that on children's programs, older women bear a disproportionate burden of negative characteristics. In our culture, the old get lumped together into a few stereotyped images: the sweet old lady, the lecherous old man, or the irascible but soft-hearted grandfather. Almost no ads and billboards feature the old. Every now and then an ad will show a grandparent figure, but then the grandparent is invariably youthful and healthy.

In *Fountain of Age,* Betty Friedan noted that the old are portrayed as sexless, demented, incontinent, toothless, and childish. Old women are portrayed as sentimental, naive, and silly gossips, and as troublemakers. A common movie plot is the portrayal of the old trying to be young—showing them on motorbikes, talking hip or dirty, or liking rock and roll. Of course there are exceptions, such as *Nobody's Fool, On Golden Pond, Mr. and Mrs. Bridge, Driving Miss Daisy, Mrs. Brown,* and *Twilight.* But we need more movies in which old people are portrayed in all their diversity and complexity.

The media is only part of much larger cultural problems. We aren't organized to accommodate this developmental stage. For example, being old-old costs a lot of money. Assisted-living housing, medical care, and all the other services the old need are expensive. And yet, most old people can't earn money. It's true that some of our elders are wealthy, but many live on small incomes. Visiting the old, I heard tragic stories involving money. I met Arlene, who, while dying of cancer, had to fear losing her house because of high property taxes. I met Shirley, who lived on noodles and white rice so that she could buy food for her cat and small gifts for her grandchildren. I met people who had to choose between pills and food or heat.

The American Obsession with Independence

Another thing that makes old age a difficult stage to navigate is our American belief that adults need no one. We think of independence as the ideal state for adults. We associate independence

...es and cultural icons such as the Marlboro man and the ... Slims woman, and we associate dependence with toxic ...es, enmeshment, and weakness. To our post-modern, ...ated ears, a psychologically healthy but dependent adult ...nds oxymoronic.

We all learn when we are very young to make our own personal declarations of independence. In our culture, *adult* means "self-sufficient." Autonomy is our highest virtue. We want relationships that have no strings attached instead of understanding, as one lady told me, "Honey, life ain't nothing but strings."

These American ideas about independence hurt families with teens. Just when children most need guidance from parents, they turn away from them and toward peers and media. They are socialized to believe that to be an adult, they must break away from parents. Our ideas about independence also hurt families with aging relatives. As people move from the young-old stage into the old-old stage, they need more help. Yet in our culture we provide almost no graceful ways for adults to ask for help. We make it almost impossible to be dependent yet dignified, respected, and in control.

As people age, they may need help with everything from their finances to their driving. They may need help getting out of bed, feeding themselves, and bathing. Many would rather pay strangers, do without help, or even die than be dependent on those they love. They don't want to be a burden, the greatest of American crimes. The old-old often feel ashamed of what is a natural stage of the life cycle. In fact, the greatest challenge for many elders is learning to accept vulnerability and to ask for help.

If we view life as a time line, we realize that all of us are sometimes more and sometimes less dependent on others. At certain stages we are caretakers, and at other stages we are cared for. Neither stage is superior to the other. Neither implies pathology or weakness. Both are just the results of life having seasons and circumstances. In fact, good mental health is not a matter of being dependent or independent, but of being able to accept the stage one is in with grace and dignity. It's an awareness of being, over the course of one's lifetime, continually interdependent.

Rethinking Dependency

In our culture the old fear their deaths will go badly, slowly, and painfully, and will cost lots of money. Nobody wants to die alone, yet nobody wants to put their families through too much stress. Families are uneasy as they negotiate this rocky terrain. The trick for the younger members is to help without feeling trapped and overwhelmed. The trick for older members is to accept help while preserving dignity and control. Caregivers can say, "You have nurtured us, why wouldn't we want to nurture you?" The old must learn to say, "I am grateful for your help and I am still a person worthy of respect."

As our times and circumstances change, we need new language. We need the elderly to become elders. We need a word for the neediness of the old-old, a word with less negative connotations than *dependency,* a word that connotes wisdom, connection, and dignity. *Dependency* could become mutuality or *interdependency.* We can say to the old: "You need us now, but we needed you and we will need our children. We need each other."

However, the issues are much larger than simply which words to use or social skills to employ. We need to completely rethink our ideas about caring for the elderly. Like the Lakota, we need to see it as an honor and an opportunity to learn. It is our chance to repay our parents for the love they gave us, and it is our last chance to become grown-ups. We help them to help ourselves.

We need to make the old understand that they can be helped without being infantilized, that the help comes from respect and gratitude rather than from pity or a sense of obligation. In our society of disposables and planned obsolescence, the old are phased out. Usually they fade away graciously. They want to be kind and strong, and, in America, they learn that to do so means they should ask little of others and not bother young people.

Perhaps we need to help them redefine kindness and courage. For the old, to be kind ought to mean welcoming younger relatives' help, and to be brave ought to mean accepting the dependency that old-old age will bring. We can reassure the old that by showing their children how to cope, they will teach them and their children how well this last stage can be managed. This information is not peripheral but rather something everyone will need to know.

Further Readings

Henry J. Aaron and Robert D. Reischauer. *Countdown to Reform: The Great Social Security Debate.* New York: Century Foundation Press, 2001.

Claude Amarnick. *Don't Put Me in a Nursing Home.* Deerfield Beach, FL: Garrett, 1996.

Dean Baker and Mark Weisbrot. *Social Security: The Phony Crisis.* Chicago: University of Chicago Press, 1999.

Margret M. Baltes. *The Many Faces of Dependency in Old Age.* Cambridge, England: Cambridge University Press, 1996.

Sam Beard. *Restoring Hope in America: The Social Security Solution.* San Francisco: Institute for Contemporary Studies, 1996.

Robert H. Binstock, Leighton E. Cluff, and Otto von Mering, eds. *The Future of Long-Term Care: Social and Policy Issues.* Baltimore: Johns Hopkins University Press, 1996.

Robert H. Binstock and Linda K. George, eds. *Handbook of Aging and the Social Sciences.* San Diego: Academic Press, 1996.

Jimmy Carter. *The Virtues of Aging.* New York: Ballantine, 1998.

Marshall N. Carter and William G. Shipman. *Promises to Keep: Saving Social Security's Dream.* Washington, DC: Regnery, 1996.

Martin Cetron and Owen Davies. *Cheating Death: The Promise and the Future Impact of Trying to Live Forever.* New York: St. Martin's Press, 1998.

William C. Cockerham. *This Aging Society.* Upper Saddle River, NJ: Prentice-Hall, 1997.

Peter A. Diamond, David C. Lindeman, and Howard Young, eds. *Social Security: What Role for the Future?* Washington, DC: National Academy of Social Insurance, 1996.

Ursula Adler Falk and Gerhard Falk. *Ageism, the Aged and Aging in America: On Being Old in an Alienated Society.* Springfield, IL: Charles C. Thomas, 1997.

Peter J. Ferrara and Michael Tanner. *A New Deal for Social Security.* Washington, DC: Cato Institute, 1998.

Arthur D. Fisk and Wendy A. Rogers, eds. *Handbook of Human Factors and the Older Adult.* San Diego: Academic Press, 1997.

Muriel R. Gillick. *Lifelines: Living Longer: Growing Frail, Taking Heart.* New York: W. W. Norton, 2000.

Margaret Morganroth Gullette. *Declining to Decline: Cultural Combat and the Politics of the Midlife.* Charlottesville: University Press of Virginia, 1997.

Charles B. Inlander and Michael A. Donio. *Medicare Made Easy.* Allentown, PA: People's Medical Society, 1999.

Donald H. Kausler and Barry C. Kausler. *The Graying of America: An Encyclopedia of Aging, Health, Mind, and Behavior.* Urbana: University of Illinois Press, 2001.

Eric R. Kingson and James H. Schulz, eds. *Social Security in the Twenty-First Century.* New York: Oxford University Press, 1997.

Thelma J. Lofquist. *Frail Elders and the Wounded Caregiver.* Portland, OR: Binford and Mort, 2001.

Joseph L. Matthews. *Social Security, Medicare, and Pensions.* Berkeley, CA: Nolo, 1999.

E. J. Myers. *Let's Get Rid of Social Security: How Americans Can Take Charge of Their Own Future.* Amherst, NY: Prometheus Books, 1996.

Evelyn M. O'Reilly. *Decoding the Cultural Stereotypes About Aging: New Perspectives on Aging Talk and Aging Issues.* New York: Garland, 1997.

S. Jay Olshansky and Bruce A. Carnes. *The Quest for Immortality: Science at the Frontiers of Aging.* New York: W. W. Norton, 2001.

Fred C. Pampel. *Aging, Social Inequality, and Public Policy.* Thousand Oaks, CA: Pine Forge Press, 1998.

Peter G. Peterson. *Gray Dawn: How the Coming Age Wave Will Transform America—And the World.* New York: Times Books, 1999.

Peter G. Peterson. *Will America Grow Up Before It Grows Old?: How the Coming Social Security Crisis Threatens You, Your Family, and Your Country.* New York: Random House, 1996.

John W. Rowe and Robert L. Kahn. *Successful Aging.* New York: Pantheon Books, 1998.

Sylvester J. Schieber and John B. Shoven. *The Real Deal: The History and Future of Social Security.* New Haven, CT: Yale University Press, 1999.

Ken Skala. *American Guidance for Seniors—And Their Caregivers.* Falls Church, VA: K. Skala, 1996.

Max J. Skidmore. *Social Security and Its Enemies: The Case for America's Most Efficient Insurance Program.* Boulder, CO: Westview Press, 1999.

Richard D. Thau and Jay S. Heflin, eds. *Generations Apart: Xers vs. Boomers vs. the Elderly.* Amherst, NY: Prometheus Books, 1997.

Dale Van Atta. *Trust Betrayed: Inside the AARP.* Washington, Regnery, 1998.

James W. Walters, ed. *Choosing Who's to Live: Ethics and Aging.* Urbana: University of Illinois Press, 1996.

David A. Wise, ed. *Facing the Age Wave.* Stanford, CA: Hoover Institutional Press, Stanford University, 1997.

Periodicals

W. Andrew Achenbaum. "Perceptions of Aging in America," *National Forum,* Spring 1998. Available from the Honor Society of Phi Kappa Phi, Box 16000, Louisiana State University, Baton Rouge, LA 70893.

America. "Keep an Eye on the Third Age," May 16, 1998.

Robert Butler. "The Longevity Revolution," *UNESCO Courier,* January 1999.

Issues and Controversies on File. "Age Discrimination," May 21, 1999. Available from Facts on File News Services, 11 Penn Plaza, New York, NY 10001-2006.

Margot Jefferys. "A New Way of Seeing Old Age Is Needed," *World Health,* September/October 1996.

Ann Monroe. "Getting Rid of the Gray: Will Age Discrimination Be the Downfall of Downsizing?" *Mother Jones,* July/August 1996.

Bernadette Puijalon and Jacqueline Trincaz. "Sage or Spoilsport?" *UNESCO Courier,* January 1999.

Jody Robinson. "The Baby Boomers' Final Revolt," *Wall Street Journal,* July 31, 1998.

Dan Seligman. "The Case for Age Discrimination," *Forbes,* December 13, 1999.

Ruth Simon. "Too Damn Old," *Money,* July 1996.

John C. Weicher. "Life in a Gray America," *American Outlook,* Fall 1998. Available from 5395 Emerson Way, Indianapolis, IN 46226.

Ron Winslow. "The Age of Man," *Wall Street Journal,* October 18, 1999.

Critical Thinking

1. Why is it that many older persons do not want to be labeled "old"?

2. Why is it that television most often casts young people as the leading characters in their shows?

3. Why is being independent and self-sufficient in American society problematic for older persons?

We Need to Fight Age Bias

Congress should act where the courts failed.

JACK GROSS

I never, never imagined when I was demoted seven years ago and then filed an age discrimination suit that I would end up in the U.S. Supreme Court, that I would testify before five congressional committees, or that my name would become associated with the future of age discrimination laws in our country. I do believe, however, that it happened for a reason.

This all began in January 2003. When my employer, Farm Bureau Financial Group (FBL) in Iowa, merged with the Kansas Farm Bureau, the company apparently wanted to purge claims employees who were over age 50. All the Kansas claims employees over 50 with a certain number of years of employment were offered a buyout, which most accepted. In Iowa, virtually every claims supervisor over 50 was demoted.

Being 54, I was included in that sweep, despite 13 consecutive years of top performance reviews. The company claimed this was not discrimination but simply a reorganization. In 2005, a federal jury spent a week hearing testimony and seeing the evidence. The jurors agreed with me, and determined that age was a motivating factor in my demotion. Since then, the case has taken on a life of its own, including an appeal to the 8th Circuit Court and a U.S. Supreme Court hearing and decision.

Since the Age Discrimination in Employment Act was passed in 1967, courts had ruled consistently that the law protected individuals if their age was a factor in any employment decision. But in my case, the Supreme Court unexpectedly changed course and ruled that age had to be the exclusive reason for my demotion, even though that wasn't the question before them. They simply hijacked my case and used it as a vehicle to water down the workplace discrimination laws passed by Congress.

This new and much higher standard of proof is clearly inconsistent with the intent of the ADEA and four decades of precedent, and will affect millions of workers. A new trial was ordered and is scheduled for November, nearly eight years after my demotion.

I did not pursue this case just for myself. From my observation, discrimination victims are usually the most vulnerable among us, those who simply cannot fight back. Thanks to my attorneys, who believed in me, my case, and now our cause, I was able to take a stand against my unjust and unlawful treatment. Many of my friends are also farm or small-town "kids" who feel like they are the forgotten minority. Many have been forcibly retired or laid off. Some have been looking for work for months, only to find doors closed when they reveal the year they graduated. Others are working as janitors despite good careers and college degrees. They all know that age discrimination is very real and pervasive.

We now look to Congress to pass the Protecting Older Workers Against Discrimination Act (H.R. 3721), to provide the same protection for older people as protection given to people of color, women or people of different faiths.

While this ordeal has been stressful, observing all levels of our judicial and congressional processes "up close and personal" has been a real education. My faith in our judicial system was shattered by the Supreme Court's errant 5–4 decision. I believe Congress, as representatives of we, the people, will rectify it. You can help by contacting your own senators and representatives to encourage their support.

I am sincerely grateful for the assistance of people and groups truly dedicated to ending workplace discrimination of any kind in our great nation.

Critical Thinking

1. How did the Supreme Court's decision in the Jack Gross age discrimination case change the rules that determined if the employers had violated the Age Discrimination in Employment Act of 1967?
2. What bill now before Congress would give older workers the same protection as are given to people of color, women, or people of different faiths?
3. Does Jack Gross believe that the U.S. Congress will pass the new Protecting Older Workers Against Discrimination Act (H.R. 3721) which would re-establish the previous rules for judging age discrimination in employment which were established in 1967?

JACK GROSS was aided by AARP in the U.S. Supreme Court's precedent-setting age discrimination case.

Friendships, Family Relationships Get Better with Age Thanks to Forgiveness, Stereotypes

AMY PATTERSON NEUBERT

Part of what makes those relationships so golden during the golden years is that people of all ages are more likely to forgive and respect one's elders, according to research from Purdue University.

"Older adults report better marriages, more supportive friendships and less conflict with children and siblings," said Karen Fingerman, the Berner-Hanley Professor in Gerontology, Developmental and Family Studies. "While physical and cognitive abilities decline with age, relationships improve. So what is so special about old age? We found that the perception of limited time, willingness to forgive, aging stereotypes and attitudes of respect all play a part. But it's more than just about how younger people treat an older person, it's about how people interact."

Fingerman and Susan T. Charles, an associate professor of psychology and social behavior at the University of California in Irvine, published their research in this month's *Current Directions in Psychological Science*.

This article is based on their earlier work, including research showing that older adults are less confrontational than younger adults when they are upset. The article also builds on studies published in 2009 in the *Journal of Gerontology: Psychological Sciences* and in 2008 in the journal *Psychology and Aging*.

One study compared young adults, ages 22–35, and older adults, ages 65–77, by asking the participants to respond to several stories about personal interactions. The study participants heard stories about how an adult committed a social transgression, such as rudeness towards a waitress or ignoring property boundaries. Half the subjects read the story with the offending character portrayed as an older adult and the other half read the same story, but the offending character was portrayed as a younger adult. When the offending character was elderly, participants of all ages indicated that the person who was offended would avoid conflict and not react, but the opposite was found if the offending character was younger. When participants read a story in which a young adult committed a social faux pas, they thought other characters should confront that person and tell them they were upset.

These assumptions play out in daily interactions that Fingerman compares to a dance.

"Each person is acting and reacting in response to his or her partner, and, in this case, each partner is anticipating the next person's move, and that determination is often based on age," she said. "People vary their behavior with social partners depending on their age. When there is a negative interaction, younger people are generally more aggressive and confrontational than older people are. But younger people often are more accommodating to older people when there is a negative interaction."

For example, an older adult may be more cordial because of the assumption that a younger person may be confrontational. At the same time, the younger adult may conform to age stereotypes that indicate they should be more patient with an older person or they may hold stereotypes that older adults cannot change and do not attempt to change this person.

"Also, with age, people get better at regulating their emotions when something upsets them," Fingerman said. "The other advantage is that older people often have more opportunity to select who they want to associate with because they are retired and do not go to work."

Other reasons for better treatment of older adults reflect care, concern and cherishing the moment. No matter the age, people are going to be more pleasant if they perceive that there is little time left in a relationship, Fingerman said. That applies not just to people who are elderly, but even young people who may not see each other because of life changes such as moving out of state or serving in the military. When time is limited, people want to make the most of their remaining interactions and enjoy the other person rather than spending time fighting.

"We've also seen this in studies when adult daughters don't want to confront their elderly mothers or discuss negative things with them because they feel there is little time left with them," Fingerman said.

Fingerman plans to study how the "need to respect one's elders" plays a role in other cultures. Her work is supported by the Department of Child Development and Family Studies.

Critical Thinking

1. Are younger people generally more or less aggressive in dealing with the negative reactions of other people with whom they interact?

2. In general do older persons' relationships with others improve or decline with age?

3. How does the perception that there is little time left in a relationship affect the quality of the interaction between people?

The Under-Reported Impact of Age Discrimination and Its Threat to Business Vitality

The Age Discrimination in Employment Act (ADEA, 29 USCA, 621) is credited with helping eliminate many blatant forms of age discrimination in employment. For example, before the ADEA was enacted 37 years ago, it was common for employment ads to list age limitations, indicating people over 40 need not apply. Across the board, mandatory retirement policies went unchallenged. Despite advancements in these areas since the founding of the Age Discrimination in Employment Act, it remains to be seen whether the ADEA has completed the job it set out to do. Has it proven to be an effective tool for eliminating the unreasonable prejudices that make it difficult for older workers to achieve their full potential? Has it provided adequate compensation for victims of discrimination? The following article takes a snapshot of the current work environment to gain a perspective. Based on extensive interviews with academics, employment lawyers, advocates for older workers, and older workers themselves, it reveals the need for reforms. It finds that, in a legal environment slanted toward employers, older workers continue to face bias and stereotyping, that most victims of discrimination are not made whole, and that society's lack of concern for this type of discrimination may prove more costly in the future as employers look more to older workers to fill projected workforce gaps.

ROBERT J. GROSSMAN

1. The ADEA: An Introduction

Thirty-seven years ago, Congress passed the Age Discrimination in Employment Act (ADEA) which makes it illegal for an employer or union to discharge, refuse to hire, or otherwise discriminate on the basis of age. Looking back, it is easy to forget the overt discrimination faced by older workers at the time. It was common for employment ads prior to 1967 to list age limitations, indicating people over 40 need not apply. Mandatory retirement policies, applicable to almost everyone but Supreme Court Justices, went unchallenged. Although some states had antidiscrimination laws on the books, they were not enforced, giving employers a free hand to discriminate. But now, almost four decades later, it bears asking whether the ADEA has done more than address age discrimination in its most blatant manifestations. Is it really effective in preventing age bias? Has it been successful in "alleviating serious economic and psychological suffering of persons between the ages of 40 and 65 caused by unreasonable prejudice?" (Polstorff v. Fletcher [1978, ND Ala] 452 F Supp 17). What role has it played in transforming the U.S. culture to be more accepting and appreciative of older workers?

2. Stereotypes Survive

Despite protestations to the contrary, there seems to be little indication that attitudes have changed significantly since the enactment of the ADEA. The notion that older people have had their day and should make room for the next generation continues to be deeply ingrained. "We think maybe it's okay because it's an economic issue, not a civil rights issue," says Laurie McCann, Senior Attorney for AARP in Washington, D.C. "Until we view it as just as wrong and serious, we may not be making the inroads we need to address the intractable, subtle discrimination that is so pervasive. I don't think employers want to discriminate; they don't hate older workers. It's the stereotypes. They may not even know they harbor these biases, but they do" (McCann, 2003).

Such attitudes are evident in the case of Ann Klingert, a 64-year-old resident of the Bronx, who recalled with astonishment the public response to an article in a local New York City newspaper regarding an EEOC lawsuit she had filed. Klingert filed with the EEOC after she was fired by Woolworths and then prohibited from applying for newly created part-time jobs which were filled mostly by student applicants. "When the lawsuit was reported in a local New York City newspaper, *Our Town,* people were outraged," she said. "They wrote letters to the editor saying things like 'why don't you just retire and just take your social security and go away'" (Klingert, 2003).

Although most employers are sensitive to the issues of sexism and racism, "the idea that you cannot teach an old dog new tricks does not seem to carry the same taboo status in society and the workplace," says Todd Maurer, Associate Professor of Industrial-Organization Psychology at the Georgia Institute of Technology. Maurer says that generalizing is dangerous in the range of older workers; perhaps even more so than in other categories. "One size does not fit all," he says. "There can be older individuals who are both interested and able when it comes to learning. Research has found large differences within older groups in things like training performance and in abilities like memory and reaction time" (Maurer, 2003). However, too often, as in the case of Maryland resident Mort Beres, employers are influenced more by stereotypes than skills or experience. When Beres, then in his late 50s, lost his job, the prior owner of small businesses and successful salesman in the auto parts manufacturing industry knew he had skills that should have been in demand, yet he was turned away repeatedly. Any offers he did receive were salaried at much less than he had earned previously, and the positions were often demeaning in nature. Beres held on as long as he could, but admitted that, out of desperation, he took some sketchy jobs. "You take every jerky job you can get just to have some income; some of them make you nauseous" (Beres, 2003).

Eventually, Beres found his niche, working as a trainer and sales rep for Irvine, California-based BDS Marketing. Assigned to the Canon account at a Best Buy in Maryland, his job was to help store personnel sell Canon printers, for which he was paid a salary plus commission. After 5 years on the job, working with a series of regional supervisors, at age 67, Beres achieved a noteworthy record by helping his store become one of the top five in the territory. However, when a new supervisor took over, Beres's star began to fall. "He'd call me and make stupid comments about my age, like 'you're too old, I think it's time for a change.'" Finally, Beres got the axe. When he asked why he had been fired, the manager told him, "I'm not telling you and I don't have to." Beres recalls hanging up and thinking about what had happened. "I got angry; really angry. It was a little, unimportant job, but they had no right

Table 1 Workers Over Age 45 Reporting Presence of Age Discrimination ($n=1500$)

Do not know	2%
No	31%
Yes	67%

Source: AARP Work and Careers Study Summary (2002).

to treat me that way." *(BDS Marketing's Vice President for Human Resources, Jeffrey Sopko, refused to comment specifically but denied Beres's version of what happened and claimed that there were other reasons for Beres's dismissal.)*

Beres's plight is not uncommon, yet society appears to be less outraged at age bias than other types of discrimination. "It seems more politically correct to discriminate against older people," says Mindy Farber, Managing Partner at Farber Taylor, LLC in Rockville, Maryland. Farber recalls hiring a new associate for the firm who was in her mid-fifties. "It was shocking. I was surprised how open people were about talking about the wisdom of my decision in light of her age. If I had hired an African American, they would have been silent. Here they told me straight out that I had made a mistake" (Farber, 2003).

3. Perspective: How Older Workers See It

From their perspectives, older workers see little evidence that they are competing on a level playing field. Sixty-seven percent of employed workers aged 45 to 74 surveyed by AARP in 2003's *Staying Ahead of the Curve* said that age discrimination is a fact of life in the workplace (AARP, 2003) (Table 1). This percentage is even higher among African Americans and Hispanics, both at 72%. Age is viewed as so critical to employees that respondents listed it, along with education, as more important in how workers are treated than are gender, race, sexual orientation or religion. Sixty percent said they believe that older workers are the first to go when employers make cuts.

A 2002 Conference Board survey of 1,600 workers aged 50 and older found that 31 percent of workers intending to retire within five years said they would stay on if given more responsibilities. Twenty-five percent said they were leaving because they were being held back or marginalized because of their age (The Conference Board, 2002). Linda Barrington, Labor Economist at The Conference Board, says the high percentage of dissatisfied workers is cause for concern. "It's twice as big as I might have expected," she says. Perceptions, of course, are not necessarily reality, but Barrington says that does not matter.

"Perceptions affect the way you work; if you're feeling undervalued, that discouragement will affect your work. Is it perception or reality? Either way, it has to be dealt with" (Barrington, 2003).

It also bears noting that far fewer of the respondents said they have suffered personally from ageism. About 9% say they believe they have been passed up for a promotion because of their age, 6% said they were fired or laid off because of age, 5% said they were passed up for a raise because of age, and 15% attributed their not being hired for a job to their age. However, the survey only queried current workers and did not include individuals in the same age category who were no longer in the workforce.

4. Advantage: Employers

Compared to its sister statutes aimed at race, religion, gender, and disability, the ADEA offers less protection. Court interpretations have proven to be less rigorous and more employer-friendly, ceding to employers the right to make bonafide business decisions even when age is linked. In practice, instead of preventing discrimination, the law serves as a roadmap for employers, enabling all but the obtuse to avoid liability and shield all but the most egregious ageist actions from public scrutiny.

Under the ADEA, if there is a valid reason for an action, it is considered acceptable if age happens to be an accompanying factor. "If you can show you would have done it anyway, you're off the hook," says Harlan Miller, an employment attorney with Miller, Billips, and Ates (Miller et al., 2003) in Atlanta, Georgia. As a result, it is almost impossible to catch a crafty employer discriminating. "I can always get around it if I'm smart. Only idiots get nailed," agrees David Neumark, a nationally recognized expert on the ADEA and Senior Fellow at the Public Policy Institute of California in San Francisco (Neumark, 2003).

Employers are not infallible, however, and they still mess up on occasion. Often when they do, it is because of retaliation: reacting badly to an employee whose initial complaint does not rise above the threshold set by the ADEA. "We tell them to go back and complain about their treatment," says James Rubin, an employment attorney with Farber Taylor. "Then the employer does something really bad. It's not the original claim; it's the reprisal. You can bring an action based on the reprisal even if the original claim is weak" (Rubin, 2003).

Employers also get caught when the rationale for their business decision falls apart. "Typically, the employer comes in with some kind of bogus selection process that says they're trying to keep the most competent," Miller says. "Gulfstream Aerospace's decision to cut from 200 to 230 of its nearly 2000 management-level employees during the period from August through December, 2000, is a case in point. Gulfstream had a rating device based on flexibility and adaptability; code words for old or young . . . and not subject to any kind of objective analysis. Our analysis showed a complete correlation between age and those factors" (Miller et al., 2003).

On the other hand, if it is legitimate, an employer's business argument can carry the day. "Is it discrimination to fire someone if it is based on economic foundations?" asks Bob Smith, Professor of Labor Economics, ILR at Cornell University in Ithaca, New York. "It's not a slam dunk that they've been mistreated just because they say they are. There may be good reasons why they're singled out. They often are paid too much and have shorter time to work, making them a poorer investment. Why should I expect my employer to invest more in me than someone who will be there longer? Just because they complain, doesn't mean there's discrimination" (Smith, 2003).

5. Avoiding Scrutiny

Employers' incentives to avoid litigation are compelling from financial and public relations perspectives. Generally, when employers get wind that employees are disgruntled and plan to complain or sue, they move to settle by enticing them into retirement with incentives and buyouts, awarded contingent upon their agreeing to confidentiality clauses that prevent discussion of the situation.

The Older Worker Protection Act clarified for employers what they need to say and do when they reach termination agreements with workers. The act requires an employer to give workers 21 days to consider a buyout proposal, to advise them of their right to seek legal counsel, and even to rescind the agreement 10 days after the fact if they have a change of heart. Until recently, a properly negotiated settlement would foreclose a former employee from further litigation. Now, there has been at least one case where the EEOC has been able to sue on behalf of workers who previously signed releases.

In a typical settlement, the employer denies discrimination, attributing the settlement to "business decisions." In a recent survey by Jury Verdict Research, plaintiffs' lawyers estimated that 84% of their clients' claims were settled, while defense lawyers reported 79% (Jury Verdict Research, 2002).

Often, employees are relieved to accept the face-saving exit. In reality, their options are meager. They are scared if they are still working or owed pensions, and lack money if they have been terminated. According to Howard Eglit,

Professor of Law at Chicago-Kent College, it costs, on average, about $50,000 for a lawyer if cases go beyond early negotiations with an employer. Most attorneys will not handle such cases on a contingent basis because they know the chances of winning are slim. Employers, on average, can count on spending $100,000 in legal fees from the time a complaint is filed with the EEOC until trial (Eglit, 2003).

Although the amounts paid to ease workers into retirement or silence complaints are private, high-profile EEOC settlements reveal just how well workers actually do when they press the ADEA to the limit. In March, 2003, the EEOC announced a class action settlement with Gulfstream Aerospace, owned by General Dynamics, on behalf of 66 workers for $2.1 million dollars, an average of approximately $33,000 for each manager the EEOC claimed had been wrongfully terminated. Ninety-three percent, many of whom may never work again full-time, accepted the deal and faded away, careers in shambles.

As meager as the settlement proved to be, there would not have been a case without former Gulfstream Aerospace manager Eddie Cosper of Rincon, Georgia. His role suggests that, behind every major class action, there is an activist who serves as a catalyst in pushing for remediation.

When Gulfstream Aerospace cut more than 200 of its nearly 2000 management employees, most of whom worked in Savannah, it had not bargained on Cosper's pride and persistence. Aged 54 and with the company for 28 years, Eddie Cosper was proud, professional, and still moving up. "I was still ambitious. Every time I put out a fire, I kept getting a promotion," he recalls. However, Cosper reached a dead-end when General Dynamics took over the company in 1999. His seasoning suddenly turned sour. "The VP would tell me, 'You're like father time; you've been here forever. Wouldn't you like to retire and do something different?'" Soon Cosper found himself reassigned to nights, with responsibility for 40 people instead of the 300 he usually had. Then, 30 days later, he was terminated. "My performance reviews were all above average," he says. "I had the highest ranking of all the four managers in my category." How did he feel when his career went up in smoke? "It's like a burning sensation in your gut. You say, why me? I put my whole life into something and it's been taken away for no reason. In the beginning, I felt sorry for myself, then I got angry. I did the numbers and realized I wasn't the only older person being targeted. So I started talking to others and built a network and database." Communication was key. "People who don't have that network have no clue," he says. "Every Joe Blow could get hit cold and not know what's happening. Probably half the people in our suit were along for the ride. If I hadn't reached them, they

wouldn't have realized they were discriminated against and would have gotten nothing."

The EEOC's settlement with Footlocker is another example of a remedy that fell short of the mark. When the company settled with 764 former Woolworth employees, the complainants, mostly low-paid hourly workers, walked off with an average of $4,000 per person. Overall, the $3.4 million was a small price to pay for a 40,000-worker retailing giant like Footlocker (EEOC, 2002). A tougher question is why they let the matter fester as long as they did. Many companies buy themselves out of trouble, right or wrong (Eglit, 2003). According to Jury Verdict Research, the median settlement for age cases from 1994 to 2000 was $65,000, $5,000 higher than the median reported for all types of discrimination, age included (Jury Verdict Research, 2002).

6. Complaints Grow

If age discrimination had been decreasing throughout the years, even allowing for more people being aware of their right to complain and more older workers proving their mettle to those who question their ability, it would be reasonable to expect the number of complaints to be trending down. Instead, there are more cases. The EEOC logged 19,921 age discrimination complaints in 2002, an increase of 14.5% from the previous year and accounting for 23.6% of all discrimination claims filed with the agency (U.S. Equal Employment Opportunity Commission, ADEA Charges, 2003).

Some EEOC complainants, either uncertain as to the true basis of the discrimination against them or believing there is more than one basis, file multiple charges. EEOC data reveals that instances of ADEA claimants who alleged an additional type of discrimination are declining. The data suggests there is no move on the part of complainants making their case on some other basis of discrimination (gender, race, religion, or national origin) to add age simply in order to bolster the case, even though it was not thought to be the primary or even substantial basis of the discrimination. For the 3-year period of 1997 to 1999, an average of 17.9% of ADEA claimants made an additional charge. From 2000 to 2003, the average percentage dropped to 15.8%. In addition, states Farber, private lawyers are seeing similar increases in age complaints in proportion to race, gender, and disability (Farber, 2003).

7. Profile

Overall, the majority of claimants tend to be white males, 55 and older at the middle management level. However,

Table 2   Age Bias Charge Filings with EEOC Nationwide by Age Group of Charging Parties Fiscal Years 1999–2002[a]

Fiscal year/age	Age 40–49	Age 50–59	Age 60–69
1999	3367	5949	3526
2000	3941	6620	4609
2001	3779	7584	4603
2002	4219	8455	5686

Source: EEOC, Office of Communications and Legislative Affairs (2003).

[a]Note. The three age ranges combined do not comprise the total ADEA charge filings with the EEOC per year, as a small number of charges which are not listed are filed by individuals 70 and older.

the number of women filing claims has doubled in the last few years, a trend that Eglit estimates will continue as women earn more, hold more desirable jobs, and can afford to hire counsel. "The ADEA offers two essential remedies: reinstatement and back pay. If you weren't getting much and your job wasn't worth much, why sue? Now, even with the glass ceiling, women have good jobs and can afford to hire an attorney and sue" (Eglit, 2003) (Table 2).

In 2002, 53% of the cases related to job loss; wrongful discharge, 8,741 and involuntary layoff, 1,463. "They're easier to prove," Eglit says. "If you've been working at a place for 20 years, look around and see five other people fired, you have a case" (Eglit, 2003). It happened in the Woolworth's/Footlocker case, says Michelle LeMoal-Grey, EEOC attorney. "When they were fired, workers spoke by phone and began to see a pattern forming in their store and beyond" (LeMoal-Grey, 2003).

Of the EEOC claimants between ages 40 and 69, 46% were in their fifties, 31% in their 60s and 23% in their 40s. About 25% of claims were based on failure to hire, an increase of 200% since 1999. As these cases are harder to prove and because damages are limited, it is difficult to find a private attorney for hire without having to pay upfront. "If you're not hired, how do you know what the reason was? It's not so easy to figure it out," Eglit observes (Eglit, 2003).

About 12% of the claimants cited harassment; antagonism, or intimidation, creating a hostile work environment; an increase of 31.5% since 1999. Constructive discharge would be an example, says Dorothy Stubblebine, an expert witness for both plaintiffs and defendants, and President of DJS Associates in Mantua, New Jersey. "Tyically, the older person is pushed out by giving him a really hard time. He's given the worst assignments 'til he can't take it any more" (Stubblebine, 2003) (Table 3).

8. Chances for Success

Whatever the claim and whomever the claimant, few gamblers would bet on the probability of prevailing in an ADEA suit. EEOC data reveals that for most claimants, the filing with the EEOC is a dead-end. Last year, of the cases before it, the agency found "reasonable cause" only 4.3% of the time, "no reasonable cause" 52% of the time, and closed cases for "administrative" reasons 33.5% of the time. Only 6.5% of cases were eventually settled. In contrast, for claimants charging all types of discrimination, age included, the EEOC found reasonable cause 7.2% of the time, found no reasonable cause 59.3% of the time, and closed cases for administrative reasons 26% of the time (U.S. Equal Employment Opportunity Commission, 2003) (Table 4 and Table 5).

For plaintiffs who win at trial, damages are legally limited to reinstatement, loss of pay, or, where there is a finding of willful discrimination, double the lost salary. In contrast, race and gender plaintiffs have the opportunity to be awarded more lucrative punitive damages. "Why shouldn't someone who's old be compensated for pain and suffering just like someone who's fired for their religion, race, or gender?" Miller asks. "There's nothing worse than, after 30 years' service, to be fired at 58" (Miller et al., 2003).

The solution for many attorneys is to bypass the ADEA and, where possible, sue under local or state statutes. "Everybody tries to stay out of Federal Court," Farber says. "Plaintiffs get their audience but they lose before they can get to a jury. It's so bad that a fellow attorney once told me that if I went to Federal Court when there were other options available, I would be guilty of malpractice." Farber says a plaintiff's chances to reach a jury brighten considerably in state or local courts. Virtually everyone on a jury can identify with the plight of an older worker. "Everybody on the jury is getting older and has a mother and father" (Farber, 2003).

If they get to a state or federal jury, Jury Verdict Research in its study, *Employment Practice Liability: Jury Award Trends and Statistics,* reports a 78% success rate overall for age cases in 2000. In Federal District Courts, from 1994 to 2000, the median verdict was $269,350, tops for all types of discrimination. However, the chances of plaintiffs getting there with the EEOC in their corner are limited. The Office of General counsel states that during the 5-year period from 1997 to 2001, the EEOC filed 205 lawsuits based on the ADEA, leaving plaintiffs who push ahead with claims the EEOC determines are without merit with the risk and expense of proceeding toward litigation on their own (Office of General Counsel, 2002). Jury Verdict Research indicates that the median verdict for more numerous privately initiated state cases was about the same (Jury Verdict Research, 2002).

Table 3   Age Discrimination Charge Filings with EEOC Nationwide Fiscal Years 1998–2002

Year[a]	FY 1998	FY 1999	FY 2000	FY 2001	FY 2002
Discharge	7054	6733	6851	7376	8741
Harassment	1871	1758	1966	2146	2311
Hiring	1953	1647	1990	3116	4889
Layoff	1036	1149	1128	1107	1810
Promotion	1547	1590	1666	1623	1463
Terms of Employment	2510	2357	2610	3440	3181
TOTAL	15,191	14,141	16,008	17,405	19,921

Source: EEOC, Office of Communications and Legislative Affairs (2003).
[a] Fiscal years run from October 1 through September 30.

Table 4   EEOC Resolution of ADEA Claims Fiscal Years 1998–2002

	FY 1998	FY 1999	FY 2000	FY 2001	FY 2002
Total ADEA Claims	15,191	14,141	16,008	17,405	19,921
Settlements (%)	4.7	5.3	7.9	6.6	6.5
Withdrawals with benefits (%)	3.6	3.7	3.8	3.6	3.6
Administrative closures (%)	26.1	23.3	22.0	26.1	33.5
No reasonable cause (%)	61.7	59.4	58.0	55.3	52.1
Reasonable cause (%)	3.9	8.3	8.2	8.2	4.3

Source: EEOC, Office of Research, Information, and Planning (2003).

Table 5   EEOC Resolution of all Discrimination Claims Fiscal Years 1998–2002

	FY 1998	FY 1999	FY 2000	FY 2001	FY 2002
Total Claims	79,591	77,444	79,896	80,840	84,442
Settlements (%)	4.6	6.2	8.5	8.1	8.8
Withdrawals with benefits (%)	3.2	3.7	4.0	4.1	4.0
Administrative closures (%)	26.7	24.1	20.5	20.7	20.6
No reasonable cause (%)	60.9	59.5	58.3	57.2	59.3
Reasonable cause (%)	4.6	6.6	8.8	9.9	7.2

Source: EEOC, Office of Research, Information, and Planning (2003).

9. Justification

Critics point out that there may be valid reasons for determining that older workers are less desirable employees. There is no question that technological changes have significantly altered the way we work, especially in white-collar jobs, explains Camille Olson, Chair of the Labor and Employment Practice Group, Seyfeith Shaw, in Chicago, Illinois. "Persons in their 20s and 30s who are comfortable with technology are more responsive and more adaptable to change. Can people in their 40s and 50s without this background feel that they belong in the workplace? You feel that time has passed you by. Does that affect your motivation, your ability to do things? It does" (Olson, 2003).

"A lot of people who think they've been screwed over have it wrong," agrees AARP's McCann. "Though I'm an advocate, I'd be the first to admit that when someone gets fired or doesn't get promoted, they yell foul. An age discrimination claim is the last resort for older white males. "If you're a 55 year old male who's lost your $70,000 job, what do you do? The odds of finding any job, let alone a comparable job, are slim, so you fight" (McCann, 2003).

"If a person has lost a step or two and doesn't project or have the kind of energy to move forward, the fact that he isn't promoted may show that's where he belongs," explains Ed King, Executive Director of the National Senior Citizen Law Center, a former EEOC mediator in Hawaii. "The question is whether the employer is stereotyping or it is legitimate" (King, 2003).

It is undeniable that age has its advantages; plusses that advocates for older workers tend to downplay. "They do better; get paid more. Their employment rates are high and they get cared for in retirement," Neumark observes. However, he says, it is not all roses and caviar for workers in their 50s or 60s. Once they are unemployed, it is hard for them to find work. They are out of work longer, have difficulty finding jobs with comparable responsibilities and wages, and tend to become disheartened and "retire" (Neumark, 2003).

Adding to the debate is the difference of opinion as to whether age 40, which seemed appropriate in the 1960s, should still be the turning point for providing a person with ADEA coverage. Some experts ask, Why not? There needs to be some beginning point, and 40 is reasonable. Others disagree, arguing that 45 or 50 are more realistic ages when discriminatory treatment is most likely to occur. Whatever the threshold, it has been clear until recently that all people from 40 on up had to be treated similarly, but no longer.

In an opinion issued February 24, 2004, on General Dynamics Land Systems versus Cline, the U.S. Supreme Court held that the ADEA does not prevent an employer from favoring older employees over younger employees. The court upheld an agreement between General Dynamics and the United Auto Workers union that provided for continued retirement health benefits for employees then over 50 years of age but eliminated that benefit for all other employees. The plaintiffs were between the ages of 40 and 50, and were denied the benefits available only to workers over the age of 50.

10. No Special Treatment

Should an employer invest extra to help support an older worker? Offer more and different training? Provide less stressful assignments? The issue, Olson says, is whether under the ADEA an employer needs to take affirmative efforts to assist individuals who do not naturally have the same skills, while at the same time paying them more. Clearly, Olson says, the law never contemplated affirmative action. The law is there only to make sure older people are not treated differently (Olson, 2003).

"The ADEA is about equal treatment, not about preferential treatment," agrees Lynn Clemens, Attorney, Office of Legal Counsel at EEOC. "There are no affirmative obligations on the employer's part. That notion goes against the act." Regardless, advocates are making the

case that there are other benefits to be gained by retaining older workers anyway, although they are paid more and have fewer skills. Olson says she does not buy it unless there is a compelling business case. "The issue is whether you need to invest in targeted training, making older workers more productive because you need them to stick around" (Olson, 2003).

11. Call for Action

Meanwhile, William Rothwell, Professor of Workforce Education and Development at Penn State University observes that Bureau of Labor Statistics projections show that while 13 percent of American workers today are 55 and older, that figure will increase to 20% by the year 2015. At the same time, the nation is expected to experience a drop in the percentage of younger workers aged 25 to 44.

With this information in mind, Rothwell says the current economic slump is the calm before the storm. When the economy turns around and there is more demand for products and services, the worker shortage will be the number one issue. "Employers in the U.S. will be forced to go back to their retiree base and deploy it more effectively than ever before. If we can't get labor from anywhere else, we'll look to the most obvious population who knows everything about our business" (Rothwell, 2003).

Unless we get serious about addressing the stereotypes and focus on reducing the alienation that older workers feel, these workers, as well as retirees, may be unreceptive and unprepared to step up when the market finally swings in their favor. Reforming the ADEA is the first step. To better combat age discrimination, we must move quickly to put more teeth into the law. If we do not, when we go to the well, it may just be dry.

References

AARP. (2003). *Staying ahead of the curve.*

Barrington, L. (2003 April 10). Telephone interview. New York, NY.

Beres M. (2003 April 22). Telephone interview. Rockville, MD.

EEOC Press Release. (2002 November 15). *EEOC settles major age bias suit; Foot Locker to pay $3.5 million to former Woolworth employees.*

Eglit, H. (2003 April 10). Telephone interview. Chicago, IL.

Farber, M. (2003 April 21). Telephone interview. Rockville, MD.

Jury Verdict Research. (2002). *Employment practice liability verdicts and settlements: Jury award trends and statistics.*

King, E. (2003 April 15). Telephone interview. Washington, D.C.

Klingert, A. (2003 May 1). Telephone interview. Bronx, NY.

LeMoal-Grey, M. (2003 April 28). Telephone interview. New York, NY.

Maurer, T. (2003 April 17). Telephone interview. Atlanta, GA.

McCann, L. (2003 April 17). Telephone interview. Washington, D.C.

Miller, Harlan, Principal, Miller, Billips & Ates. (2003). Atlanta, GA. (18 April).

Neumark, D. (2003 April 8). Telephone interview. San Francisco, CA.

Office of General Counsel. (2002, August 13). The U.S. Equal Employment Opportunity Commission. *Study of the litigation program fiscal years 1997–2001,* Table 2.

Olson, C. (2003 April 10). Telephone interview. Chicago, IL.

Rothwell, W. (2003 April 17). Telephone interview. University Park, PA.

Rubin, J. (2003 April 21). Telephone interview. Rockville, MD.

Smith, B. (2003 April 17). Telephone interview. Ithaca, NY.

Stubblebine, D. (2003 April 4). Telephone interview. Mantua, NJ.

The Age Discrimination in Employment Act of 1967. (1967). Pub. L. 90–202, as amended. Volume 29 of the United States Code beginning at section 621.

The Conference Board. (2002). *Voices of experience: Mature workers in the future workplace.*

United States Supreme Court. (2004, February 24). *General Dynamics Land Systems v. Cline,* No. 02–1080.

U.S. Equal Employment Opportunity Commission. (2003). *Age discrimination in employment act charges,* FY 1992-FY 2002.

Critical Thinking

1. Did most older workers surveyed by AARP in 2002 believe that age discrimination in the workplace was no longer a problem?

2. Of age, gender, race, sexual orientation, or religion, which is seen as the factor that resulted in most discrimination and unfair treatment in the workplace?

3. What changes in the age composition of the American population will force employees to retain older workers in forthcoming years?

UNIT 4

Problems and Potentials of Aging

Unit Selections

Learning Outcomes

After reading this Unit, you will be able to:

- Cite the risk factors that are most likely to cause a person to have a heart attack.

- List the six steps a person could take to appreciably reduce the chance of ever having a heart attack.

- Distinguish the difference between embryonic stem cells and adult stem cells in terms of their origins and availability.

- Explain why adult stem cells are more frequently used and acceptable in treating a host of diseases and health problems than embryonic stem cells.

- Cite the reason why some older persons might be reluctant to turn over their finances and property to their children.

- Explain why many elderly persons who have been abused financially by their children don't take their claims to court.

- Discuss the advantages that both the European and American studies found for persons age 50 and older who started and maintained a regular exercise program.

- Compare the advantage of a moderate exercise program over a light exercise program in terms of the death rates of the participants.

Student Website
www.mhhe.com/cls

Internet References

AARP Health Information
    www.aarp.org/bulletin
Alzheimer's Association
    www.alz.org
A.P.T.A. Section on Geriatrics
    http://geriatricspt.org
Caregiver's Handbook
    www.acsu.buffalo.edu/~ drstall/hndbk0.html
Caregiver Survival Resources
    www.caregiver.com
International Food Information Council
    www.ific.org
University of California at Irvine: Institute for Brain Aging and Dementia
    www.alz.uci.edu

Viewed as part of the life cycle, aging might be considered a period of decline, poor health, increasing dependence, social isolation, and—ultimately—death. It often means retirement, decreased income, chronic health problems, and death of a spouse. In contrast, the first 50 years of life are seen as a period of growth and development.

For a young child, life centers around the home, and then the neighborhood. Later, the community and state become a part of the young person's environment. Finally, as an adult, the person is prepared to consider national and international issues—wars, alliances, changing economic cycles, and world problems. During the later years, however, life space narrows. Retirement may distance the individual from national and international concerns, although he or she may remain actively involved in community affairs. Later, even community involvement may decrease, and the person may begin to stay close to home and the neighborhood. For some, the final years of life may once again focus on the confines of home, be it an apartment or a nursing home.

Many older Americans try to remain masters of their own destinies for as long as possible. They fear dependence and try to avoid it. Many are successful at maintaining independence and the right to make their own decisions. Others are less successful and must depend on their families for care and to make critical decisions. However, some older people are able to overcome the difficulties of aging and to lead comfortable and enjoyable lives.

In "Never Have a Heart Attack," Gina Kolata points out the factors that are most likely to cause a person to have a heart attack and the steps that an individual could take to significantly

© Ronnie Kaufman/Blend Images LLC

reduce their chance of having a heart attack. In "Adult Stem Cell Research Far Ahead of Embryonic Innovative Treatments," the article points out how successful the stem cell treatments are for treating a variety of ailments. In "Trust and Betrayal in the Golden Years," the author addresses the problems confronted by many older persons when they turn over control of their finances and property to their children. In addition, the almost insurmountable difficulties that older persons encounter when trying to resolve these problems are pointed out. In "Never Too Late: Exercise Helps Late Starters," the article points out how a regular exercise program even after age 50 helps to improve the health and longevity of older persons.

Never Have a Heart Attack

Reduce your risk to almost zero by following these six proven steps.

Gina Kolata

TAKE A GUESS:

Which of the following people is likely to suffer a heart attack?

- Chris Conway, 54, is thin, eats a healthy diet, takes a baby aspirin every day, and exercises regularly.
- Howard Wainer, 66, has diabetes. Until recently, his blood pressure and blood sugar were too high.
- Naomi Atrubin, 79, has already had two heart attacks.

So who's at risk? Surprise—it's all three of them.

Wainer and Atrubin have obvious risk factors, but Conway has to contend with family history—his father had a heart attack in his mid-40s, and died of one at 66. All these people, however, share a common concern about their health: about 1.1 million Americans will suffer a heart attack this year, and some 500,000 will not survive it.

Despite the risks, most people don't understand what causes a heart attack. The common view is that it's simply a plumbing problem—cholesterol builds up, clogging arteries like sludge in a pipe. When an artery supplying blood to the heart becomes completely obstructed, portions of the heart, deprived of oxygen, die. The result is a heart attack, right?

Not quite, say heart experts. Heart disease involves the gradual buildup of plaque. And plaque is like a pus-filled pimple that grows within the walls of arteries. If one of those lesions pops open, a blood clot forms over the spot to seal it and the clot blocks the artery. Other things can stop your heart, but *that's* what causes a heart attack.

The bigger issue is how to stop it from happening. There's no way to predict where an artery-blocking clot will originate, so prying open a section of an artery with a stent will not necessarily prevent a heart attack. Stents relieve chest pain, but people who have

no symptoms—such as Howard Wainer—are better off adhering to tried-and-true measures to slow plaque growth and prevent the lesions from bursting. Those measures, says Peter Libby, M.D., chief of cardiovascular medicine at Brigham and Women's Hospital in Boston, "are things no one wants to hear: keep your weight down, make physical activity a part of your life, stop smoking if you smoke." And, of course, keep your blood pressure and cholesterol under control, taking medications if necessary.

About 1.1 million of us will have a heart attack this year.

Few people are following that advice. Twenty-five percent of Americans over age 50 have at least two risk factors, such as high blood pressure or cholesterol levels, or an elevated blood-sugar level. Only 10 percent of Americans have every risk factor under control.

"In the majority of cases when someone has a heart attack, at least two or three risk factors might have been avoided," says Valentin Fuster, M.D., a cardiologist at Mount Sinai School of Medicine in New York City.

In the majority of cases when someone has a heart attack, most risk factors might have been avoided.

In fact, a 50-year-old man with none of the risk factors has only a 5 percent chance over the next 45 years of ever having a heart attack, according to Daniel Levy, M.D., director of the Framingham Heart Study, a federal study of heart disease in Framingham, Massachusetts. But if that man has even one risk factor, such as high cholesterol, his chance of having a heart attack soars to 50 percent. For a woman with no risk factors, the chance of having a heart attack is 8 percent; with just one risk factor, it goes to 38 percent. (Assess your own ten-year risk at hp2010.nhlbihin.net/atpiii/calculator.asp.)

By focusing on a few key risk factors, most people can significantly reduce their odds of ever having a heart attack. "There's a lot we can do," says Libby.

Keep Your Cholesterol in Check

Excess cholesterol gets stuck in artery walls. The walls become inflamed with white blood cells of the immune system, and those cells release chemicals that cause plaque. The normal level of so-called bad cholesterol, or LDL cholesterol, is 60 to 130. But if you are at high risk of a heart attack—because you have diabetes, for example—your level should be below 100 and, ideally, no higher than 70. Diet and weight loss are the preferred way to control your cholesterol, say heart-disease experts. If that doesn't work, statins—a class of cholesterol-lowering drugs—can reduce your LDL enough to help prevent heart attacks. Two decades of large and rigorous studies have shown that statins are safe for almost everyone.

Exercise Regularly

For optimal heart health, heart researchers recommend 30 minutes of moderate exercise—such as brisk walking—most days of the week. Exercise can help you control your weight, and it can also help you avoid diabetes if your blood sugar is inching up.

Lower Your Blood Pressure

High blood pressure can damage artery walls, causing them to become stiff and narrow. Ideally your blood pressure should be below 120/80. If you can get it that low with diet and exercise, great; if not, medications may do the job. Studies have shown that blood-pressure medications can reduce heart attack risk by 27 percent.

Control Your Weight

Obesity increases the likelihood that your cholesterol, blood pressure, and blood sugar will be too high; losing weight can often bring these numbers down. Being even slightly overweight also boosts your risk of heart attack, particularly if you tend to gain weight around your middle.

Stop Smoking

Smokers are two to three times more likely to die from heart disease than nonsmokers, says the American Heart Association. In addition to raising blood pressure and lowering HDL (good) cholesterol, smoking injures blood vessels, boosting your risk of having a heart attack. Even if you've been smoking for years, kicking the habit will help your heart. Studies have found that within one year of quitting, your heart attack risk is cut almost in half; within 15 years, it's like that of a nonsmoker.

Control Your Blood Sugar

High blood sugar can promote the growth of plaque. To be safe, your blood sugar level, tested after fasting, should be from 70 to 130 milligrams per deciliter of blood. Your doctor can order this test as part of a physical exam.

"I witness the cholesterol story time and time again," says Elliott Antman, M.D., director of the cardiac-care unit at Brigham and Women's Hospital. "People come to me for a second opinion after having a heart attack and I ask them, 'Have you ever been told what your cholesterol levels were?' The person will say, 'Yes, I was told they were normal.' That's not good enough anymore," if you've already had a heart attack. If you can get your LDL cholesterol level below 70, he says, you are unlikely to have another heart attack.

An LDL of less than 70 is also a good goal for people who have never had a heart attack, says Daniel Rader, M.D., head of preventive cardiovascular medicine at the University of Pennsylvania. Rader offers extra tests, including one for the blood protein CRP; if this protein is elevated, it indicates an increased heart-disease risk. Rader also offers heart scans to assess the extent of plaque in a person's arteries. If the tests reveal additional risk, he will suggest drugs to drive an LDL level down to 70. With an LDL level that low, Rader says, "your lifetime risk of heart disease will be reduced dramatically." It may not reach zero, he says, but it will be a lot lower.

Naomi Atrubin is counting on it. Her LDL cholesterol level, with medication, is currently 69; she's taking another drug to control her blood pressure, and she exercises. "I feel good," she says, though she's knows what's at stake: that only an aggressive approach on all fronts will help her avoid a third—and potentially fatal—heart attack.

Critical Thinking

1. What is the chance that a 50-year-old man who has none of the risk factors for a heart attack having a heart attack in the next 45 years?

2. If a 50-year-old man has one risk factor for a heart attack, such as high cholesterol, what are his chances of having a heart attack in the next 45 years?

3. What do doctors recommend as the safest level of a person's LDL or bad cholesterol in order to avoid a heart attack?

4. List the risk factors that are identified as problems that can lead to a heart attack.

GINA KOLATA is a science writer for *The New York Times*.

Reprinted from *AARP The Magazine*, January/February 2010, pp. 22–23. Copyright © 2010 by Gina Kolata. Reprinted by permission of Gina Kolata and AARP.

Adult Stem Cell Research Far Ahead of Embryonic Innovative Treatments

MALCOLM RITTER

A few months ago, Dr. Thomas Einhorn was treating a patient with a broken ankle that wouldn't heal, even with multiple surgeries. So he sought help from the man's own body.

Einhorn drew bone marrow from the man's pelvic bone with a needle, condensed it to about four teaspoons of rich red liquid, and injected that into his ankle.

Four months later the ankle was healed. Einhorn, chairman of orthopedic surgery at Boston University Medical Center, credits "adult" stem cells in the marrow injection. He tried it because of published research from France.

Einhorn's experience isn't a rigorous study. But it's an example of many innovative therapies doctors are studying with adult stem cells. Those are stem cells typically taken from bone marrow and blood—not embryos.

For all the emotional debate that began about a decade ago on allowing the use of embryonic stem cells, it's adult stem cells that are in human testing today. An extensive review of stem cell projects and interviews with two dozen experts reveal a wide range of potential treatments.

Adult stem cells are being studied in people who suffer from multiple sclerosis, heart attacks and diabetes. Some early results suggest stem cells can help some patients avoid leg amputation. Recently, researchers reported that they restored vision to patients whose eyes were damaged by chemicals.

Apart from these efforts, transplants of adult stem cells have become a standard lifesaving therapy for perhaps hundreds of thousands of people with leukemia, lymphoma and other blood diseases.

"That's really one of the great success stories of stem cell biology that gives us all hope," says Dr. David Scadden of Harvard, who notes stem cells are also used to grow skin grafts.

"If we can recreate that success in other tissues, what can we possibly imagine for other people?"

That sort of promise has long been held out for embryonic stem cells, which were first isolated and grown in a lab dish in 1998. Controversy over their use surrounded the 2001 decision by former President George W. Bush to allow only restricted federal funding for studying them.

Proponents over the past decade have included former first lady Nancy Reagan and actors Michael J. Fox and the late Christopher Reeve. Opponents object that human embryos have to be destroyed to harvest the cells.

Embryonic cells may indeed be used someday to grow replacement tissue or therapeutic material for diseases like Parkinson's or diabetes. Just on Friday, a biotech company said it was going ahead with an initial safety study in spinal cord injury patients. Another is planning an initial study in eye disease patients later this year.

But in the near term, embryonic stem cells are more likely to pay off as lab tools, for learning about the roots of disease and screening potential drugs.

Observers say they're not surprised at the pace of progress.

As medical research goes, the roughly 10 years since the embryonic cells were discovered "is actually a very short amount of time," said Amy Rick, immediate past president of the Coalition for the Advancement of Medical Research. The group has pushed for embryonic stem cell research for about that long. Hank Greely, a Stanford University law professor who works in bioethics and has followed stem cells since the 1990s, said: "Give it another five years and I'll be surprised if we don't have some substantial progress" beyond initial safety studies.

The Pro-Life Secretariat of the U.S. Conference of Catholic Bishops continues to oppose embryonic work. Deirdre McQuade, an official there, said that compared to adult stem cell research, work on embryonic cells is proving "fruitless."

Adult cells have been transplanted routinely for decades, first in bone marrow transplants and then in procedures that transfer just the cells. Doctors recover the cells from the marrow or bloodstream of a patient or a donor, and infuse them as part of the treatment for leukemia, lymphoma and other blood diseases. Tens of thousands of people are saved each year by such procedures, experts say.

But it is harnessing these cells for other diseases that has encouraged many scientists lately.

In June, for example, researchers reported they had restored vision to people whose eyes were damaged by caustic chemicals. Stem cells from each patient's healthy eye were grown and multiplied in the lab and transplanted into the damaged eye, where they grew into healthy corneal tissue.

A couple of months earlier, the Vatican announced it was funding adult stem cell research on the intestine at the University of Maryland. And on Friday, Italian doctors said they'd transplanted two windpipes injected with the recipients' own stem cells.

But these developments only hint at what's being explored in experiments across the United States.

Much of the work is early, and even as experts speak of its promise, they ask for patience and warn against clinics that aggressively market stem-cell cures without scientific backing.

Some of the new approaches, like the long-proven treatments, are based on the idea that stem cells can turn into other cells. Einhorn said the ankle-repair technique, for example, apparently works because of cells that turn into bone and blood vessels. But for other uses, scientists say they're harnessing the apparent abilities of adult stem cells to stimulate tissue repair, or to suppress the immune system.

"That gives adult stem cells really a very interesting and potent quality that embryonic stem cells don't have," says Rocky Tuan of the University of Pittsburgh.

One major focus of adult stem cell work for about a decade has been the ailing heart. While researchers remain committed, much of the early enthusiasm from patients, doctors and investors has slacked off because results so far haven't matched expectations, says Dr. Warren Sherman of Columbia University.

"Everyone, including myself, is impatient and would like to see positive results appear quickly," said Sherman, who hosts an annual international meeting of researchers. But he called for patience.

In treating heart attack, for example, studies show stem cell injections help the heart pump blood a bit better, Sherman said. But the research has not yet established whether injections cut the risk of death, more heart attacks or future hospitalizations, he said.

Sherman said he hopes a large study of those patient outcomes can be done in the next couple of years, and is "very optimistic that patients will benefit."

Similarly, in heart failure, research indicates stem cells can ease symptoms but larger studies are still needed to show how much good the treatments provide, he said. He noted that current studies are testing stem cells taken not only from bone marrow and leg muscle, but also from fat.

Another heart-related condition under study is critical limb ischemia, where blood flow to the leg is so restricted by artery blockage it causes pain and may require amputation. The goal here is to encourage growth of new blood vessels by injecting stem cells into the leg.

Sherman said limb ischemia research is moving fast and the results "are very, very encouraging."

The injected cells may serve as building blocks while also stimulating local tissue to grow the vessels, said Dr. Douglas Losordo of Northwestern University. His own preliminary work suggests such a treatment can reduce amputation rates.

Dr. Gabriel Lasala of TCA Cellular Therapy also has reported positive preliminary results. One success is Rodney Schoenhardt of Metairie, La.

Schoenhardt had already had surgery on both legs for the disease, and his surgeon was talking about amputating his left leg. Schoenhardt suffered so much pain in his left leg while standing that he used a wheelchair instead.

For Lasala's research, Schoenhardt got 40 shots in each leg about 18 months ago, with stem cells going into his left calf and a placebo dose into the other. Soon, he said, the pain in his left leg was gone.

Schoenhardt, 58, now mows his lawn, and he remodeled his living room to fix damage from Hurricane Katrina. "My wheelchair is in my garage, collecting dust," he said.

"I'm even thinking about taking up a little tennis again."

With all the heart-related stem cell studies, the former president of American Heart Association says, "We should be enthusiastic, but cautiously so." Beyond the promising indications of early studies, researchers need definitive evidence that the treatments not only make patients better but also don't cause unintended harm, says Dr. Clyde Yancy.

Among the other diseases being studied for stem cell treatments:

- Multiple sclerosis. In MS, the body's immune system repeatedly assaults brain and spinal cord tissues, which can cause numbness in the limbs, paralysis or vision loss.
- Last year, Dr. Richard Burt of Northwestern reported a small trial in patients with early MS that was aimed at rebooting the immune system to stop the attacks. He removed stem cells from the patient's blood, destroyed their immune systems, and then re-injected them with their own cells to build a new immune system.
- To his surprise, most patients actually improved. He's now conducting another trial to provide firmer evidence of improvement.
- Dr. Jeffrey Cohen of the Cleveland Clinic is trying a different and less-researched approach. In a preliminary trial he is just starting, he'll use a different kind of stem cell from patients' marrow that he hopes can slow nervous system damage but also promote repair.
- Lessons learned from this approach might eventually reveal some clues for treating other conditions like Parkinson's or spinal cord injury, he said.
- Type 1 diabetes. It's also caused by a misguided attack by the immune system, this time on insulin-producing cells. Burt and colleagues reported last year that the "rebooting" strategy allowed some patients to go without insulin for four years. However, some experts call his approach too risky for that disease. Burt is now doing another study in newly diagnosed adults.
- Another study, at about a dozen medical centers around the country, is testing whether an off-the-shelf preparation of marrow stem cells can calm the immune system of diabetics. It's still early work, says C. Randal Mills, chief executive officer of Osiris Therapeutics.

- Cancers such as melanoma and kidney cancer. The idea is to transplant cells to produce a new immune system that will attack the diseases. Earlier work around a decade ago failed to give lasting benefit, but new approaches aim for better results, said Dr. Michael Bishop of the National Cancer Institute.

- Even as scientists hope adult stem cells will produce new treatments, they are concerned about clinics that make claims about unproven stem cell therapy.

- "Clinics have sprung up all over the world . . . that are essentially selling snake oil, that are preying on the hopes of desperate patients," said Sean Morrison, a stem cell expert at the University of Michigan.

- Morrison suggests patients consult their own doctors about going to a clinic.

More information

- Stem cell clinic website: www.closerlookatstemcells.org
- General stem cell information: http://stemcells.nih.gov/info/basics/
- Adult stem cells: www.isscr.org/public/adultstemcells.htm

Critical Thinking

1. Why have stem cell implants worked on repairing injured ankles?
2. Currently how are stem cells used to repair eye damage?
3. Comparing adult stem cell research with embryonic stem cell research, which is currently proving most effective?

As seen in *Terre Haute Tribune-Star,* August 12, 2010. Copyright © 2010 by Associated Press. Reprinted by permission via YGS Group.

Trust and Betrayal in the Golden Years

Just when they're needed most, a growing number of children are turning on aging parents—taking away their nest eggs and their independence.

Kyle G. Brown

Concerned about her mother's mental health, Sarah took decisive action. She helped 82-year-old Celia move to a retirement community, she set up accounts for her at a local health-food store and an upscale clothing boutique. She also took over her financial affairs.

But at the mention of her daughter, Celia says: "I swear to God, she should be in jail."

Since 2004, when an Alberta court granted her daughter guardianship of her mother and control of her $400,000 in savings and stocks, Celia claims Sarah has taken almost all of her possessions—and left her without a bank account, or even identification. (Both of their names have been changed to protect their privacy.) While her daughter claims to be acting in her best interests, Celia feels betrayed and helpless.

And she is hardly alone. Toronto lawyer Jan Goddard, who has worked on elder-abuse issues for 17 years, says financial exploitation of seniors is now "endemic across the country." This can range from snatching a few dollars from grandma's purse to transferring property.

Brenda Hill, the director of the Kerby Rotary House Shelter in Calgary, agrees. "We've had people who have had their homes sold, who have been virtually on the street with no food and no money because their children have taken all their assets," she says. "It happens quite often."

And the problem is likely to get worse before it gets better. People 65-plus are the fastest-growing segment of the Canadian population—but cuts to health services in the 1990s have meant that fewer seniors are living in public institutions.

This, in turn, has placed increased pressure on family members, which a Statistics Canada report in 2002 suggested could lead to a rise in the abuse of older adults.

South of the border, taking money from mom and dad is also seen as a serious issue. So much so, that the Elder Financial Protection Network predicts that it will become the "crime of the century."

Ageism is partly to blame. As is a culture of entitlement—where the money parents spend can be seen as a "waste" of the child's future inheritance.

Charmaine Spencer, a gerontologist at B.C.'s Simon Fraser University, says both are particularly prevalent in North America. Although she adds, "I have not seen a single culture in which abuse of the elderly does not take place—it's financial and psychological abuse, and when that doesn't work, it's physical."

But addressing such exploitation is anything but straightforward. How do legal and medical professionals determine when adult children are taking advantage of aging parents—and when they are enforcing necessary restrictions on those no longer able to care for themselves? How do they intervene, either to stop abuse or to help elderly parents cope with newly dependent roles, when seniors are enmeshed in painful power struggles with grown sons and daughters?

Take one of Ms. Goddard's eightysomething clients. The increasingly frail woman complained that she needed more support than her son—who lives in her house—was providing. She decided to revoke his power of attorney.

But, according to Ms. Goddard, when the woman told her son about the meeting, he was furious. The next day, she called Ms. Goddard to cancel everything. As she spoke nervously on the phone, Ms. Goddard could hear the woman's son in the background, telling her what to say.

Though lawyers like Ms. Goddard can call in the police in such situations, getting seniors to make formal complaints against their children can be difficult. Ultimately, she says, clients have to face the repercussions of confronting their families and "keep wavering whenever they go back home."

Seniors' own shame can also keep them from reporting that their children are taking advantage of them. Although abuse seems to cut across socio-economic lines (even New York socialite Brooke Astor made headlines recently because of her son's alleged neglect), older adults often feel guilty talking publicly about private matters.

As for those who do brave action against their children, many do not make it very far. While money is in their children's hands, victims of financial abuse cannot afford the fees to take a case to court—which can run at a minimum of $10,000. And legal aid is rarely awarded to seniors involved in civil cases.

Ms. Hill tells the story of a Calgary widow who sold her house and moved into her daughter's home. Her children transferred money from her account to theirs, borrowed her bank card and charged her for "services" such as rides and errands.

A few months later, the woman fled to the Kerby Rotary House Shelter with a small fraction of her savings. But at the age of 87 she could not face the idea of spending what little time and money she had left in the courts. Now, she resides in a seniors' lodge with just enough cash to live out her days—though her daughter will never be brought to justice.

Dr. Elizabeth Podnieks, the founder of the Ontario Network for the Prevention of Elder Abuse, conducted the first national survey on elder abuse in 1990. She says that even when lawyers do take seniors' cases, complainants have difficulty convincing the court that they are the victims of theft and exploitation. For example, their memory is often called into question, as they struggle to recall "giving" money to defendants.

Family members who question their parents' ability to look after their finances may consult a capacity assessor—a health professional with special training in assessing mental capacity.

Tests vary from province to province, but Larry Leach, a psychologist at Toronto's Baycrest centre for geriatric care, says they generally set out to answer the tricky question of whether elderly adults "appreciate all the risks of making an investment and giving gifts to people."

If a parent is deemed incapable, the government may then become the guardian of property until a family member applies to the courts to gain guardianship.

This is what soured the relationship between Celia and her daughter. In 2004, Celia was diagnosed with dementia and deemed "unable to care for herself." Her daughter then won guardianship over Celia's affairs.

Celia hotly disputes the doctor's findings—but now the onus is on her to prove that she is mentally fit or to appoint a new guardian.

Meanwhile, she is no longer speaking to Sarah. Once in charge of her own health-food store, she feels humiliated taking "handouts" from her daughter. "I can't do anything. Where can I go with no money?" she says.

As for more cut and dried cases, where neither dementia nor family dynamics is in play, Dr. Podnieks says: "Older people don't understand why the police can't just 'go in and get my money back.' They know it's a crime, you know it's a crime, the abuser knows it's a crime—so where is the law, where is the protection?"

Detective Tony Simioni, who is part of the Edmonton Police Force's Elder Abuse Intervention Team, says senior abuse is about 20 years behind child abuse, both in terms of public awareness and government and police resources. "Financial-abuse cases rarely see the top of the agenda," he says. "It's low on the totem pole of crimes."

Still, Judith Wahl, who has been working at the Advocacy Centre for the Elderly in Toronto for more than 20 years, remains optimistic. She believes that public education campaigns on elder abuse are making an impact. The rising number of reported incidents, she says, is partly due to a growing willingness to talk openly about abuse.

A 75-year-old Winnipeg woman is a case in point. She was coerced for years into paying her daughter's bills, rent and grocery tabs.

"I would come home and cry and sort of tear my hair, and think, 'Where do I turn to for help? Who do I go to?'" she says.

But eventually her friends encouraged her to contact a seniors support centre. With their help, she gained the confidence to confront her daughter—and to grant her son power of attorney.

These days, she gives gifts to her granddaughter, but when her daughter asks her for more, she tells her to talk to her "attorney."

Critical Thinking

1. What are the difficulties confronting an older person who is being abused financially by his/her children?

2. How do finances impede an older person from taking their abusing children to court?

3. What impact have public education campaigns on elder abuse had in Canada?

KYLE G. BROWN is a freelance writer based in Calgary.

Never Too Late: Exercise Helps Late Starters

HARVARD MEN'S HEALTH WATCH

The Industrial Revolution changed America forever, and the Information Era has changed it still further. More than ever before, men are working with their brains instead of their backs. It's great progress, but it does have unintended consequences, including global economic competition and unprecedented levels of stress. Another consequence is diminished physical activity. Now that most men don't need to exercise to earn their keep, many view exercise as kids' stuff, the fun and games that fill childhood—or used to in the days before video games and flat-screen TVs.

America has become a nation of spectators. That deprives men of the exercise that improves cholesterol levels, lowers blood sugar, burns away body fat, strengthens muscles and bones, improves mood and sleep, and protects against diabetes, dementia, certain cancers, and especially heart attacks and strokes.

Men who stay physically active throughout life reap these benefits and more. But what about men who slide into sloth once they're too old for school sports? Can a late start make up for years of sedentary living?

Second chances are rare in this life. But when it comes to exercise, research reinforces earlier studies that tell older men not to act their age.

Starting Late in Sweden

A 35-year study from Sweden provides strong evidence that starting to exercise late in life is better than never starting at all—much better, in fact.

The subjects were 2,205 male residents of the municipality of Uppsala. All the men were between the ages of 49 and 51 when they volunteered for the study between 1970 and 1973. During the course of the investigation, the men were evaluated five times, at ages 50, 60, 70, 77, and 82. At each evaluation, the men submitted detailed information about their exercise, smoking, and drinking habits, and the researchers measured body height and weight, blood sugar and cholesterol levels, and blood pressure.

The researchers divided the men into three groups based on their exercise levels. At age 50, most of the men rated their own health as good, and there was little difference in body mass index, blood pressure, or cholesterol between the low-, moderate-, and high-exercise groups, but smoking was less prevalent in high- versus low-level exercisers (47 percent vs. 61 percent). Over the next 35 years, though, major differences in health emerged. Most importantly, men who were highly physically active at age 50 were 32 percent less likely to die during the study than those who were least active; moderately active men enjoyed a smaller, but still respectable, 13 percent lower death rate than the least active gents.

The protective effect of regular exercise comes as no surprise. But the long-term nature of the Swedish study allowed the scientists to follow men who were sedentary at age 50 but who increased their exercise level between ages 50 and 60. For the first five years, the major result was disappointment, since these men continued to die at the same high rate as men who remained inactive. But over the next five years, the benefit kicked in; by 10 years of follow-up, the men who adopted exercise in middle age enjoyed the same low mortality rate as men who began before age 50. All in all, men who adopted exercise after 50 had a 49 percent lower death rate than the men who remained inactive, a benefit even greater than the 40 percent risk reduction experienced by men who quit smoking after age 50. And the protective effect of exercise remained significant even after the scientists adjusted their results for the impact of smoking, drinking, obesity, diabetes, cholesterol, blood pressure, and socioeconomic status.

Men looking for an excuse to stay on the couch may suspect a catch, wondering if they have to become long-distance runners to benefit from taking up exercise in midlife. Quite the reverse. According to the Swedish

Turning Back the Clock

Ponce de Leon learned it the hard way: There is no fountain of youth. But an interesting study tells us that exercise can make arteries act younger.

As people age, their arteries tend to constrict (narrow), reducing the tissue's supply of oxygen-rich blood. To find out if exercise can improve age-related vascular function, scientists compared 13 healthy men with an average age of 27 and 15 healthy men with an average age of 62. As expected, the older gents' arteries were more prone to constrict and less apt to dilate (widen). But for the next three months, eight of the older men began an exercise program, averaging nearly five hours a week of moderate aerobic training. At the end of that time, the arterial function tests were repeated, and the men who began to exercise in their 60s scored younger.

The great 17th-century physician Thomas Sydenham said, "A man is as old as his arteries." Twenty-first-century research suggests older men can use their legs to turn back the hands of their arterial clock.

study, men were classified as moderate exercisers if they simply took frequent walks or often went cycling for pleasure. And high-level exercise involved a minimum of just three hours of serious gardening or recreational sports a week. And in case you're tempted to cook up another excuse, you'll soon see that this important study does not stand alone.

Late Bloomers in Britain

Between 1978 and 1980, scientists evaluated 7,735 men from 24 British towns. In 1992, researchers were able to re-evaluate 5,934 of the men, who then had an average age of 63 years. The scientists tracked these men for an additional four years, comparing their risk of illness and death to their amount of physical activity.

At each evaluation, the researchers collected information about recreational and occupational exercise, smoking, drinking, social class, obesity, and health status, but they did not measure cholesterol, blood pressure, or blood sugar levels.

As in the Swedish study, the British research revealed a strong link between exercise and survival. Even light exercise was protective, reducing the rate of death by 39 percent; moderate exercise was even better, cutting the mortality rate by 50 percent. Most importantly, exercise was beneficial for men who were sedentary in 1978–80 but who began exercising sometime during the next 12 to

14 years; men who began to exercise later in life enjoyed a 45 percent lower mortality rate than men who remained sedentary throughout. And the benefits of late-life exercise were evident in men who already had heart disease by the time they became active as well as in men who were still healthy when they began to exercise.

News from Norway

A third European study, this time from Norway, confirms the findings from Sweden and England. Beginning in 1972, researchers evaluated 2,014 healthy men who were 40 to 60 years old. When the study began, each man got a comprehensive medical work-up and an exercise test. The evaluations were repeated between 1980 and 1982, and the scientists continued to keep track of the men through 1994.

As in the other studies, men who were physically fit enjoyed substantial protection from cardiovascular disease and early death; in all, the most fit men had a 55 percent lower mortality rate than the least fit. In addition, men who took up exercise and improved their fitness

Not By Exercise Alone

Men who become physically active later in life enjoy better health and a lower death rate than men who remain sedentary. That's good news for couch potatoes everywhere—but will reforming other health habits in midlife also help?

A study of 15,708 American men and women ages 45 to 64 says the answer is an emphatic yes. At the start of the study, only 1,344 people had all four of these healthy lifestyle habits: eating five or more servings of fruits and vegetables daily, not being obese, not smoking, and exercising regularly. But over the next six years, another 970 people adopted the healthful habits. The late adopters were quickly rewarded with improved health; over the next four years they enjoyed a 35 percent lower risk of cardiovascular events and a 40 percent lower death rate than their peers who failed to reform.

Exercise was one of the newly acquired health habits, but since the benefits of starting to exercise later in life take five years to kick in, exercise itself can't account for these rapid improvements. Better late than never, and better all than one.

It's a simple but powerful message, but it seems to fall on deaf ears. Only 8 percent of Americans between the ages of 40 and 74 have all four of these health habits plus moderate alcohol use— and that percentage has actually declined from a still woeful 15 percent in 1988.

levels between 1972 and 1982 reduced their risk of dying during the study—but men who let their exercise slide lost the protective effect of physical fitness.

American Veterans

The benefits of catch-up exercise are not confined to Europeans. A 2010 study of 5,314 male veterans ages 65 to 92 shows that fitness pays off on both sides of the Atlantic. All the volunteers underwent exercise tolerance testing at VA Medical Centers in Washington, D.C., and Palo Alto, Calif. Researchers followed the men for up to 25.3 years. During that time, the men who were most fit enjoyed a 38 percent lower mortality rate than those who were least fit. But the men who began to exercise during the follow-up period nearly caught up with the men who were in shape at the start of the study; unfit individuals who improved their fitness had a 35 percent lower mortality rate than their peers who remained unfit.

Harvard Men, Too

These four studies that show it's never too late to get fit confirm and extend the findings of an earlier American investigation that focused on middle-aged men. A 1993 report evaluated 10,269 Harvard alumni who were 45 or older when the study began in 1977. Over the next eight years, researchers tracked the effects of lifestyle changes on mortality. Previously sedentary men who began exercising after age 45 clearly benefited, enjoying a 23 percent lower rate of death than their classmates who remained inactive. The maximum benefits were linked to an amount of exercise equivalent to walking for about 45 minutes a day at a pace of about 17 minutes per mile. Not surprisingly, the Harvard study found that other lifestyle changes also helped, even if they did not occur until after age 45; quitting cigarette smoking, maintaining normal blood pressure, and avoiding obesity were all associated with less heart disease and longer life.

Which changes matter most? To find out, researchers evaluated some 36,500 male Harvard graduates and 21,000 male and female graduates of the University of Pennsylvania. All in all, sedentary individuals gained 1.6 years of life expectancy from becoming active later in life, smokers gained 1.8 years from quitting, and those who maintained normal blood pressure gained 1.1 years. Best of all was a combination of changes; sedentary smokers gained 3.7 years from quitting and becoming active.

Never Too Late

From both sides of the Atlantic, the message is clear: exercise is beneficial for all stages of life, and it's never too late to start. But men who start exercising after age 50 also need to exercise caution. Here are some tips:

- Get a check-up to be sure that you're healthy. In addition to checking for diabetes, hypertension, abnormal cholesterol levels, and evidence of cardiovascular disease, your doctor should be sure your joints and muscles don't merit special precautions.

- Pick an activity that's right for you. For many older gents (and for younger guys, too), walking is ideal. Biking and swimming are also excellent sports, and physically active hobbies such as serious gardening fill the bill, too.

- Set a realistic goal. Aim for 30 to 40 minutes of moderate exercise, such as brisk walking, nearly every day. But don't try to morph from couch potato to jock all at once. Instead, start out gradually and build up to your goal slowly but steadily. For example, you may want to begin exercising for 15 minutes three times a week, and then add minutes and days as you improve. And even when you're in top shape, it's always smart to alternate hard workouts with easier ones and to vary your routine.

- For best results, add stretching exercises, which are ideal for warming up before and cooling down after your workout. Remember, too, that strength training will complement aerobic training to build a balanced exercise program; all it takes is two to three sessions a week.

- Once you find yourself enjoying exercise, don't be afraid to extend yourself. Walkers, for example, might try a little jogging, golfers should walk the course, and doubles tennis players could switch to singles (or find younger partners).

- Get practical advice from friends and relatives who enjoy exercise and know the tricks of the trade. Consider professional guidance from a trainer or pro, and don't hesitate to spend a few bucks on good shoes or other gear.

- Make exercise part of a comprehensive health makeover. It's particularly important to avoid tobacco in all its forms and to eat right, control your weight, reduce stress, get enough sleep, and get regular medical care. But just as you've eased your way into exercise, make the other lifestyle changes you need gradually, and don't get down on yourself if you backslide.

- Above all, listen to your body. In most cases, you'll hear sounds of improvement, but if you detect distress signals—particularly chest pain or pressure, undue fatigue or breathlessness, or an irregular heartbeat or lightheadedness—back off and report it to your physician.

It's never too late to start taking care of yourself, and it's never too early, either. Whether you started early or later, keep going throughout life. And spread the gospel of exercise for health to the younger generations, who have grown distressingly fat and lazy. One of the best ways to lead is by example.

Critical Thinking

1. In the Harvard study of men over 45, what were the lifestyle changes other than exercise that were associated with less heart disease and a longer life?

2. In a study of American veterans age 65 and older, how much did unfit veterans who exercised to improve their fitness lower their mortality rate?

3. How much did men in the British study who began exercises lower their mortality rate?

UNIT 5

Retirement: American Dream or Dilemma?

Unit Selections

Learning Outcomes

After reading this Unit, you will be able to:

- Describe the major concerns of the baby boomer generation as they approach retirement age.

- Identify the keystone to the baby boomers having an adequate retirement income.

- Explain why waiting until your late 70s or early 80s is the best time to begin buying or cashing in on a monthly annuity.

- Enumerate the advantages of waiting until age 70 to begin drawing your Social Security check rather than starting to draw it at 62.

- Discuss the advantages and disadvantages of beginning to withdraw from the Social Security Program at age 62.

- Describe the conditions which would qualify a person who never worked to receive a Social Security check.

- Describe the difference between a "defined benefit" pension plan and a "defined contribution" pension plan.

- Discuss why 45 percent of working-age households are at risk for being unable to maintain their pre-retirement standard of living.

- List the six lifestyle choices that older persons may choose from when they arrive at retirement age.

- Discuss the reasons why older persons may make different choices of what they prefer to do at the age of retirement.

Student Website

www.mhhe.com/cls

Internet References

American Association of Retired People
  www.aarp.org
Health and Retirement Study (HRS)
  www.umich.edu/~hrswww

Since 1900, the number of people in America who are age 65 years and over has been increasing steadily, but a decreasing proportion of that age group remains in the workforce. In 1900, nearly two-thirds of those over the age of 65 worked outside the home. By 1947, this figure had declined to about 48 percent, and in 1975, about 22 percent of men age 65 and over were still in the workforce. The long-range trend indicates that fewer and fewer people are employed beyond the age of 65. Some people choose to retire at age 65 or earlier; for others, retirement is mandatory. A recent change in the law, however, allows individuals to work as long as they want with no mandatory retirement age.

Gordon Strieb and Clement Schneider (*Retirement in American Society,* 1971) observed that for retirement to become an institutionalized social pattern in any society, certain conditions must be present. A large group of people must live long enough to retire; the economy must be productive enough to support people who are not in the workforce; and there must be pensions or insurance programs to support retirees.

Retirement is a rite of passage. People can consider it either as the culmination of the American Dream or as a serious problem. Those who have ample incomes, interesting things to do, and friends to associate with often find the freedom of time and choice that retirement offers very rewarding. For others, however, retirement brings problems and personal losses. Often, these individuals find their incomes decreased; they miss the status, privilege, and power associated with holding a position in the occupational hierarchy. They may feel socially isolated if they do not find new activities to replace their previous work-related ones. Additionally, they might have to cope with the death of a spouse and/or their own failing health.

Older persons approach retirement with considerable concern about financial and personal problems. Will they have enough retirement income to maintain their current lifestyle? Will their income remain adequate as long as they live? Given their current state of health, how much longer can they continue to work? The next articles deal with changing Social Security regulations and changing labor demands that are encouraging older persons to work beyond the age of 65. In "Uncertain Future," the problems and concerns of the baby boomer generation concerning whether they have saved enough money to retire are presented. Jane Bryant Quinn in "Do-It-Yourself Financial Freedom," describes 12 easy steps that a person needs to take throughout their life to ensure an adequate income. In "Top 25 Social Security Questions," the author explains numerous question or concern someone may have about their qualifications

© John Lund/Drew Kelly/Blend Images LLC

to receive Social Security in their retirement years. In "Color Me Confident," the author discusses the problem of having an adequate retirement income with the new 401(k) defined contribution plans that most businesses have now implemented. And in "Work/Retirement Choices and Lifestyle Patterns of Older Americans," the authors examine six different work, retirement, and leisure patterns that older people may choose to determine which is most satisfying to the individual.

Uncertain Future

Poll reveals baby boomers' retirement fears. Many think they will have to work longer than planned, one-quarter have no savings at all.

ALAN FRAM

Baby boomers facing retirement are worried about their finances, and many believe they'll need to work longer than planned or will never be able to retire, a new poll finds.

The 77 million-strong generation born between 1946 and 1964 has clung tenaciously to its youth. Now, boomers are getting nervous about retirement. Only 11 percent say they are strongly convinced they will be able to live in comfort.

A total of 55 percent said they were either somewhat or very certain they could retire with financial security. But another 44 percent express little or no faith they'll have enough money when their careers end.

Further underscoring the financial squeeze, 1 in 4 boomers still working say they'll never retire. That's about the same number as those who say they have no retirement savings.

The Associated Press-LifeGoesStrong.com poll comes as politicians face growing pressure to curb record federal deficits, and budget hawks of both parties have expressed a willingness to scale back Social Security, the government's biggest program.

The survey suggests how politically risky that would be: 64 percent of boomers see Social Security as the keystone of their retirement earnings, far outpacing pensions, investments and other income.

The survey also highlights the particular retirement challenge facing boomers, who are contemplating exiting the work force just as the worst economy in seven decades left them coping with high jobless rates, tattered home values and painfully low interest rates that stunt the growth of savings.

"I have six kids," said Gary Marshalek, 62, of South Abington Township, Pa., who services drilling equipment and says he has repeatedly refinanced his home and dipped into his pension to pay for his children's college. His inability to afford retirement "sounds like America at the moment," Marshalek said. "Sounds like the normal instead of the abnormal."

Marshalek was among the 25 percent in the poll who say they plan to never retire. People who are unmarried, earn under $50,000 a year, or say they did a poor job of financial planning are disproportionately represented among that group.

Overall, nearly 6 in 10 baby boomers say their workplace retirement plans, personal investments or real estate lost value during the economic crisis of the past three years. Of this group, 42 percent say they'll have to delay retirement because their nest eggs shrank.

Though the first boomers are turning 65 this year, the poll finds that 28 percent already consider themselves retired. Of those still working, nearly half want to retire by age 65 and about another quarter envision retiring between 66 and 70.

Two-thirds of those still on the job say they will keep working after they retire, a plan shared about evenly across sex, marital status and education lines, the survey finds. That contrasts with the latest Social Security Administration data on what older people are actually doing: Among those age 65–74, less than half earned income from a job in 2008.

"I'm going to keep working after I retire, if nothing else for the health care," said Nadine Krieger, 58, a food plant worker from East Berlin, Pa. Citing $50,000 in retirement savings that she says won't go far, she added, "We probably could have saved more, but you can't when you have a couple of kids in the house."

About 6 in 10 married boomers expect a comfortable retirement, compared with just under half of the unmarried. Midwesterners are most likely to express confidence in their finances.

"I'm a good planner," said Robert Rivers, 63, a retired New York State employee in Ravena, N.Y. He still works seasonally for the federal government and collects a modest military pension. A recreational pilot, he says he has scaled back his lifestyle by flying and driving less.

"I'm spending money I have, not spending it and trying to repay it," he said.

Among boomers like Rivers who plan to continue working in retirement, 35 percent say they'll do so to make ends meet. Slightly fewer cite a desire to earn money for extras or to simply stay busy.

Excluding their homes, 24 percent of boomers say they have no retirement savings. Those with nothing include about 4 in 10 who are non-white, are unmarried or didn't finish college.

At the other end, about 1 in 10 say they have banked at least $500,000. Those who have saved at least something typically have squirreled away $100,000, with about half putting away more than that and half less.

Despite the worries and dearth of savings cited by many, only about a third of boomers say it's likely that they'll have to make do with a more modest lifestyle once they retire. Only about 1 in 4 expect to struggle just to pay their expenses.

Financial experts say such expectations are often not realistic.

"Most families have to make a significant adjustment from their working lives to their retirement years," said financial planner Sheryl Garrett, who runs the Garrett Planning Network. Ads that show silver-haired couples strolling off into the sunset do not represent the typical retirement, she added.

The AP-LifeGoesStrong.com poll was conducted from March 4–13 by Knowledge Networks of Menlo Park, Calif., and involved online interviews with 1,160 baby boomers born between 1946 and 1964. The margin of sampling error is plus or minus 3.5 percentage points.

Knowledge Networks used traditional telephone and mail sampling methods to randomly recruit respondents. People selected who had no Internet access were given it for free.

Critical Thinking

1. How has the economic downturn of the last three years affected the retirement plans of many of the baby boom generation?

2. What are the characteristics of the baby boomers who have no retirement income?

3. What percentage of the baby boom generation believe they will have to adjust to a more modest lifestyle after they retire?

Do-It-Yourself Financial Freedom

JANE BRYANT QUINN

Safety nets fray when times get hard. Retirements that once looked secure are hanging by a thread. The message for those in their 50s is clear: Mend the nets while there's still time. Those in their 60s and 70s have fewer options. Still, there are ways of making sure your money lasts for life. **Here's how to do it in 12 easy steps:**

1 Get rid of debt.

Nothing is more destructive of retirement than carrying debt when your paycheck stops. If you're in your early 50s, start debt reduction now. Try to prepay your mortgage, too, so you'll own your home free and clear. If you're retiring now and prepaying would use up too much cash, consider the other extreme: Reduce your payments by taking a new, 30-year mortgage. It's counterintuitive, but it works. Or use your equity to buy a smaller place that will leave you with no house payment or a much smaller one.

Don't fall prey to the slimy promises of commercial debt consolidators. Here are two legitimate and low-cost places to go for help with debt reduction: The National Foundation for Credit Counseling (www.nfcc.org, 1-800-388-2227) and the Association of Independent Consumer Credit Counseling Agencies (www.aiccca.org, 1-800-703-8787).

In the worst case, consider bankruptcy. Never tap retirement accounts to cover unpayable debts. IRAs and 401(k)s are protected in bankruptcy. You'll need those funds for a fresh start.

2 Build a better budget.

When you're thinking about retirement, nothing is more important than knowing how far your income will stretch. What will your expenses be? How much income will you have, including prudent withdrawals from your savings? Get your spending under control sooner rather than later. The longer you kid yourself, the greater your chance of running out of money.

3 Increase your savings.

Save, save, save—even if it means changing your lifestyle or not helping your grandchildren with tuition. The kids have a lifetime to repay their student loans, but you're running out of time. If you arrive at retirement with too little money, you're cooked.

4 Wise up on investments.

Among older people, there's a stampede to safety. Money poured out of stock-owning mutual funds after the panic of 2008-09, and into funds invested in bonds. Many older investors still don't want to take a risk in stocks.

But inflation and taxes will cut the real returns on your bonds and bond funds down to practically nothing. In your 50s and 60s—with 30 or 40 years of retirement ahead—you need to keep some money invested in stocks for long-term growth.

I don't mean individual stocks. For safety reasons, get rid of them—every single share. You have no idea what is going on inside companies, including the one you work for. Even blue chips can be laid low—look what happened to the country's leading banks. Are you holding on to individual stocks to avoid paying tax on capital gains? That tax is probably lower today than it ever will be. Bite the bullet, sell now and diversify.

As a first step, divide your nest egg into three parts:

- Money you'll need within four or five years. Keep it in a bank or a money market fund—any account that is readily accessible when the need arises.
- Money you won't have to touch for 15 years or more. Keep it in well-diversified stock index funds, which track the market as a whole rather than trying to pick individual companies. Low-cost stock index funds are offered by Vanguard and Fidelity Investments. T. Rowe Price has index funds, too, but they cost a little more.
- In-between money. Keep it in bond mutual funds. When interest rates rise (as most people expect to

happen in coming years), the value of bond fund shares will fall. But managers will be snapping up those new, higher-interest bonds, so the income from your fund will rise. When rates fall again, in the next recession, the value of your shares will go back up. If you reinvested your dividends, you'll have more shares working for you, too.

5 Keep your job, if possible.

Or get one, if you've already retired. Every extra year of work improves your Social Security benefit, increases your savings (assuming you save) and reduces the number of years that your nest egg has to last. It might bring you health insurance, too. Public schools, hospitals and government agencies offer benefits. Some private companies—including Costco, Home Depot and Wal-Mart—give benefits even to part-timers (usually with a waiting period).

6 Do whatever you can to keep health insurance.

If your company offers retiree coverage, don't even think of moving to another city or state until you find out if you can take your coverage with you. Most plans won't follow you or will charge you more at a new location.

If you need individual coverage, check with local health insurance agents who can round up plans suitable for you (you can find an agent through the National Association of Health Underwriters). For the lowest premium, pick a policy with a high deductible. You may pay more out of pocket if you become sick, but you're protected from catastrophic, bankruptcy-inducing costs. Once you have signed up, you're in the insurer's PPO network, which gives you discounts of up to 50 percent or so, even on bills you pay yourself.

Health care reform would be helpful for those not yet in Medicare. Any new law is likely to bar rejection for preexisting conditions (at my age, life is a preexisting condition) and provide faster access to generic drugs and subsidies to help cover costs. Those on Medicare will likely see the "doughnut hole"—which requires them to pay some Medicare Part D costs—close over the next few years.

7 Be smart about Social Security.

Draw from your 401(k) or IRA first, and claim Social Security benefits later. If you can wait until 70, your check will be about 76 percent higher than if you had started at 62, and will improve the protection for your spouse as well.

8 Be smart about retirement funds, too.

If you're with a large employer, consider leaving your 401(k) money in your company plan, provided that it offers flexible withdrawal options. Your money will be managed at a much lower cost than you'll find elsewhere, and the funds have been chosen carefully for people in your situation. If you have a traditional pension and take it as a lump sum, don't hand it to a broker or planner who wants to sell you products. Choose index funds yourself or work with a fee-only financial planner (see below).

9 Put off reverse mortgages.

When you turn 62, salespeople come out in force, urging you to strip the equity out of your home to support your spending now. Don't do it. The fees and effective interest rates are high, and the proceeds are low. Save the reverse mortgage option for your late 70s or early 80s, when other money might be running low. AARP has tons of good information at www.aarp.org/money/personal/reverse_mortgages/.

10 Annuities.

When you're retired, there's nothing like receiving a regular check. One way to get it is with an immediate annuity. You take a sum of money and use it to buy an income for life. Your state of health doesn't matter. The fixed payments are based entirely on your age and the type of benefit you want (for cost comparisons, see www.immediateannuities.com). But fixed payments will be whittled away by inflation, so don't buy an annuity too early. Buy in your late 70s or early 80s, when they won't have to last as long.

Stay away from the fancy, tax-deferred annuities that make big promises about future income benefits. They're too complicated to dissect here, so I'll say only that the cost is much higher than you think and the odds are good that they won't perform as you expect. My personal rule is, "if it's complicated, forget it." Deferred annuities with income benefits fit that bill.

11 Work with a financial planner.

Planners are very helpful in working with budgets and projecting how much you can afford to spend when you retire. But work with fee-only planners, who don't sell products and who charge only for their advice. Planners who take commissions on products could steer you wrong (for example, by selling you those awful, complex annuities). Three places to find a fee-only planner near you: GarrettPlanningNetwork.com, the Alliance of Cambridge Advisors (CambridgeAdvisors.com), and the National Association of Personal Financial Advisors (www.napfa.org).

12 Move in with your kids.

The last resort, if all else fails. That should be motivation enough to get moving on your own plan for financial success.

Critical Thinking

1. Why is it unwise to take a reverse mortgage on your house at 62?

2. When retired, what is the advantage of keeping a large share of your money invested in stocks rather than in bonds?

3. Why is it wise, if you retire from a large employer who has your retirement money in a 401K plan, to leave it in the plan rather than drawing it out and reinvesting?

Jane Bryant Quinn is a financial columnist and the author of *Making the Most of Your Money Now.*

Top 25 Social Security Questions

Confused about when to claim or whether you're eligible for benefits? We have answers.

STAN HINDEN

Here are the most frequently asked questions about Social Security that AARP has received from you.

1. **I am about to turn 62 and plan to file for Social Security. How do I get started?**

   You should apply three months before you want to start collecting. Sign up online or call 1-800-772-1213. Here are some documents you may have to produce: your Social Security card or a record of the number; your birth certificate; proof of U.S. citizenship or lawful alien status; military discharge papers if you served before 1968; and last year's W-2 tax form or tax return if you're self-employed.

2. **How is my Social Security benefit calculated?**

   Benefits are based on the amount of money you earned during your lifetime—with an emphasis on the 35 years in which you earned the most. Plus, lower-paid workers get a bigger percentage of their preretirement income than higher-paid workers. In 2010, the average monthly benefit for retirees is $1,172.

3. **If I remarry, can I still collect Social Security benefits based on my deceased first husband's record?**

   You can—subject to several rules. In general, you cannot receive survivor benefits if you remarry before age 60 unless that marriage ends, too, whether by annulment, divorce or death of your new husband. If you remarry after age 60 (50 if disabled), you can still collect benefits on your former spouse's record. After you reach 62, you may get retirement benefits on the record of your new spouse if they are higher.

4. **Why won't retirees get a cost-of-living adjustment for 2011? Many of us count on this for food, medicine and other bills.**

   COLAs are based on the consumer price index, which tracks inflation. Because inflation has been flat, according to the CPI, there will be no benefit increase—for the second year in a row. AARP is calling on Congress to provide beneficiaries with financial relief.

5. **I am 56 and receive Social Security disability benefits. At what point will I switch to regular Social Security? Will the monthly amount change?**

   When you reach full retirement age, your disability benefits will automatically convert to retirement benefits. The amount will remain the same.

6. **My friend died at 66. She worked full time and had not applied for benefits. What happens to the money she contributed to Social Security? Can her children claim benefits?**

   The money people contribute goes into a fund from which benefits are paid to eligible workers and their families. These include a widower, a surviving divorced husband, dependent parents, disabled children, and children if they have not aged out.

7. **My husband and I are getting a divorce. He wants the settlement agreement to say I will not get his Social Security benefits. Can he do that?**

   No, he has no control over your future benefits. You can qualify for a divorced spouse's benefits if you were married at least 10 years, are now unmarried, are 62 or older, and if any benefit from your own work record would be less than the divorced spouse's benefit.

8. **Cleaning out my mother's home after her death, we found Social Security checks from the 1980s. Can we cash them?**

   No. The checks are negotiable for only 12 months after issue.

9. **My man and I have lived together for over seven years. If he dies, can I collect his Social Security benefits?**

   If your state recognizes your common-law marriage, then you'll likely be eligible for survivor benefits. But you'll have to provide evidence that includes sworn statements, mortgage or rent receipts, or insurance policies.

10. **Do my Social Security contributions go into a personal retirement account for me and earn interest?**

Although many people think so, the answer is no. Social Security operates under a pay-as-you-go system, which means that today's workers pay for current retirees and other beneficiaries. Workers pay 6.2 percent of their wages up to a cap of $106,800; employers pay the same. The money that younger people contribute will pay for our benefits when we retire.

11. **How much money does the U.S. government owe to the Social Security trust fund, and will it be repaid?**

To prepare for the boomers' retirement, Social Security has collected more in taxes than it pays in benefits. Surplus funds go into the trust fund and are invested in U.S.-guaranteed Treasury bonds. In 2009, the trust fund held $2.5 trillion in bonds and earned 4.9 percent in interest. These bonds are just as real as U.S. Treasury bonds held by mutual funds or foreign banks. Ultimately, it's up to the American people to ensure the government keeps its promise to retirees, just as it would to other investors.

12. **I have a pension from the Army. Will that affect my Social Security benefits?**

It will not. You can get both your Social Security benefits and your military pension. If you served in the military before 1957, you did not pay Social Security taxes, but you will receive special credit for some of that service. Special credits also are available to people who served from 1957 to 1967 and from 1968 to 2001.

13. **I didn't work enough to qualify for Social Security. My husband gets it, but he is ill and may not live much longer. Will I be able to collect benefits?**

Yes, but your benefit will depend on your age and situation: If you are at full retirement age or older, you'll get 100 percent of your deceased husband's benefit. A widow or widower between 60 and full retirement age receives a reduced benefit.

14. **Is it true that some people are collecting Social Security benefits who never paid into the system?**

Social Security is an earned benefit. In order to collect a retirement benefit, a worker must pay into the system for at least 10 years. In some cases, nonworking family members, such as a spouse, may be eligible for benefits based on the worker's record. Tough rules in place assure that only legal residents can collect Social Security benefits.

15. **I filed for Chapter 13 bankruptcy after being laid off. Do Social Security benefits count as income in bankruptcy, or are they protected?**

Your benefits are protected. Social Security is excluded from the calculation of disposable income when setting up a debtor repayment plan.

16. **My husband died recently. Can I choose between my own benefit and that as a widow? Can I collect both?**

Eligibility for a widow's benefit begins at age 60, or 50 if you are disabled. If you are full retirement age, your survivor benefit will be 100 percent of his benefit; if you take it early, the amount will be reduced. You can switch to your own benefit as early as 62. In any event, you can only get one benefit, whichever is higher.

17. **I began drawing Social Security at age 62 in 2006, but I'm still working. Since I'm still paying Social Security taxes, will my benefits increase?**

If your latest work years are among your highest-earning years, the SSA refigures your benefit and pays you any increase due. This is automatic, with new benefits starting in December of the following year.

18. **My wife is 62 and collects Social Security based on her own work record. Can she receive spousal benefits based on my record when I retire in a few years?**

If she is eligible for both benefits, yours and hers, Social Security will pay her own benefits first. If she is due additional benefits, she will get a combination of benefits equaling the higher spouse's benefit.

19. **Why would changes in Social Security be considered as a way to help balance the federal budget?**

Some policymakers say all spending, including Social Security, should be cut. Social Security has not contributed to the deficit. In fact, the trust fund is projected to reach $4.3 trillion by 2023. AARP believes that Social Security benefits should not be targeted to reduce the deficit.

20. **If I retire to a foreign country, can I have my Social Security benefits sent there?**

If you are a U.S. citizen, you may receive your benefits in most foreign countries, usually by check or direct deposit. If you are not a U.S. citizen, the answer is more complicated, with certain rules applying to certain countries. For specifics, see the Social Security publication "Your Payments While You Are Outside the United States."

21. **I started collecting Social Security at 62. I heard that if I changed my mind, I could pay back the amount I'd collected and get a higher payment. Is that possible?**

Yes, but the sum you'd be paying back may be quite large, perhaps prohibitive. You must repay all benefits that you and your family received, plus any money withheld from your checks for Medicare Parts B, C and D; also, any tax withheld. For specifics, you'll need to contact Social Security.

22. **Can I collect Social Security and unemployment compensation at the same time?**

Yes. Unemployment benefits aren't counted as wages under Social Security's annual earnings test, so you'd still receive your benefit. However, the amount of your unemployment benefit could be cut if you receive a pension or other retirement income, including Social Security and railroad retirement benefits. Contact your state unemployment office for information on whether your state applies a reduction.

23. **I am 63 and collecting Social Security. If I work, will my benefit be cut?**

It depends on your income. Between age 62 and the start of the year when you reach full retirement age, $1 in benefits is withheld for every $2 you earn above a limit, which is $14,160 in 2010. In the year you reach full retirement age, $1 is withheld for every $3 above another limit, $37,680 in 2010. In your birthday month, the limits go away—and your benefit will be recalculated upward to compensate for the money that was withheld.

24. **I'm 50. Will Social Security be there when I retire?**
The Social Security trust fund, where accumulated assets are held, currently contains about $2.5 trillion. According to the system's board of trustees, that money and continuing tax contributions will allow payment of all benefits at current rates until 2037. After that, there still will be enough tax revenue coming in to pay about 78 percent of benefits. Congress is being urged to make financial fixes to Social Security to ensure it will be there for you.

25. **I know I can start collecting Social Security at age 62. But should I?**
That depends. If you're healthy and can afford it, you should consider waiting until you reach your full retirement age of 66, or even 70. Here's why. By law, the age when workers can qualify for full benefits is gradually increasing, from 65 to 67. (It will be 67 for anyone born after 1960.) If you claim benefits before reaching full retirement age, they'll be reduced. That's because the goal set by Congress is to pay the same lifetime benefits to an individual regardless of when they're initially claimed. So let's say you claim benefits at age 62 and get $1,000 a month. If you can wait until you're 66, you'll get at least 33 percent more ($1,333). And if you can wait until you're 70, you'll get at least 75 percent more ($1,750). Social Security determines the amount of your benefits based, in part, on your highest 35 years of earnings. So you may get a larger monthly benefit if your extra years of work are your top earning years.

Critical Thinking

1. Should the surplus of funds in the social security account be used by the federal government to reduce the deficit and balance the budget?

2. Can a person receive a social security and an unemployment check at the same time?

3. Is it possible for a wife to receive her husband's social security benefits after his death?

STAN HINDEN is a retired Washington Post financial writer and author of How to Retire Happy: The 12 Most Important Decisions You Must Make Before You Retire.

Color Me Confident

Why many Americans may be working when they retire.

PAUL MAGNUSSON

Despite everything, Susan Buer, a 46-year-old South Dakota homemaker, is confident that she'll have enough money to retire on. She's in the process of getting divorced, a situation that affects nearly half of all married couples, and one that usually leaves both partners worse off financially. She has less than $10,000 in savings. Credit card debt and a car loan cloud her future. She hasn't yet calculated how much she'll need to retire, although she's "very confident" she can do the math. "Eventually, I'll talk to a financial planner about all this, but I just haven't had the time yet," Buer says.

In her approach to retirement, Buer reflects the best and worst of many Americans—a can-do spirit and procrastination. According to a recent *AARP Bulletin* poll, many people are confident that they can meet their basic retirement expenses, yet have not done basic planning or calculated what funds they'll need. Many fear their employers will cut back on their health and pension benefits but have not begun to save adequately for the costs they'll face.

The poll, which surveyed 1,096 workers and 686 retirees age 40 and older, indicates that many Americans may not have adjusted to the new economic reality: that the responsibility for funding retirement is shifting from business and the federal government onto the shoulders of workers themselves.

This is happening gradually, as traditional "defined benefit" pensions, which are based on salary, are being replaced by more chancy "defined contribution" plans, such as a 401(k), that require employees to contribute a percentage of pay and bear much of the risk of investing the principal. In 1980, 83 percent of workers with pension plans were enrolled in a defined benefit plan. Today, that figure has shrunk to 21 percent, according to the U.S. Department of Labor.

A recent *Bulletin* poll indicates that many American workers may not have adjusted to the new economic reality: that responsibility for funding retirement is shifting from business and government onto workers themselves—and many have not begun to save for the costs they'll face.

Workers may not yet fully grasp their own increasing role in retirement planning or the implications of what Yale professor Jacob Hacker calls "the great risk shift." (see "Retirement Insecurity," *AARP Bulletin,* March). Although 68 percent of workers (or their spouses) said they've saved some money for retirement, 31 percent have not saved a dime. The most common reasons were "not enough income" and "high everyday expenses." Thirty percent also said that a lack of financial discipline was a contributing factor.

Just last month, the Center for Retirement Research at Boston College released a study that painted an equally gloomy picture of retirement, saying that 45 percent of working-age households are "at risk" of being unable to maintain their preretirement standard of living.

"Unless Americans change their ways, many will struggle in retirement," said CRR Director Alicia H. Munnell. "There is no silver bullet; the answer is saving more and working longer. Even relatively modest adjustments—working two extra years or saving 3 percent more—can substantially improve retirement security."

Rose-colored glasses seem to be particularly characteristic of the 75 percent of all workers who define themselves as "very confident" or "somewhat confident" about having enough money to live comfortably in their retirement years. Of that group, 48 percent haven't tried to calculate their retirement savings needs; 22 percent have saved no money so far for retirement; and 43 percent have less than $25,000 in savings and investments, excluding the value of their homes and defined benefit plans. Most worrisome, a third of them have no money in a 401(k), and 45 percent have no IRA savings.

However, when it comes to specifics like pensions, health care and debt, respondents express serious concerns. Among the findings:

Pensions. Forty percent of those who are employed—or whose spouses are employed—worry that their employers will reduce or eliminate pension or health care benefits before or during their retirement. In fact, some reported that such changes had already occurred in the last five years: elimination of a traditional defined benefit pension plan (10 percent) or the plan's benefits frozen or reduced (9 percent); traditional pension plan converted into a 401(k)-type defined contribution plan (15 percent); and health care benefits reduced (44 percent).

Social Security may help fill in the gaps. Thirty-nine percent of workers say they expect Social Security to be a major source of their retirement income—this compares with 58 percent of current retirees who report that Social Security is a major source of their income.

Health care. Twenty-eight percent of workers and 13 percent of retirees said they were concerned about not having enough money in retirement to pay for their medical expenses. And 40 percent of workers and 33 percent of retirees are worried about their ability to meet long-term care expenses.

Debt. Debt is a serious issue for both workers and retirees. More than half of workers see their (or their spouse's) current level of debt as a problem, compared with 30 percent of retirees. Workers are also more likely than retirees to carry a mortgage, credit card debt or a car loan, or even medical or dental debt.

So how much does it take to retire? There is no single answer. One rule of thumb is that workers should plan on replacing 60 to 70 percent of pretax employment income with savings and investments. Some may need less if all debts, mortgages and other loans are paid off and health care is covered.

And if there's a financial shortfall, continued employment may be a last resort. Two in 10 workers in the *Bulletin* poll say they plan to draw a major portion of their retirement income from a job. The back-to-work crew may just be the most realistic of all.

86% of retirees and 75% of workers age 40-plus are at least somewhat confident they have or will have enough money for retirement.

31% of workers age 40 or older have not yet saved any money for their retirement.

28% of current retirees also acknowledge not saving any money for their retirement years before they retired.

58% of retirees report that Social Security is a major source of their income.

28% of workers and 13% of retirees are not confident they'll have enough money for retirement medical expenses.

40% of workers and 33% of retirees are not confident they can pay for long-term care.

53% of workers see their current level of debt as a problem, compared with 30% of retirees.

Critical Thinking

1. What percent of the current workers 40 and over have not yet saved any money for retirement?
2. What percent of the current retirees report that Social Security is their major source of income?
3. How many of the current workers say they plan to draw a major portion of their retirement income from a job?

PAUL MAGNUSSON is a freelance writer in Washington.

Work/Retirement Choices and Lifestyle Patterns of Older Americans

Harold Cox et al.

This study examined the work, retirement, and lifestyle choices of a sample of older Indiana residents. The six lifestyles examined in this study were:

1. *to continue to work full-time;*
2. *to continue to work part-time;*
3. *retire from work and become engaged in a variety of volunteer activities;*
4. *to retire from work and become involved in a variety of recreational and leisure activities;*
5. *to retire from work and later return to work part-time; and*
6. *to retire from work and later return to work full-time*

These findings indicate that health was not a critical factor in the older person's retirement decision, and that those who retired and engaged in volunteer or recreational activities were significantly more satisfied with their lives than those who continue to work. Those who retired and engaged in volunteer or recreational activities scored significantly higher on life satisfaction than those who had returned to work full or part-time. There was no significant difference between those who had retired and those who had continued working in terms of how they were viewed by their peers. Of those who retired and then returned to work, the most satisfied with their lives were the ones who returned to work in order to feel productive. Those least satisfied with their lives were the ones that returned to work because they needed money.

Introduction

There are basically six different choices of lifestyles from which older Americans choose when they reach retirement age. They can (1) continue to work full-time, (2) reduce work commitments but continue to work part-time, (3) retire from work and become engaged in a variety of volunteer activities that provide needed services but for which they will receive no economic compensation or (4) retire from work and become involved in a variety of recreational and leisure activities, (5) retire from work and later return to work part-time, (6) retire from work and return to work full-time.

There are a multitude of life experiences and retirement patterns that may ultimately lead older persons to choose among the diverse ways of occupying themselves during their later years. Some enjoy their work as well as the income, status, privilege, and power that go with full-time employment and never intend to retire. Some retire intending to engage in recreational and leisure activities on a full-time basis only to find this lifestyle less satisfying than they imagined and ultimately return to work. The need to feel productive and actively involved in life is often a critical factor inducing some retirees to return to work. Some retirees who have become widowed, divorced, or never married find themselves too socially isolated in retirement. They return to work either full-time or part-time because their job brings them into contact with a variety of people, and therefore they are less isolated. Thus, there are a variety of reasons why older persons may continue to work or to become active volunteers during their later years. On the other hand, many persons retire, dedicate themselves to recreation and leisure activities, and are most satisfied doing so.

The purpose of this study was to determine which of these six groups were better off in terms of their health, life satisfaction, retirement adjustment and the respect they received from their peers.

A second factor, which will be examined in this study, is the advisability for both government and industry of encouraging older workers to remain in the labor force longer. Changes in Social Security regulations after the year 2000 are going to gradually increase the age of eligibility for Social Security payment from 62 to 64 for early retirement and from 65 to 67 for full retirement benefits. Will changes in the age of eligibility for retirement income derived from Social Security regulations be good or bad for older Americans?

Review of Literature
Work

The meanings of such diverse activities as work, leisure, and retirement to a member of a social system are often quite complex. Paradoxically, the relevance of work and leisure activities for an individual is often intertwined in his or her thinking. Consequently, the concept of work or occupation has been difficult for sociologists to precisely define.

For some time sociologists have struggled to come up with an adequate definition of work. Dubin (1956), for example, defined work as continuous employment in the production of goods and services for remuneration. This definition ignores the fact that there are necessary tasks in society carried out by persons who receive no immediate pay. Mothers, fathers, housewives, and students do not receive pay for their valued activities.

Hall (1975) attempts to incorporate both the economic and social aspects of work in his definition: "An occupation is the social role performed by adult members of society that directly and/or indirectly yields social and financial consequences and that constitutes a major focus in the life of an adult." Similarly Bryant (1972) tries to include both the economic and social aspects of work life in his definition of labor: "Labor is any socially integrating activity which is connected with human subsistence." By *integrating activity* Bryant means sanctioned activity that presupposes, creates, and recreates social relationships. The last two definitions seem to take a broader view of work in the individual's total life. Moreover, they could include the work done by mothers, fathers, housewives, and students. The advantage of definitions that attach strong importance to the meaning and social aspects of a work role is that they recognize the importance of roles for which there is no, or very little, economic reward. The homemaker, while not receiving pay, may contribute considerably to a spouse's career and success. College students in the period of anticipatory socialization and preparation for an occupational role may not be receiving any economic benefits, but their efforts are crucial to their future career.

The most appropriate definitions of work, therefore, seem to be those that emphasize the social and role aspects of an occupation, which an individual reacts to and is shaped by, whether or not he or she is financially rewarded for assuming these roles. From the perspective of sociology, one's work life and the roles one assumes during the workday will, in time, shape one's self-concept, identity, and feelings about oneself, and therefore strongly affect one's personality and behavior. Moreover, from this perspective, the individual's choice of occupations is probably strongly affected by the desire to establish, maintain, and display a desired identity.

Individual Motivation to Work

Vroom (1964) has attempted to delineate the components of work motivation. The first component is wages and all the economic rewards associated with the fringe benefits of the job. People desire these rewards, which therefore serve as a strong incentive to work. Iams (1985), in a study of the post-retirement work patterns of women, found that unmarried women were very likely to work at least part-time after retirement if their monthly income was below $500. Hardy (1991) found that 80 percent of the retirees who later re-entered the labor force stated that money was the main reason they returned to work. The economic inducement to work is apparently a strong one.

A second inducement to work is the expenditure of physical and mental energy. People seem to need to expend energy in some meaningful way, and work provides this opportunity. Vroom (1964) notes that animals will often engage in spontaneous activity as a consequence of activity deprivation.

A third motivation, according to Vroom, is the production of goods and services. This inducement is directly related to the intrinsic satisfaction the individual derives from successful manipulation of the environment.

A fourth motivation is social interaction. Most work roles involve interaction with customers, clients, or members of identifiable work groups as part of the expected behavior of their occupants.

The final motivation Vroom mentions is social status. An individual's occupation is perhaps the best single determinant of his or her status in the community.

These various motivations for work undoubtedly assume different configurations for different people and occupational groups. Social interaction may be the most important for some, while economic considerations may be most important for others. For still others the intrinsic satisfaction derived from the production of goods and services may be all-important. Thus, the research by industrial sociologists has indicated that there are diverse reasons why individuals are motivated to work.

The critical questions for gerontologists is whether the same psychological and social factors that thrust people into work patterns for the major part of their adult life can channel them into leisure activities during their retirement years. Can people find the same satisfaction, feeling of worth, and identity in leisure activities that they did in work-related activities? Streib and Schneider (1971) think they can. They argue that the husband, wife, grandmother, and grandfather's roles may expand and become more salient in the retirement years. Simultaneously, public service and community roles become possible because of the flexibility of the retiree's time. They believe that the changing activities and roles, which accompany retirement, need not lead to a loss of self-respect or active involvement in the mainstream of life.

Retirement Trends

Demographic and economic trends in American society have resulted in an ever-increasing number of retired Americans. Streib and Schneider (1971) observed that for retirement to become an institutionalized social pattern in any society, certain conditions must be met. There must be a large group of people who live long enough to retire, the economy must be sufficiently productive to support segments of the population that are not included in the work force, and there must be some well-established forms of pension or insurance programs to support people during their retirement years.

There has been a rapid growth in both the number and percentage of the American population 65 and above since 1900.

In 1900, there were 3.1 million Americans 65 and over, which constituted four percent of the population. Currently, approximately 31 million Americans are in this age category, which makes up 12.5 percent of the population. While the number and proportion of the population over

Table 1   Civilian Labor Force Participation Rates: Actual and Projected*

	Men			Women		
Year	45–54	55–64	65 and Over	45–54	55–64	65 and Over
1950	95.8	86.9	45.8	37.9	27.0	9.7
1960	95.7	86.8	33.1	49.8	32.2	10.8
1970	94.2	83.0	26.8	54.4	43.0	9.7
1980	91.2	72.3	19.1	59.9	41.5	8.1
1986	91.0	67.3	16.0	65.9	42.3	7.4
1990*	90.7	65.1	14.1	69.0	42.8	7.0
2000*	90.1	63.2	9.9	75.4	45.8	5.4

Source: For the rates from 1950–1970: U.S. Department of Labor (1980:224). For the rates from 1980–2000: Bureau of Labor Statistics (unpublished data).
*Values are projections from the Bureau of Labor Statistics middle growth path.

65 have been increasing steadily, the proportion of those who remain in the work force has decreased steadily. In 1900, nearly two thirds of those 65 worked. Sammartino (1979) reports that by 1947 this figure had declined to 47.8 percent. By 1987 only 16.5 percent of those 65 and older were still in the work force. In the past 20 years the decline in labor force participation in later years has extended into the 55–64 year old age group. Clark (1988) observed that between 1960 and 1970 the labor force participation of men (55–64) dropped from 86.8% to 83%. By 1990 the labor force participation rate of men in this age group (55–64) had dropped to 65.1% (see Table 1). Table 1 indicates that the labor force participation rates of women 55–64 rose from 27% to 43% from 1950 to 1970 but has remained relatively stable since 1970. Thus, while the labor force participation rate of 55-years and -older women has remained relatively stable since 1970, the labor force participation rate of women 45–54 has grown from 54.4% in 1970 to 69% in 1990. It would appear from these figures that, while younger women are in increasing numbers entering the labor force, women 55 and above are following the same path as their male counterparts and choosing to retire early.

Similarly, there appears to be a somewhat greater convergence in the work and retirement patterns of men and women when comparing 1900 with 1970. The earlier pattern of work histories seemed to be for men to enter the work force earlier and retire later; women tended to enter later and retire earlier. Current trends indicate that women are entering the work force earlier and working longer.

Men, on the other hand, enter the work force later and retire earlier. Thus, the work histories of men and women are becoming very similar, although men as a group still have longer work histories than women. Today, more women are both entering the labor force and also remaining in the labor force throughout their adult lives.

The trend for both men and women for the past 30 years has been for larger numbers to choose to claim Social Security benefits prior to age 65. Allen and Brotman (1981) point out that in 1968, 48 percent of all new Social Security payment awards to men were to claimants under 65; by 1978 this figure had increased to 61 percent. In 1968, 65 percent of all new Social Security awards to women were to claimants under 65; in 1978, the figure was 72 percent.

Simultaneously, fewer persons are choosing to remain in the labor force beyond the age of 65. Soldo and Agree (1988) report that 62 percent of the men and 72 percent of the women who received Social Security benefits in 1986 had retired prior to age 65 and therefore were receiving reduced benefits. The General Accounting Office reports that almost two-thirds of those receiving private retirement benefits in 1985 stopped working prior to age 65. Of those who do remain in the labor force after age 65, Soldo and Agree (1988) report that 47 percent of the men and 59 percent of the women held part-time positions.

Quinn and Burkhauser (1990) report that probably the most critical factor in the decision to retire early is adequate retirement income. They found that between 1975 and 1990 the proportion of workers covered by two pension plans had risen from 21 percent to 40 percent. Moreover, Gall, Evans, and Howard (1997) report a number of studies that found that those with higher incomes, or at least adequate finances, were more satisfied with their life in retirement (Fillenbau, George, and Palmore 1985; Seccombe and Lee 1986; Crowley 1990; Dorfman 1992).

There is a multiplicity of problems confronting the individual at retirement: the lowering of income; the loss of status, privilege, and power associated with one's position in the occupational hierarchy; a major reorganization of life activities, since the nine-to-five workday becomes meaningless; a changing definition of self, since most individuals over time shape their identity and personality in line with the demands of their major occupational roles; considerable social isolation if new activities are not found to replace work-related activities; and a search for a new identity, new meaning, and new values in one's life. Obviously, the major reorganization of one's life that must take place at retirement is a potential source of adjustment problems. Critical to the adjustment is the degree to which one's identity and personality structure was attached to the work role. For those individuals whose work identity is central to their self-concept and gives them the greatest satisfaction, retirement will represent somewhat of a crisis. For others, retirement should not represent a serious problem.

Work and Retirement Patterns in Later Life

Beck (1983) identified three different work and retirement patterns of older persons which include:

1. the fully retired
2. the partially retired
3. the formerly retired

What could be added to Beck's pattern are "the never retired."

There are a number of different studies and authors who have attempted to identify the critical factor determining who will or will not work during their later years. Beck (1983) found that individuals with high job autonomy and high demand jobs were most likely to return to work after formal retirement. Those with the greatest financial need—service workers and laborers—were less likely to return to work despite financial limitations. Beck concludes that income was the critical factor in the motivation of workers who were very poor to return to work. Those in other income categories were less likely to return to work because of actual financial benefits as much as for other factors.

A number of other studies tended to support Beck's analysis of work and retirement patterns. Tillenbaum (1971) found that those with higher levels of education were more likely to continue working beyond age 65 or to return to work after retiring if they chose to do so. Quinn (1980) found the self-employed were much more likely to work beyond retirement age. Streib and Schneider (1971) found that white collar workers were significantly more likely than blue collar workers to return to work. They found no relationship between income and post-retirement work. Howell (1988) reports that those who formally retire and engage in no substantial work during the next three years are more likely to have been unemployed before retirement and to have lower incomes after retirement. They are also more likely to be nonwhite urban dwellers in poor health.

The past research has indicated then that those who either continue to work after retirement age or return to work after retiring are most likely to:

1. have stable employment patterns throughout their adult life;
2. be in white collar occupations;
3. have higher incomes;
4. have a higher number of years of education;
5. be self-employed.

Those least likely to either work after retirement age or return to work after retirement age:

1. those who experienced periods of unemployment throughout their adult life;
2. those in blue collar occupations;
3. those with low incomes;
4. those who have a lower number of years of education;
5. those who are of minority status (Tillenbaum 1971; Quinn 1980; Howell 1988).

These findings support the idea that many people who continue to work after retirement do so for other than financial reasons. If work was stable and both social and psychologically meaningful to the individual, he/she is much more likely to be found working during the retirement years.

As a rule, retirees do not return to jobs with low autonomy, poor working conditions, and difficult physical labor. Those who most need to continue working during the retirement years for financial reasons are least likely to be able to do so. This is most probably related to their inability to find gainful employment.

Volunteer Work in Retirement

Social integration refers to the individual being actively involved in a variety of groups and organization and thus integrated into the web of community activity. The active older person is likely to be involved in a variety of groups ranging from family to social clubs to church and community organizations. While work and career often place the individual in disparate groups and organizations throughout much of his/her adult life, active engagement in voluntary organizations is likely to keep the individual socially involved during their retirement years.

Moen, Dempster-McClain, and Williams (1992) report that studies as early as 1956 reporting that older persons participating in volunteer work on an intermittent basis and belonging to clubs and organizations were positively related to various measures of health. They concluded that occupying multiple roles in the community was positively related to good health.

A number of studies have found a positive relationship between social integration (in the form of multiple roles) and health in later life (Berkman and Breslow 1983; House, Landes, and Umberson 1988; Moen et al.; Williams 1992).

The researchers were unable to determine if multiple roles lead to improved health or if healthy people were more likely to engage in multiple roles. Moen et al. (1992), however, once again found that being a member of a club or organization appeared to be a critical factor in the current health of the individual, after previous health had been controlled. Paid work over the life course, while positively related to multiple roles in later life, was negatively related to measures of health. However, any volunteer activity at any time during adult life appears to promote multiple role occupancy, social integration, and health in later life.

Mobert (1983) observes that church affiliation itself was not considered a volunteer group or activity; however, membership in groups sponsored by the church such as choir, Old Timers, etc. was considered a volunteer activity. Moreover, church members generally remain active participants in church-related activities long after dropping participation from other voluntary associations (Gray and Moberg 1977). Markides (1983) and Ortega, Crutchfield, and Rusling (1983) argue that the church serves as a focal point for individual and community integration of the elderly and that this is crucial to their sense of well-being. Both of these studies found that church attendance was significantly correlated with life satisfaction.

Productivity in Later Life

Older workers who remain in the work force have been found to be just as productive as younger workers. An industrial survey conducted by Parker (1982) found that older workers were most often regarded as superior to younger workers. Adjectives used by employers to describe older workers were responsible, reliable, conscientious, tolerant, reasonable, and loyal. Older workers have greater stability, they miss work less frequently, change jobs less frequently, and are more dedicated and loyal to the employing organization. Welford (1988) found that performance on production jobs tends to increase with age. While this is true, employers generally offer incentive plans to encourage older workers to retire early. Older workers are generally higher on salary schedules, have accumulated more vacation time and fringe benefits. Thus, many employers see younger workers as cheaper. The fact that they are untested does not seem critical to the employer.

Fyock in discussing the early retirement policies of the 1970's states that:

Employers liked it because it enabled them to hire and promote younger, more recently trained and lower paid workers. The public liked it because it didn't appear to cost anything and because at age 62 or earlier they could expect to retire; older workers for obvious reasons loved it. (Fyock 1991:422)

Fyock (1991) warns however that we currently have an aging work force and that in the near future employers may find it to their advantage to encourage older workers to remain in the work force longer. She believes that employers often find that retirement appeals to their best, instead of the most expendable, employee.

Projected job growth coupled with a declining number of younger workers has raised concern about possible labor shortages. If these projections prove accurate and labor shortages do develop, the answer to the problem would seem to be the retention of older workers—the very workers employers are currently encouraging to retire. Dennis (1986), Sheppard (1990), and Fyock (1991) all argue that an aging labor force can be a source of opportunity for employers. The smart employers, they believe, will be the ones who know how to take advantage of the opportunity.

McShulski (1997) reports the need for a "soft landing" program which eases older workers out of the labor force on a very gradual basis. Encouraging retiring employees to work a reduced number of hours and handle more limited duties for less pay, helps both the company and the employee. Future retirees can impart relevant job information to their coworkers and teach less experienced employees about specific tasks and customer needs. Thus, working for reduced hours and more limited responsibilities results in a gradual transition to retirement, which is good for the company and the employee according to McShulski.

Retirement Policies and Older Workers

Industrialized societies traditionally have low fertility rates and long life expectancy, resulting in an ever-growing number and percentage of our population that is over 65. Thus, industrialized nations very early began to shift social welfare programs from younger persons to older persons. Many economists are questioning the willingness of society to continue to support an ever-growing number of older persons through public-funded retirement incomes.

Initially, in 1935 when Social Security was passed, both management and labor were anxious to get older persons out of the labor force. Management believed that older workers were too expensive since they were high on salary schedules and had accumulated considerable fringe benefits. Labor unions believed that removing older workers would create jobs for younger workers. The public was happy since they were given economic help in support of their older family members and ultimately they looked forward to being able to retire themselves.

The post-WWII era saw major expansions in Social Security programs. Social Security was extended to cover nearly all wage earners and self-employed persons. The permissible retirement age was lowered to 62, and a national disability income program was added to Social Security. A legal interpretation of the Taft-Hartley Act resulted in private pension plans becoming legitimate items of collective bargaining. The result was that private pension plans have grown substantially from 1950 to present. As a result of these and related activities, a retirement norm has emerged in America. Most people now plan to retire and to live some part of their life out of the labor force.

Congress, with the passage of new Social Security legislation in 1983, began, for the first time, to question the desirability of removing seniors from the labor force. Concern about the financial solvency of the Social Security program led Congress and the President to increase Social Security taxes, to increase taxes on earned income of older persons, to tax Social Security benefits, and to raise the eligible age of Social Security benefits after the year 2000.

Retirement age will go up very gradually during the first quarter of the next century. Early retirement will be increased from 62 to 64 years of age. Full retirement will be increased from 65 to 67. Reduction in pension benefits for those who retire early will go up from 20% to 30% of their full retirement income. Those who stay at work after 65 will get a pension boost of 8% for each extra year of work instead of today's 3%.

The changes in Social Security benefits are clearly designed to encourage people to work longer and retire later. The question that remains, given the trend toward younger retirements, is will these changes really keep older workers in the work force longer or merely mean that more retirees will earn less and therefore more will fall below the poverty line.

Economists and labor planners have never been able to establish the fact that for every older worker who retires, a job is created for a younger worker. Changing technologies and the creation of new jobs have at different times created a greater or lesser demand for more workers. Morris (1986) states that:

If financial and social policy disincentives to employment could be reduced there is no prior reason to believe that the economy would be unable to expand gradually to accommodate more retired persons especially in part-time, self-employed, and service capacities (Morris 1986:291).

Morris (1986) argues that half of the Social Security recipients abruptly leave the labor force and the other half engage in some short-term labor force participation after they retire.

The critical question raised by Congress in changing Social Security benefits in 1983 is can government policies change the age at which people choose to retire. If the older person is to be encouraged to remain in the labor force longer, both the individual worker and the business/industrial community must be convinced of the advantages of keeping older persons in the labor force longer. There seems to be no question that older persons can be productive members of the labor force beyond the retirement age if they have the opportunity and choose to do so.

Hypothesis

1. Those working full-time or part-time will be in better health than those who have retired.
2. Those people who have retired will score higher on measures of life satisfaction than those working full or part-time.
3. Those retirees engaged in volunteer or leisure activities will score higher on measures of life satisfaction than those returning to work.
4. Those people working full-time or part-time during their later years will be more highly regarded by their peers.

Methodology

The questionnaire utilized in this study included the standard demographic variables, as well as measures of attitude toward retirement, the respondent's perceived state of health, life satisfaction, retirement adjustment, and his/her perceived status among friends.

The questionnaire was mailed to 597 members of the Older Hoosiers Federation and 200 Green Thumb workers in Indiana. The Older Hoosiers Federation is a volunteer groups of senior citizens who lobby for or against various state and federal legislation which they perceive would affect older Americans. They are primarily retired Americans over the age of 55. The Green Thumb workers are persons 55 and older who work on various parks, roads, and community projects. They are employed by the federal government in community service projects in order to raise their income above the poverty level. A limitation of this study is that the sample was an available sample and not a random sample. It was the best available sample that the researchers could find at this time. There were 342 valid returns, which represented 42.91% of those surveyed.

Findings

The first hypothesis stated that those persons working full or part-time will be in better health than those who are retired. This hypothesis was not supported by the data. As Table 2 indicates, calculating the mean score on the subjects' perceived state of health for those working full-time, those working part-time, those retired and engaged in volunteer activities, and those retired and engaged in leisure activities and then performing a one-way analysis of variance resulted in a finding of no significant difference in the means of the four groups. While past studies of when people retire have indicated that perceived health and subjects' belief that they have adequate income to retire are often identified as the critical variables in the decision of when to retire, that would not appear to be the case with this sample. There were no significant differences in the perceived state of health for those subjects who were working in comparison to those subjects who were retired (Table 2).

Table 2 One-Way Analysis of Variance: Mean Perceived Health Scores for Older Workers and Retirees

	Mean	N = 329
Work Full-Time	3.4706	51
Work Part-Time	3.2970	101
Retired/Engaged in Volunteer Activities	3.2867	143
Retired/Engaged Leisure Act.	3.2647	34

Source	D.F.	Sum of Squares	Mean Squares	F-Ratio	F-Probability
Between Groups	3	1.4682	.4891	.9956	.3951
Within Groups	325	159.6574	.4913		
Total	328	161.1246			

Table 3 One-Way Analysis of Variance: Mean Life Satisfaction Scores
for Older Workers and Retirees

	Mean	N = 318
Work Full-Time	7.6372	49
Work Part-Time	7.1875	96
Retired/Engaged in Volunteer Activities	7.9928	139
Retired/Engaged in Leisure Activities	8.0000	34

Source	D.F.	Sum of Squares	Mean Squares	F-Ratio	F-Probability
Between Groups	3	40.4064	13.4688	8.2667	.0015
Within Groups	314	803.0056	2.5573		
Total	317	843.4119			

Table 4 One-Way Analysis of Variance: Mean Life Satisfaction Scores
for Older Workers and Retirees

	Mean	N = 268
Returned to Work Full-Time	2.2000	5
Returned to Work Part-Time	2.0333	90
Retired/Engaged in Volunteer Activities	2.3885	139
Retired/Engaged in Leisure Activities	2.2941	34

Source	D.F.	Sum of Squares	Mean Squares	F-Ratio	F-Probability
Between Groups	3	6.9659	2.3220	5.9067	.0006
Within Groups	264	103.7804	.3931		
Total	267	110.7463			

Hypothesis Two stated that those persons who have retired will score higher on measures of life satisfaction than those who are working full or part-time. The mean scores on life satisfaction were calculated for those working full-time, those working part-time, those retired and engaged in volunteer activity, and those retired and engaged in leisure activity. The data indicated that those retired and engaged in volunteer activities and those retired and engaged in leisure activity scored significantly higher on measures of life satisfaction than those working either full or part-time (Table 3). The hypothesis was supported by the data (Table 3).

Hypothesis Three stated that those retirees engaged in volunteer or leisure activities will score higher on measures of life satisfaction than those who retired and then returned to work on a full-time or part-time basis. Mean life satisfaction scores were calculated for those who had retired and then returned to work full-time, those who had retired and then returned to work part-time, those who had retired and were engaged in volunteer activities, and those who had retired and were engaged in leisure activities. Those retired and engaged

in volunteer or leisure activity scored significantly higher on life satisfaction than those who had retired and returned to work full or part-time. As Table 4 indicates there were only five people in this sample who had retired and returned to work full-time. Returning to work full-time was rare in this sample of people.

Hypothesis Four stated that those retirees who returned to work full or part-time will be more respected by their peers than those who have retired and engaged in volunteer or leisure activities.

In terms of their perceived respect by friends, those retired and returning to work full-time scored highest with a mean of 3.0. Those who retired and were engaged in volunteer activities scored second with a mean of 2.86. Those who retired and were engaged in leisure activities scored third with a mean of 2.76. Those who had retired and returned to work part-time perceived they were least respected by their friends with a score of 2.68. While the analysis of variance did not find significant differences in these means at the .05 level of significance, they were

Table 5 One Way Analysis of Variance: Mean Scores for Perceived Respect of Older Workers and Retirees by Their Peers

	Mean	N = 277
Returned to Work Full-Time	3.00006	4
Returned to Work Part-Time	2.6869	99
Retired/Engaged in Volunteer Activities	2.8643	140
Retired/Engaged in Leisure Activities	2.7647	34

Source	D.F.	Sum of Squares	Mean Squares	F-Ratio	F-Probability
Between Groups	3	2.0236	.6745	2.4254	.0657
Within Groups	272	75.8326	.2778		
Total	276	77.8556			

Table 6 One Way Analysis of Variance: Mean Scores on Life Satisfaction Based on the Reasons Individuals Returned to Work

	Mean	N = 130
Needed the money	6.7027	74
Wanted to feel productive	8.2703	37
Lonely & bored	7.2632	19

Source	D.F.	Sum of Squares	Mean Squares	F-Ratio	F-Probability
Between Groups	2	60.6360	30.3180	10.7420	.0000
Within Groups	127	358.4410	2.8224		
Total	129	419.0769			

significant at the .07 level of significance. Since the .05 level of significance is the normal level of acceptance of the significance of difference between groups, this hypothesis was not supported by the data (Table 5).

In order to clarify how the retirees' decision to return to work would affect their life satisfaction, an additional calculation was done. One question asked those who had returned to work was why they had done so. The choices to this question were: I needed the money, I needed to do something that makes me feel productive, and I was lonely and bored and work gave me something interesting to do. Mean scores and measures of life satisfaction were calculated for each of these three groups (Table 6). The highest mean score was for the group who returned to work in order to feel productive, and their score was 8.27. The second highest mean score was for those who had returned to work because they were lonely and bored, and their score was 7.26. The lowest mean score on life satisfaction was 6.7 for those who had been forced to return to work because they needed the money (Table 6). Thus, most of the people that returned to work did so because they needed the money, but they were the least satisfied with their lives.

Conclusion

The data from this study indicate that those who retire and engage in volunteer or recreational activities score higher on measures of life satisfaction than those that never retired. Of those that retired and then returned to work, those that did so because they wanted to feel productive scored highest on life satisfaction. Those that returned to work because they needed the money scored lowest on life satisfaction.

These findings would suggest that if the goal of the federal government is to keep older people in the labor force longer, some means must be found by which the older workers are kept at jobs in which they feel productive and needed. For the business community to continue, primarily for economic reasons, to encourage older workers to retire from highly skilled jobs in which they are more productive than younger workers does not seem desirable.

One possible solution to this problem might be for the federal government to give a tax incentive to businesses employing older workers so that the economic advantage business sees for retiring older workers and employing younger ones would diminish.

A major break in the cost of employing older workers in business would be for the federal government to develop a national health insurance program. One of the major costs to the employer of older workers is the amount of money they must put into health insurance for them. For the federal government to assume this cost would be a major reduction in the business cost of continuing to employ older workers.

Perhaps businesses could continue to utilize the talents of older workers by developing reduced and flexible work schedules which would pay them a lower salary but keep them involved in critical tasks for the industry, as suggested by McShulski (1997).

Since the trend of the last thirty years has been for an ever increasing number of workers to retire prior to age 65, perhaps the government's attempts to keep people in the workforce longer by increasing the age at which they can draw a Social Security check will not be successful. It is possible that through private savings, private investment programs, and pension programs financed by their employers, older workers will continue to retire prior to age 65.

On the other hand, improving technology may mean that business and industry will need fewer employees to produce the nations' goods and services, and therefore they will continue to encourage their workers to retire at younger ages.

The complexity and unpredictability of the factors involved makes predicting future employment and retirement patterns for older Americans at best hazardous and at worst impossible. Observing the results of economic and political pressures placed on both business and government by an ever increasing number of the baby boom generation arriving at retirement age in the next 25 years should prove interesting.

References

Allen, Carole and Herman Brotman. 1981. *Chartbook on Aging.* Washington, D. C.: Administration on Aging.

Beck, S. 1983. "Determinants of Returning to Work after Retirement." Final Report for Grant No. 1R23AG035:65–101, Kansas City, MO.

Berkman, Lisa F. and Lister Breslow. 1983. *Health and Ways of Living: The Alameda Country Study.* New York: Oxford University Press.

Clark, Robert. 1988. "The Future of Work and Retirement." *Research on Aging* 10:169–193.

Clifton, Bryant. 1972. *The Social Dimensions of Work.* Upper Saddle River, NJ: Prentice Hall.

Crowley, J. E. 1990. "Longitudinal Effects of Retirement on Men's Well-Being and Health." *Journal of Business and Psychology* 1:95–113.

Dennis, Helen. 1986. *Fourteen Steps to Managing an Aging Work Force,* edited by Helen Dennis, Lexington, MA: Lexington Books.

Dorfman, L. T. 1992. "Academics and the Transition to Retirement." *Educational Gerontology* 18:343–363.

Dubin, Robert. 1956. "Industrial Workers' Word: A Study of the Central Life Interests of Industrial Workers." *Social Problems* 3:131–142.

Fillenbau, G. G., L. K. George, and E. B. Palmore. 1985. "Determinants and Consequences of Retirement." *Journal of Gerontology* 39:364–371.

Fyock, Catherine. 1991. "American Work Force Is Coming of Age." *The Gerontologist* 31:422–425.

Gall, Terry, David Evans, and John Howard. May 1997. "The Retirement Adjustment Process; Changes in Well-Being of Male Retirees Across Time." *The Journal of Gerontology* 52B(3):110–117.

Gray, Robert M. and David O. Moberg. 1977. *The Church and the Older Person,* revised edition. Grand Rapids, MI: Ermanns.

Hall, Richard. 1975. *Occupations and the Social Structure.* Englewood Cliffs, NJ: Prentice Hall.

Hardy, Melissa. 1991. "Employment After Retirement." *Research on Aging* 13(3):267–288.

House, James S., Karl R. Landes, and Debra Umberson. 1988. "Social Relationships and Health." *Science* 241:540–545.

Howell, Nancy Morrow. 1988. "Life Span Determinants of Work in Retirement Years." *International Journal of Aging and Human Development* 27(2):125–140.

Iams, Howard M. 1985 "New Social Security Beneficiary Women." Correlates of work paper read at the 1985 meeting of the American Sociological Association.

Markides, Kyrakos S. 1983. "Aging, Religiosity and Adjustment: A Longitudinal Analysis." *Journal of Gerontology* 38:621–625.

McShulski, Elaine. 1997. "Ease Employer and Employee Retirement Adjustment with 'Soft Landing' Program." *HR Magazine,* Alexandria: 30–32.

Mobert, David D. 1983. "Compartmentalization and Parochialism in Religion and Voluntary Action Research." *Review of Religious Research* 22(4):318–321.

Moen, Phyllis, Donna Dempster-McClain, and Robin Williams. 1992. "Successful Aging: A Life Course Perspective on Women's Multiple Roles and Health." *American Journal of Sociology* 97(6):1612–1633.

Morris, Malcolm. 1986. "Work and Retirement in an Aging Society." *Daedalus* 115:269–293.

Ortega, Suzanne T., Robert D. Crutchfield, and William A. Rusling. 1983. "Race Differences in Elderly Personal Well-Being, Friendship, Family and Church." *Research on Aging* 5(1):101–118.

Parker, Stanley. 1982. *Works and Retirement.* London: Allen & Unwin Publishers.

Quinn, Joseph and Richard Burkhauser. *1990 Handbook of Aging and the Social Sciences,* edited by Richard Beinstock and Linda K. Gorge. Academic Press.

Quinn, J. F. 1980. *Retirement Patterns of Self-Employed Workers in Retirement Policy on an Aging Society,* R. L. Clark ed., Durham, NC: Duke University Press.

Soldo, Beth J. and Emily M. Agree. 1988. *Population Bulletin* 43(3). Population Reference Bureau.

Sammartino, Frank. 1979. "Early Retirement." in *Monographs of Aging,* No. 1, Madison: Joyce MacBeth Institute on Aging and Adult Life, University of Wisconsin.

Seccombe, K. and G. R. Lee. 1986. "Gender Differences in Retirement Satisfaction and Its Antecedents." *Research on Aging* 8:426–440.

Sheppard, Harold. 1990. *The Future of Older Workers.* International Exchange Center on Gerontology, University of South Florida, Tampa. FL.

Streib, G. F. and C. J. Schneider. 1971. *Retirement in American Society.* Cornell University Press, Ithaca, NY.

Tillenbaum, G. C. 1971. "The Working Retired." *Journal of Gerontology* 26:1:82–89. U. S. Department of Labor, Civilian Labor Force Participation Rates: Actual and Projected 1980.

Vroom, Victor. 1964. *Work & Motivation.* New York: John Wiley.

Welford, A. T. 1988. "Preventing Adverse Changes of Work with Age." *American Journal of Aging and Human Development* 4:283–291.

Critical Thinking

1. Of the life choices a person could have at retirement age, which group scored highest on life satisfaction?

2. Of those who retired and returned to work, who were the most satisfied?

3. Which group scored lowest in life satisfaction after retirement?

UNIT 6

The Experience of Dying

Unit Selections

Learning Outcomes

After reading this Unit, you will be able to:

- Explain how and when hospice care was started in the United States.
- Explain the health care philosophy of the hospice program in the United States in 1973.
- Describe the main function of denial in the grieving process.
- Explain why confusion is normal for those whose social world has been destroyed.
- List the areas of congruence regarding the end of life preferences between the terminally ill and their family caregivers.
- Identify the areas of incongruence between the terminally ill and their families.
- List the six thematic areas that the terminally ill spoke of concerning the parts of their lives over which they felt they had control.
- Indicate the two areas of control that the severely ill could not control.

Student Website

www.mhhe.com/cls

Internet References

Agency for Health Care Policy and Research
    www.ahcpr.gov
Growth House, Inc.
    www.growthhouse.org
Hospice Foundation of America
    www.HospiceFoundation.org

Modern science has allowed individuals to have some control over the conception of their children and has provided people with the ability to prolong life. However, life and death still defy scientific explanation or reason. The world can be divided into two categories: sacred and secular. The sacred (that which is usually embodied in the religion of a culture) is used to explain all the forces of nature and the environment that can neither be understood nor controlled. On the other hand, the secular (defined as "of or relating to the world") is used to explain all the aspects of the world that can be understood or controlled. Through scientific invention, more and more of the natural world can be controlled. It still seems highly doubtful, however, that science will ever be able to provide an acceptable explanation of the meaning of death. In this domain, religion may always prevail. Death is universally feared. Sometimes, it is more bearable for those who believe in a life after death. Here, religion offers a solution to this dilemma. In the words of anthropologist Bronislaw Malinowski (1884–1942):

> Religion steps in, selecting the positive creed, the comforting view, the culturally valuable belief in immortality, in the spirit of the body, and in the continuance of life after death. (Bronislaw Malinowski, *Magic, Science and Religion and Other Essays,* Glencoe, IL: Free Press, 1948)

The fear of death leads people to develop defense mechanisms in order to insulate themselves psychologically from the reality of their own death. The individual knows that someday he or she must die, but this event is nearly always thought to be likely to occur in the far distant future. The individual does not think of himself or herself as dying tomorrow or the next day, but rather years from now. In this way, people are able to control their anxiety about death.

Losing a close friend or relative brings people dangerously close to the reality of death. Individuals come face to face with the fact that there is always an end to life. Latent fears surface. During times of mourning, people grieve not only for the dead, but also for themselves and for the finiteness of life.

The readings in this section address bereavement, grief, and adjustments to the stages of dying. Stephen Connor, in "Development of Hospice and Palliative Care in the United States," points out the things that need to be done and the changes that need to be made to improve the quality of palliative care in this country. In "The Grieving Process," the authors list and describe the stages of grief that the individual will experience following the death of a loved one.

© Getty Images / Mark Thornton

The authors of "End-of-Life Concerns and Care Preferences: Congruence among Terminally Ill Elders and Their Family Caregivers" attempt to distinguish the similarities and differences in the beliefs and preferences of these two groups. In "The Myriad Strategies for Seeking Control in the Dying Process," the authors examine the strategies and means used by dying persons to maintain control of their lives in the final days.

Development of Hospice and Palliative Care in the United States

STEPHEN R. CONNOR

Introduction

More than 30 years have passed since palliative care was introduced in the United States, and what began as a small rebellion has evolved into a fairly large health care industry. Although the palliative care movement has considerably improved the care given to those at the end of life, many challenges remain for palliative care providers in the United States. Some of these challenges have arisen out of the seeds planted in the early years of the U.S. hospice movement.

Early U.S. Hospice History

Palliative care began in the United States through an effort to transplant hospice care from the United Kingdom to the United States. In 1963, Florence Wald, then Dean of the School of Nursing at Yale, invited Dr. Cicely Saunders from London to give a series of lectures on hospice care. Cicely Saunders, matriarch of the worldwide hospice movement, had developed approaches to managing pain and the total needs of the dying patients based on the philosophy of using a team to treat the whole person. Cicely's visit eventually led to the formation of the first U.S. hospice in Branford, Connecticut, which began serving patients at home in 1973.

It is significant that in the United States great emphasis was placed on care in the home, in contrast to the United Kingdom, where hospice care began primarily in inpatient settings. This reflected a number of U.S. factors including a desire for independence, a distrust of medical institutions, and a lack of resources for non-profit hospices operating outside mainstream medicine.

Although some have said that hospice began in the United States as an anti-physician movement, this is not precisely accurate. There was certainly, from the beginning, a strong involvement in hospice from nurses, chaplains, and psychosocial professionals. However, early pioneers in hospice care also included many physicians who, like their other professional colleagues, shared a concern for how the health care system was caring—or more accurately, not caring—for the dying.

Much has been written about the institutionalization of the U.S. health care system—the pervasive attitude of denial and the view of death as the enemy. What was happening in the middle 1970s in the United States as the nescient hospice movement was beginning, reflected the U.S. society as a whole. A consumer movement was underway to take back control of various social institutions, including churches, community services, and health care, from birth to death.

Another significant feature of hospice's development in the United States was the involvement of volunteers. In the beginning everyone was essentially a volunteer, either lay or professional. As hospice has progressed in the United States, lay volunteers have continued to play an important role and have been fundamental in establishing hospice. Today, approximately 400,000 volunteers work in U.S. hospices.

To nurture those in the hospice field, a series of national meetings were convened in Connecticut in 1975, in Boonton, New Jersey in early 1977, and in Marin County in early 1978. These meetings led to the formation of the National Hospice Organization (NHO) in 1978. The first large national NHO conference was held in Washington, D.C. in October 1978 and the first Standards of a Hospice Program of Care were published by NHO in 1979. In 1999, NHO changed its name to the National Hospice and Palliative Care Organization to reflect the melding of traditional hospice care with palliative care in the United States.

Even at this early stage of development, hospice leaders were working with key legislative leaders to develop a system to reimburse hospice care in the United States. Before reimbursement could occur, however, data had to be collected to demonstrate what hospice actually did and what costs were involved. The Health Care Finance Administration (now Center for Medicaid and Medicare Services) conducted a national demonstration project involving 26 hospices throughout the United States to study the effect of reimbursed hospice care. The results of this demonstration project enabled government and hospice representatives to develop a model for how hospice care could be organized and funded, and a bill was introduced to Congress creating a new Medicare entitlement for hospice care.

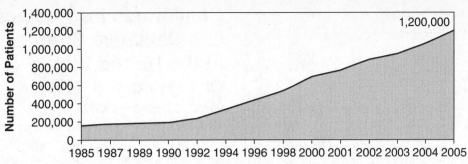

Figure 1 Hospice patients served 1985–2005.

Medicare Hospice Benefit

The Hospice Medicare Benefit (MHB), which was established in 1982 through amendments to the Social Security Act, was included in the Tax Equity and Fiscal Responsibility Act (TEFRA). It was the only new benefit added to Medicare under President Ronald Reagan's administration, and included a three-year sunset provision requiring a report back to Congress on hospice's impact and reauthorization before becoming a permanent benefit in 1985.

The MHB was a unique addition to the U.S. health care system. Prior to implementation of the MHB, the government "reimbursed" providers for their cost in delivering care. With the MHB, a provider was paid a set amount under a prospective reimbursement system. By creating a set payment for hospice care, the government was sharing the risks with a provider. If a patient's cost exceeded the MHB payment, the hospice lost money or had to find other sources of payment. If the MHB payment exceeded a patient's cost, the hospice was allowed to keep the gain even though all hospices originally were not-for-profit organizations.

The set MHB payments were based on the cost of care in the original hospice demonstration project and assumed that each hospice was in compliance with all the standards of hospice care at the time. These standards were changed into Medicare *Conditions of Participation* or regulations that had to be met for a provider to receive payment. Key provisions of the *Conditions of Participation* required hospices to:

- admit eligible patients with a terminal illness with a prognosis of six months or less who chose not to continue curative treatment and agree to hospice care;
- re-certify surviving patients as being terminally ill at specified intervals;
- meet administrative requirements including a governing body, an interdisciplinary team, a plan of care for each patient, a medical record for each patient, a medical director, regular training, quality assurance, use of volunteers, and maintenance of professional management of the program; and
- provide core services by hospice employees including a physician, nurse, counselor, and medical social worker; and provide other non-core services including physical, occupational, and speech therapy, home health

aides/homemakers, medical equipment and supplies, medications, and short term inpatient care for symptom management and respite.

MHB payment is made for each day of hospice care on a per diem basis at one of four rates: routine home care; continuous home care for crisis periods in lieu of hospitalization; general inpatient care for severe symptom management; and inpatient respite care to give up to five days break for caregivers.

Growth of Hospice and Palliative Care in the United States

Over the last 25 years, since the enactment of the MHB, hospice has grown considerably and is now the fastest growing benefit in the Medicare program. Even with that, it still represents less than 3% of Medicare expenditures. For the first 10 years following implementation of the benefit, there was slow growth as community-based hospices learned to adapt to meeting regulatory requirements. However, growth in the 1990s and through 2005 was enormous (see Figure 1) and in 2005 more than 1.2 million people received hospice care in the United States. That same year NHPCO estimates that at least one of every three deaths, of all causes, in the United States was under hospice care.

There have been a number of significant changes to the hospice population over the last 25 years. Initially, more than 90% of hospice patients had a primary diagnosis of malignancy. In 2005, the percent of hospice admissions with a cancer diagnosis had dropped to less than 50%. Also, length of service in hospice dropped from an average of around 70 days to less than 50 days. More concerning is that the median time in hospice dropped to around 20 days, with more than 30% of patients receiving service for seven days or less. These lengths of service have improved slightly in the last few years (see Figure 2), but are still historically low.

The number of sites where hospice care is delivered has grown significantly in recent years (see Figure 3). Over a 20-year period, from 1985 to 2005, the number of hospice sites has increased from around 1,500 to more than 4,000. This growth has been fueled both by the MHB and by increased acceptance of hospice in the U.S. health care system. Also contributing to the growth of hospice has been the growth of for-profit hospices, with over a third of U.S. hospice organizations being for-profit corporations today.

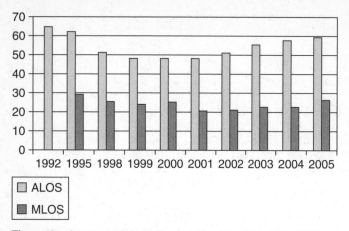

Figure 2 Average and median length of service 1992–2005.

In the last 10 years, there has been considerable growth in programs that deliver palliative care in hospitals and in the community. These programs mostly developed outside of hospices and were the result mainly of limitations on hospice eligibility and the need to provide palliative care more broadly to those who had symptom control problems and serious illness but who were not yet terminally ill. A study of end-of-life care in teaching hospitals in the United States (SUPPORT, 1995) revealed that hospitalized patients often had unmet needs for pain control and that treatment wishes were often unknown or ignored, even when useful information was readily accessible to physicians and specially trained nurses were available for patients and families.

The growth in specialist palliative care in the United States has been dramatic. The Center to Advance Palliative Care reports that the number of palliative care programs increased from 632 (15% of hospitals) in 2000 to 1,240 (30% of hospitals) in 2006—a 96% increase in only five years. Also, NHPCO reports that 64.6% of hospice providers now report the provision of some palliative care outside their hospice program.

A number of additional new developments have shown that palliative care, including hospice, is becoming more accepted in the U.S. health care system. Recently, the American Board of Medical Specialties approved hospice and palliative medicine as a recognized sub-specialty. So far, 10 specialties have indicated their interest in allowing their members to sub-specialize in this field, including: Psychiatry and Neurology, Internal Medicine, Family Medicine, Radiology, Surgery, Anesthesiology, Physical Medicine & Rehabilitation, Obstetrics/Gynecology, Pediatrics, and Emergency Medicine.

Also, the Accreditation Council for Graduate Medical Education has begun to accredit fellowship programs in palliative medicine and the Hospice and Palliative Nurses Association offers certification for advanced practice nurses, registered nurses, and nursing assistants. The American Academy for Hospice and Palliative Medicine is growing into a professional society for physicians and the Center to Advance Palliative Care has initiated a National Palliative Care Research Center. While these developments indicate that hospice and palliative care are coming of age in the United States, there remain many challenges and inequities.

Challenges for Hospice and Palliative Care in the United States

Changes to the Hospice Medicare Benefit

Medicare reimbursement has been the driving force behind hospice's tremendous success in reaching people at the end-of-life in the United States. At the same time, however, regulatory requirements of the MHB have limited the provision of palliative care primarily to those near death. Palliative care services can be provided to patients under existing general Medicare requirements but do not facilitate interdisciplinary care that is essential to palliative care. Physicians and physician surrogates can bill for evaluation and management, licensed psychologists and social workers can bill for some psychological services, and home health agencies can provide general home care, but only under hospice is interdisciplinary care reimbursed as a package.

Some have called for the creation of a specific palliative care benefit in the United States that is separate from hospice. There is concern that creating a parallel palliative care benefit in the United States could result in competition between hospice and palliative care providers. What is needed most are payment provisions that reinforce provisions of good palliative care at various points in the continuum of care for patients with life-threatening illnesses.

Hospice and palliative care leaders in the United States acknowledge that a change is needed in the payment system for palliative care. There is also an understanding that changes to health care reimbursement will occur incrementally and not all at once. What seems to be needed is careful study of the impact of changes and additions to the payment system so that unintended negative consequences can be mitigated.

There is, for instance, a growing consensus that the current restriction on "curative" treatment is not helpful and is the primary cause of late referral to hospice. This treatment restriction was imposed on hospice providers by the director of the Reagan administration's budget office, out of fear that giving patients palliative care and allowing them to continue chemotherapies and other treatments would be too expensive.

While hospice providers at the time did not want to encourage patients to continue treatments that would make their symptom management more difficult and their quality of life poor, patient autonomy and each patient's right to make their own personal decisions about treatment was respected. In fact, the first National Hospice Organization standard for hospice programs of care in 1979 stated that hospice care was "appropriate" care and went on to define appropriate care as a combination of palliative and curative therapies.

A number of studies conducted through the Robert Wood Johnson Foundation's Promoting Excellence in End-of-Life Care program have demonstrated in various settings that removing the curative treatment restriction under the MHB would not in fact be more expensive to the Medicare program (see http://www.promotingexcellence.org/i4a/pages/index.cfm?pageid=1).

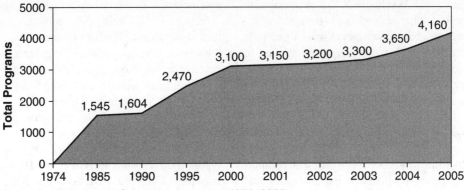

Figure 3 Growth in U.S. hospice programs 1974–2005.

Current hospice providers have a considerable amount of flexibility in how they define curative and palliative treatments. Under Medicare regulations each hospice team determines whether a treatment is curative or not. Very few of the newer treatments available to cancer patients and others with life-threatening conditions can be viewed as curative. A growing number of hospices are implementing "open access" policies wherein all patients with limited prognoses are admitted without regard to their current treatment choices. The hospice then works with the patient and treating physicians to decide which are appropriate to continue based on the patient's goals for care. This approach usually results in earlier hospice referral and enough increased reimbursement to cover the added treatment costs.

Another significant regulatory barrier is the requirement that hospice patients have a prognosis of six months or less if the disease runs its normal course. This requirement is a barrier to timely hospice palliative care. However, to eliminate the six-month prognosis requirement necessitates replacing it with "something else" and that "something else" should not be more onerous than the original requirement.

This problem can be placed on a continuum, with one end being complete reliance on the use of physician judgment and the other end being the use of objective measurable criteria with no judgment involved. There are problems with either of these approaches. Physician judgment has been shown to be notably inaccurate (Christakis, 1999) and many problems are associated with the use of rigid criteria, notably with the application of home health skilled need or homebound criteria and rigid application of local coverage determinations by the Medicare fiscal intermediaries on who is eligible for hospice care.

Some have suggested expanding the six-month criteria to 12 months. This could make it easier for patients to acknowledge the possibility of their approaching death and physicians might find it easier to agree to making such a prognosis, much like the surprise question of "would you be surprised if this patient were alive a year from now?" However, expanding the prognostic criteria doesn't fundamentally change the issue of having to make a determination that death is approaching. Moreover, the federal government has indicated that such a change would be scored as a potential doubling of the cost of hospice care. Therefore, this approach is not likely to occur.

What is needed then is an expansion of hospice benefits to include reimbursement for interdisciplinary consults at an earlier stage of the illness and for care management services prior to admission to a formal hospice service. Such consults and services could be tied to the existence of a life-threatening diagnosis, rather than requiring a prognosis and would require a referral. Such consults are being done now on a limited basis in hospitals, nursing facilities, and residences. Care management programs are emerging; however, to be most effective, the provider needs to have the capacity to do more than just talk on the phone and give advice. To prevent hospitalization, it is sometimes necessary to go to the patient even if it is 2 A.M. Currently, hospices have the most well developed after-hour service delivery capacities.

Workforce Issues

Such an expansion of palliative care will require a substantial increase in a competent workforce. Now that hospice and palliative medicine has been accepted as a recognized sub-specialty, there may be increased incentive for new and existing physicians to enter the field. However, as seen in the sub-specialty of geriatrics, which has not grown in spite of a growing and recognized need, there need to be adequate incentives to attract competent physicians to the field.

Similarly for nursing, which will soon confront a much more significant shortage than has been reported due to large scale retirements, palliative care needs to attract caring and competent professional nurses and skilled nursing assistants. Certification by the National Board for Certification of Hospice and Palliative Nurses is growing and helping to ensure basic competency for nursing professionals. There are currently no recognized certification programs in hospice and palliative care for psychosocial professionals, chaplains, or hospice administrators.

Social workers have been providing the bulk of psychosocial services in hospice programs. This is due to the fact that social work is a required core hospice service and that social workers, if adequately trained in mental health, can also meet the hospice's required need for counseling services. However, there is growing concern that hospices and palliative care programs are not devoting adequate resources to psychosocial services, which are thought to be one of the defining characteristics of the field.

Certainly all team members, including physicians, nurses, and volunteers, can provide some psychosocial care, but social workers, psychologists, and psychiatrists are necessary to address the often complex dynamics and needs of families facing a death. Also, there has been much new knowledge in the field of mental health that may not be adequately applied to the dying and their families. Just providing active listening or providing "supportive" care is not enough. Opportunities for healing relationships and promoting growth at the end of life are major outcomes of good hospice care.

Spiritual and religious services are not as well developed as they could be in hospice and palliative care. Some hospices employ staff chaplains while most coordinate care with community clergy. Most clergy report that their seminarian training was wholly inadequate to prepare them to minister to the dying. Few clergy have undertaken chaplaincy training and when ministering to patients and families are at risk of doing as much harm as good; for example, when patients are left feeling their illness is punishment for misdeeds or lack of faith. Still, spiritual support is generally better in hospice care than in the general health care system and opportunities to help patients find meaning are among the most important of hospice interventions.

If current projections are correct, then more than twice as many hospice professionals and volunteers will be needed in the next 20 years to meet the unmet need for palliative care and the growing numbers of older people in our society. Already, hospices do not have enough physicians to provide optimal care and could use many more to enhance the quality of services.

Access and Quality

The challenge for hospice and palliative care providers can be boiled down to achieving unfettered access to quality palliative care for all who need it. Initially, hospice care in the United States was limited to mainly white suburban cancer patients. Over the past 30 years access has improved considerably and is close to but not yet at parity with population needs. A recent report (Connor et al., in press) demonstrates that blacks are now 7% less likely to receive hospice care than whites. Data for other minority groups is difficult to analyze and the U.S. society is growing increasingly multi-racial.

Significant improvement has been made in improving access to hospice for patients with non-cancer diagnoses, and hospice is now caring for about 60% of all patients who die from cancer. However, access to hospice for patients with solid organ failure, dementia, and frailty still has a long way to go and is limited by current regulatory requirements and prognostic uncertainties. Determining prognosis in non-cancer populations remains a challenge, though recent efforts to improve NHO's original prognostic guidelines are underway.

There remains considerable geographic disparity in access to hospice care (Connor et al., under review), with rates of hospice use ranging from 11% of all deaths in Alaska to 49% of all deaths in Arizona in 2002. Access to hospice and palliative care in very rural areas is a considerable concern.

Most users of hospice care report higher ratings of satisfaction than those dying in other settings (Teno et al., 2004). However, consumer expectations for end-of-life care are low to begin with

and there is a general tendency toward leniency bias. Considerable work is now being done to develop sensitive and specific measures for providers of end-of-life care. As hospice and palliative care have grown in the United States, there has not been as much attention to quality as in the rest of the health care system.

Initial focus was on improving the quality of nursing home care, which has generated the most concern about poor quality. However, hospitals, home health agencies, physician practices, and other Medicare providers have now had to develop accountability measures, many of which are now publicly reported on websites such as Home Health Compare and Nursing Home Compare. Hospice will join their ranks before long.

Most current efforts to measure quality in hospice and palliative care are aimed at drawing out from patients and families feedback about their perception and evaluation of the care they have received. This is only fair as these are important outcomes that we can't risk manage and are inherently important to consumers. We also need to look beyond this feedback to look at how our organizations are functioning, how our workforce is improving, and how we measure changes in the patient's condition in an increasingly electronic world of medical records.

In summary, the hospice and palliative care experiment in the United States is continuing to evolve and grow. While we were wrong to believe that the need for specialized palliative care would be eliminated by now, we can hope that in another 20 years we may see a health care system that provides easy access to palliative care throughout the continuum of care for all those with life-threatening illnesses and, in Cicely's words, is provided by people who can give with both their minds and hearts.

References

Christakis, N. (1999). *Death foretold: Prophecy and prognosis in medical care.* Chicago: University of Chicago Press.

Connor, S., Elwert, F., Spence, C., & Christakis, N. (under review). Racial disparity in hospice use in the United States in 2002. *Social Science and Medicine.*

Connor, S., Elwert, F., Spence, C., & Christakis, N. (in press). Geographic variation in hospice use in the United States in 2002. *Journal of Pain and Symptom Management.*

SUPPORT Investigators. (1995). A controlled trial to improve care for seriously ill patients. *Journal of the American Medical Association, 274*(20), 1591–1598.

Teno, J., Clarridge, B., Casey, V., Welch, L., Wetle, T., Sheild, R., & Mor, V. (2004). Family perspectives on end of life care at the last place of care. *Journal of the American Medical Association, 291*(1), 88–93.

Critical Thinking

1. Originally, how did hospice care in the United States differ from hospice care in England?

2. What was the only new program added to Medicare under President Ronald Reagan's administration?

3. What different kinds of medical problems led to the development of palliative care rather than hospice?

The Grieving Process

Michael R. Leming and George E. Dickinson

Grief is a very powerful emotion that is often triggered or stimulated by death. Thomas Attig makes an important distinction between grief and the grieving process. Although grief is an emotion that engenders feelings of helplessness and passivity, the process of grieving is a more complex coping process that presents challenges and opportunities for the griever and requires energy to be invested, tasks to be undertaken, and choices to be made (Attig, 1991, p. 387).

Most people believe that grieving is a diseaselike and debilitating process that renders the individual passive and helpless. According to Attig (1991, p. 389):

It is misleading and dangerous to mistake grief for the whole of the experience of the bereaved. It is misleading because the experience is far more complex, entailing diverse emotional, physical, intellectual, spiritual, and social impacts. It is dangerous because it is precisely this aspect of the experience of the bereaved that is potentially the most frustrating and debilitating.

Death ascribes to the griever a passive social position in the bereavement role. Grief is an emotion over which the individual has no control. However, understanding that grieving is an active coping process can restore to the griever a sense of autonomy in which the process is permeated with choice and there are many areas over which the griever does have some control. . . .

Coping with Grief

The grieving process, like the dying process, is essentially a series of behaviors and attitudes related to coping with the stressful situation of changing the status of a relationship. . . . Many have attempted to understand coping with dying as a series of universal, mutually exclusive, and linear stages. However, because most will acknowledge that not all people will progress through the stages in the same manner, we will list a number of coping strategies used as people attempt to resolve the pain caused by the loss of a significant relationship.

Robert Kavanaugh (1972) identifies the following seven behaviors and feelings as part of the coping process: shock and denial, disorganization, volatile emotions, guilt, loss and loneliness, relief, and reestablishment. It is not difficult to see similarities between these behaviors and Kübler-Ross's five stages (denial, anger, bargaining, depression, and acceptance) of the dying process. According to Kavanaugh (1972, p. 23), "these seven stages do not subscribe to the logic of the head as much as to the irrational tugs of the heart—the logic of need and permission."

Shock and Denial

Even when a significant other is expected to die, at the time of death there is often a sense in which the death is not real. For most of us our first response is, "No, this can't be true." With time our experience of shock diminishes, but we find new ways to deny the reality of death.

Some believe that denial is dysfunctional behavior for those in bereavement. However, denial not only is a common experience among the newly bereaved, but also serves positive functions in the process of adaptation. The main function of denial is to provide the bereaved with a "temporary safe place" from the ugly realities of a social world that offers only loneliness and pain.

With time the meaning of loss tends to expand, and it may be impossible for one to deal with all of the social meanings of death at once. For example, if my wife dies, not only do I lose my spouse, but also I lose my best friend, my sexual partner, the mother of my children, a source of income, the person who writes the Christmas cards, and so on. Denial can protect me from some of the magnitude of this social loss, which may be unbearable at one point in time. With denial, I can work through different aspects of my loss over time.

Disorganization

Disorganization is that stage in the bereavement process in which one may feel totally out of touch with the reality of everyday life. Some go through the 3-day time period just prior to the funeral as if on "automatic pilot" or "in a daze." Nothing normal "makes sense," and they may feel that life has no inherent meaning. For some, death is perceived as preferable to life, which appears to be devoid of meaning.

This emotional response is also a normal experience for the newly bereaved. Confusion is normal for those whose social world has been disorganized through death. When my father died, my mother lost not only all of those things that one loses with a death of a spouse, but also her caregiving role—a social role and master status that had defined her identity in the 5 years that my father lived with cancer. It is only natural to experience confusion and social disorganization when one's social identity has been destroyed.

Volatile Reactions

Whenever one's identity and social order face the possibility of destruction, there is a natural tendency to feel angry, frustrated, helpless, and/or hurt. The volatile reactions of terror, hatred, resentment, and jealousy are often experienced as emotional manifestations of these feelings. Grieving humans are sometimes more successful at masking their feelings in socially acceptable behaviors than other animals, whose instincts cause them to go into a fit of rage when their order is threatened by external forces. However apparently dissimilar, the internal emotional experience is similar.

In working with bereaved persons over the past 15 years, I have observed that the following become objects of volatile grief reactions: God, medical personnel, funeral directors, other family members, in-laws, friends who have not experienced death in their families, and/or even the person who has died. I have always found it interesting to watch mild-mannered individuals transformed into raging and resentful persons when grieving. Some of these people have experienced physical symptoms such as migraine headaches, ulcers, neuropathy, and colitis as a result of living with these intense emotions.

Guilt

Guilt is similar to the emotional reactions discussed earlier. Guilt is anger and resentment turned in on oneself and often results in self-deprecation and depression. It typically manifests itself in statements like "If only I had . . . ," "I should have . . . ," "I could have done it differently . . . ," and "Maybe I did the wrong thing." Guilt is a normal part of the bereavement process.

From a sociological perspective, guilt can become a social mechanism to resolve the **dissonance** that people feel when unable to explain why someone else's loved one has died. Rather than view death as something that can happen at any time to any one, people can **blame the victim** of bereavement and believe that the victim of bereavement was in some way responsible for the death—"If he had been a better parent, the child might not have been hit by the car," or "If I had been married to him I might also have committed suicide," or "No wonder he died of a heart attack, her cooking would give anyone high cholesterol." Therefore, bereaved persons are sometimes encouraged to feel guilt because they are subtly sanctioned by others' reactions.

Loss and Loneliness

As we discussed earlier, loss and loneliness are the other side of denial. Their full sense never becomes obvious at once; rather, each day without the deceased helps us to recognize how much we needed and depended upon those persons. Social situations in which we expected them always to be present seem different now that they are gone. Holiday celebrations are also diminished by their absence. In fact, for some, most of life takes on a "something's missing" feeling. This feeling was captured in the 1960s love song "End of the World."

> Why does the world go on turning?
> Why must the sea rush to shore?
> Don't they know it's the end of the world
> 'Cause you don't love me anymore?

Loss and loneliness are often transformed into depression and sadness fed by feelings of self-pity. According to Kavanaugh (1972, p. 118), this effect is magnified by the fact that the dead loved one grows out of focus in memory—"an elf becomes a giant, a sinner becomes a saint because the grieving heart needs giants and saints to fill an expanding void." Even a formerly undesirable spouse, such as an alcoholic, is missed in a way that few can understand unless their own hearts are involved. This is a time in the grieving process when anybody is better than nobody and being alone only adds to the curse of loss and loneliness (Kavanaugh, 1972, p. 118).

Those who try to escape this experience will either turn to denial in an attempt to reject their feelings of loss or try to find surrogates—new friends at a bar, a quick remarriage, or a new pet. This escape can never be permanent, however, because loss and loneliness are a necessary part of the bereavement experience. According to Kavanaugh

(1972, p. 119), the "ultimate goal in conquering loneliness" is to build a new independence or to find a new and equally viable relationship.

Relief

The experience of relief in the midst of the bereavement process may seem odd for some and add to their feelings of guilt. My mother found relief in the fact that my father's battle with cancer had ended, even though this end provided her with new problems. I have observed a friend's relief 6 months after her husband died. This older friend of mine was the wife of a minister, and her whole life before he died was his ministry. With time, as she built a new world of social involvements and relationships of which he was not a part, she discovered a new independent person in herself whom she perceived was a better person than she had ever been.

Although relief can give rise to feelings of guilt, like denial, it can also be experienced as a "safe place" from the pain, loss, and loneliness that are endured when one is grieving. According to Kavanaugh (1972, p. 121):

> The feeling of relief does not imply any criticism for the love we lost. Instead, it is a reflection of our need for ever deeper love, our quest for someone or something always better, our search for the infinite, that best and perfect love religious people name as God.

Reestablishment

As one moves toward reestablishment of a life without the deceased, it is obvious that the process involves extensive adjustment and time, especially if the relationship was meaningful. It is likely that one may have feelings of loneliness, guilt, and disorganization at the same time and that just when one may experience a sense of relief something will happen to trigger a denial of the death. What facilitates bereavement and adjustment is fully experiencing each of these feelings as normal and realizing that it is hope (holding the grieving person together in fantasy at first) that will provide the promise of a new life filled with order, purpose, and meaning.

Reestablishment never occurs all at once. Rather, it is a goal that one realizes has been achieved long after it has occurred. In some ways it is similar to Dorothy's realization at the end of The Wizard of Oz—she had always possessed the magic that could return her to Kansas. And, like Dorothy, we have to experience our loss before we really appreciate the joy of investing our lives again in new relationships.

The Four Tasks of Mourning

In 1982 J. William Worden published Grief Counseling and Grief Therapy, which summarized the research conclusions of a National Institutes of Health study called the Omega Project (occasionally referred to as the Harvard Bereavement Study). Two of the more significant findings of this research, displaying the active nature of the grieving process, are that mourning is necessary for all persons who have experienced a loss through death and that four tasks of mourning must be accomplished before mourning can be completed and reestablishment can take place.

According to Worden (1982, p. 10), unfinished grief tasks can impair further growth and development of the individual. Furthermore, the necessity of these tasks suggests that those in bereavement must attend to "grief work" because successful grief resolution is not automatic, as Kavanaugh's (1972) stages might imply. Each bereaved person must accomplish four necessary tasks: (a) accept the reality of the loss, (b) experience the pain of grief, (c) adjust to an environment in which the deceased is missing, and (d) withdraw emotional energy and reinvest it in another relationship (Worden, 1982).

Accept the Reality of the Loss

Especially in situations when death is unexpected and/or the deceased lived far away, it is difficult to conceptualize the reality of the loss. The first task of mourning is to overcome the natural denial response and realize that the person is dead and will not return.

Bereaved persons can facilitate the actualization of death in many ways. The traditional ways are to view the body, attend the funeral and committal services, and visit the place of final disposition. The following is a partial list of additional activities that can assist in making death real for grieving persons.

1. View the body at the place of death before preparation by the funeral director.
2. Talk about the deceased and the circumstances surrounding the death.
3. View photographs and personal effects of the deceased.
4. Distribute the possessions of the deceased among relatives and friends.

Experience the Pain of Grief

Part of coming to grips with the reality of death is experiencing the emotional and physical pain caused by the loss. Many people in the denial stage of grieving attempt to avoid pain by choosing to reject the emotions and feelings that they are experiencing. Some do this by avoiding places and circumstances that remind them of the deceased. I know of one widow who quit playing golf and quit eating at a particular restaurant because these were activities that she had enjoyed with her husband. Another widow found it extremely painful to be with her dead husband's twin, even though he and her sister-in-law were her most supportive friends.

J. William Worden (1982, pp. 13–14) cites the following case study to illustrate the performance of this task of mourning:

One young woman minimized her loss by believing her brother was out of his dark place and into a better place after his suicide. This might have been true, but it kept her from feeling her intense anger at him for leaving her. In treatment, when she first allowed herself to feel anger, she said, "I'm angry with his behavior and not him!" Finally she was able to acknowledge this anger directly.

The problem with the avoidance strategy is that people cannot escape the pain associated with mourning. According to Bowlby (cited by Worden, 1982, p. 14), "Sooner or later, some of those who avoid all conscious grieving, break down—usually with some form of depression." Tears can afford cleansing for wounds created by loss, and fully experiencing the pain ultimately provides wonderful relief to those who suffer while eliminating long-term chronic grief.

Adjust to an Environment in which the Deceased is Missing

The third task, practical in nature, requires the griever to take on some of the social roles performed by the deceased, or to find others who will. According to Worden (1982, p. 15), to abort this task is to become

helpless by refusing to develop the skills necessary in daily living and by ultimately withdrawing from life.

I knew a woman who refused to adjust to the social environment in which she found herself after the death of her husband. He was her business partner, as well as her best and only friend. After 30 years of marriage, they had no children, and she had no close relatives. She had never learned to drive a car. Her entire social world had been controlled by her former husband. Three weeks after his funeral she went into the basement and committed suicide.

The alternative to withdrawing is assuming new social roles by taking on additional responsibilities. Extended families who always gathered at Grandma's house for Thanksgiving will be tempted to have a number of small Thanksgiving dinners after her death. The members of this family may believe that "no one can take Grandma's place." Although this may be true, members of the extended family will grieve better if someone else is willing to do Grandma's work, enabling the entire family to come together for Thanksgiving. Not to do so will cause double pain—the family will not gather, and Grandma will still be missed.

The final task of mourning is a difficult one for many because they feel disloyal or unfaithful in withdrawing emotional energy from their dead loved one. One of my family members once said that she could never love another man after her husband died. My twice-widowed aunt responded, "I once felt like that, but I now consider myself to be fortunate to have been married to two of the best men in the world."

Other people find themselves unable to reinvest in new relationships because they are unwilling to experience again the pain caused by loss. [A] quotation from John Brantner . . . provides perspective on this problem: "Only people who avoid love can avoid grief. The point is to learn from it and remain vulnerable to love."

However, those who are able to withdraw emotional energy and reinvest it in other relationships find the possibility of a newly established social life. Kavanaugh (1972, pp. 122–123) depicts this situation well with the following description.

At this point fantasies fade into constructive efforts to reach out and build anew. The phone is answered more quickly, the door as well, and meetings seem important, invitations are treasured and any social gathering becomes an opportunity rather than a curse. Mementos of the past are put away for occasional family gatherings. New clothes and new places promise dreams instead of only fears. Old friends are important for encouragement and permission to rebuild one's life. New friends can offer realistic opportunities for coming out from under the grieving mantle. With newly acquired friends, one is not a widow, widower, or survivor—just a person. Life begins again at the point of new friendships. All the rest is of yesterday, buried, unimportant to the now and tomorrow.

Critical Thinking

1. When one's identity and social order face the possibility of being destroyed by the death of a loved one, what are some of the most volatile reactions?
2. What are the results of feeling guilty when grieving over a loved one?
3. What are the four tasks of mourning according to Kavanaugh (1972)?

End-of-Life Concerns and Care Preferences: Congruence among Terminally Ill Elders and Their Family Caregivers

Daniel S. Gardner, PhD and Betty J. Kramer, PhD

Introduction

In the past several decades, it has become clear that there are substantial disparities between the way older Americans wish to die and the way their last days are realized. This discrepancy is due, in part, to well-documented gaps in the quality of care that people receive at the end of life (Field & Cassel, 1997; SUPPORT, 1995). Although most people prefer to die in their own homes (Higginson & Sen-Gupta, 2000; Tang & McCorkle, 2003; Thomas, Morris, & Clark, 2004), a majority of deaths occur in hospitals or nursing homes (Gallo, Baker, & Bradley, 2001; Pritchard, Fisher, Teno, Sharp, Reding, Knaus, et al., 1998). And despite considerable advances in medical and supportive approaches to pain management, a significant number of older adults with advanced and terminal illness experience serious pain and discomfort (SUPPORT, 1995; Teno, Clarridge, Casey, Welch, Wetle, Shield, et al., 2004). In an effort to better understand the needs and enhance the care of dying individuals and their families, end-of-life researchers have explored these and other disparities between end-of-life preferences and outcomes.

Barriers to quality end-of-life care include the unpredictable nature of terminal illness, communication difficulties in familial and social relationships, and the complex care needs of dying patients and their families (Kramer & Auer, 2005). Quality care is also hindered by systemic-level factors, including the emphasis on curative and life-sustaining intervention over quality of life and supportive care, health care financing and service delivery structures that move patients between multiple care settings with minimal coordination and poor continuity of care, a lack of providers trained in the fundamentals of palliative care (e.g., biopsycho-social-spiritual aspects of grief and loss, effective clinical communication, attention to family systems), and the absence of evidence-based practice knowledge in this area (Emanuel, von Gunten, & Ferris, 2000; Field & Cassel, 1997; Morrison, 2005). Further, end-of-life care models that represent the standard of care—hospice and palliative care—are underutilized and often inaccessible to the poor, racial and ethnic minorities, and elders with uncertain disease pathways.

Less is known about the subjective end-of-life experiences, concerns, and preferences of older patients and their family members (Cohen & Leis, 2002; Singer, Martin & Kellner, 1999; Vig, Davenport, & Pearlman, 2002). Recently there have been calls for research to better understand factors that affect patients' and families' perceptions of quality of life and quality of care at the end of life (Field & Cassel, 1997; Kramer, Christ, Bern-Klug, & Francoeur, 2005; NIH, 2004; SUPPORT, 1995). This study explores the challenges, concerns, and preferences of low-income elders receiving palliative care, and focuses on congruence and incongruence between the elders and their primary family caregivers.

Quality of Life and Care at the End of Life

The Institute of Medicine defined a "good death" as one with minimal suffering, which satisfies the wishes of dying patients and their families, while adhering to current medical, cultural and ethical standards (Field & Cassel, 1997). Researchers often operationalize a good death as the degree to which an individual's dying experiences correspond with their preferences for quality of life and quality of care at the end of life (Engelberg, Patrick, & Curtis, 2005). A growing literature has sought to shed light on the aspects of care that are most important to terminally ill elders and their family members (Heyland, Dodek, Rocker, Groll, Gafhi, Pichora et al., 2006; Laakkonen, Pitkala, & Strandberg, 2004).

When faced with advanced life-threatening illness, most people wish to be free of pain and symptoms (Heyland et al., 2006; Vig & Pearlman, 2004), to be treated with dignity and respect (Chochinov, Hack, Hassard, Kristjianson, McClement, & Harlos, 2002; Steinhauser, Christakis, Clipp, McNeilly, McIntyre, & Tulsky, 2000), and to maintain a sense of autonomy and control over their last days (Singer et al., 1999; McSkirmning, Hodges, Super, Driever, Schoessler, Franey, et al., 1999; Vig & Pearlman, 2004). Nearly all prefer to be informed of their prognoses and have time to put their affairs in order (Heyland et al., 2006; McCormick & Conley, 1995; Terry, Olson, Wilss, & Boulton-Lewis, 2006). Dying elders hope to avoid becoming burdens to their families (McPherson, Wilson, & Murray, 2007; Vig & Pearlman, 2004) and typically eschew the use of artificial means to prolong life (Heyland et al., 2006; Singer et al., 1999; see Steinhauser et al., 2000 for divergent findings). There is, however, a great deal of heterogeneity in what constitutes a "good death." Ultimately, end-of-life preferences are individual, dynamic and multidimensional, and vary across contexts such as age, gender, disease course, care setting, financial resources, and social and familial relationships (Thomas et al., 2004).

Congruence in Patient and Family Perspectives

During the course of advanced and terminal illness, elders increasingly rely on family members to identify and communicate their emotional and physical needs and concerns (McPherson, Wilson, Lobchuk, & Brajtman, 2008; Waldrop, Kramer, Skretny, Milch, & Finn, 2005). Much of the research on patients' end-of-life care preferences is also based on the report of family surrogates or healthcare proxies (Teno et al., 2004). However, the accuracy of family members' assessments of dying patients' concerns and preferences is uncertain. Studies have documented significant incongruence between patients and family members on their evaluations of quality of life (Farber, Egnew, Herman-Bertch, Taylor, & Guldin, 2003; McPherson & Addington-Hall, 2003), frequency and severity of pain and other physical and psychological symptoms (McPherson et al., 2008; Mularski, Curtis, Osborne, Engelberg, & Ganzini, 2004; Sneeuw, Sprangers, & Aaronson, 2002), and end-of-life preferences (Engelberg et al., 2005; Moorman & Carr, 2008; Shalowitz, Garret-Myer, & Wendler, 2006; Steinhauser et al., 2000). Farber and colleagues (2003) describe these differences as reflecting the often highly divergent "cultural perspectives" of patients and their formal and informal caregivers around death and dying.

Although findings have been inconsistent, congruence in the end-of-life preferences and perceptions of elders and their family caregivers has been found to range from moderate to poor. There is some evidence of greater agreement around objective and measurable factors such as patient functioning and mobility, and less regarding subjective factors such as pain and depression (Desbiens & Mueller-Rizner, 2000; Engelberg et al., 2005; McPherson & Addington-Hall, 2003; Tang & McCorkle, 2003). Congruence may be more likely when surrogate decision-makers are younger and female (McPherson & Addington-Hall, 2003; Zettel-Watson, Ditto, Danks, & Smucker, 2008), family income is higher (Desbiens & Mueller-Rizner, 2000), the illness is of longer duration, or the patient is closer to death (Sneeuw et al., 2002). Notably, there is evidence that families who have had explicit discussions about dying and the patient's wishes are more likely to agree with each other about end-of-life care preferences (Engelberg et al., 2005; Sulmasy, Terry, Weisman, Miller, Stallings, Vettese et al., 1998).

Despite gaps in our understanding of the correspondence between individual and family experiences of dying and preferences for end-of-life, very few studies have focused on congruence among paired patient-family caregiver dyads (Engelberg et al., 2005). And there remains a critical lack of knowledge about the shared and distinct challenges, concerns, and preferences of older adults and their family caregivers at the end of life (Vig et al., 2002). Empirical inquiry in this area may help to enhance familial understanding of older patients' concerns and the accuracy of surrogate decision-making, and to ultimately improve the quality of life at the end of life. The study described here uses qualitative methods to delve more deeply into the subjective experiences of terminally ill elders and their family caregivers, describe their end-of-life preferences and identify areas of congruence and incongruence.

Methods
Study Design

These data were collected as part of a larger longitudinal research study exploring the process and experience of end-of-life care provided to frail elders with advanced chronic disease enrolled in an innovative, fully "integrated" managed care program (Kramer & Auer, 2005). The design was an embedded case study (Scholz & Tietje, 2002), involving in-depth data collection with multiple sources of data. Case study research design makes it possible to examine processes, perceptions and outcomes regarding naturalistic phenomena of which the researcher seeks multiple perspectives (Yin, 2003). The results reported here address the congruent and incongruent end-of-life perceptions, challenges, concerns, and care preferences of elders and their primary family caregivers.

Research Site and Sample

Elder Care of Dane County, a not-for-profit organization, has provided community-based health and social services for older adults since 1976. The Elder Care Partnership (ECP) program, the largest program offered by this organization, provides comprehensive, fully integrated health, psychosocial, and long-term care to low-income frail elders. The program integrates practices that are consistent with clinical practice guidelines for quality palliative care (National Consensus Project, 2004). Detailed descriptions of the study and site can be found elsewhere (Kramer & Auer, 2005).

Study participants were purposively selected by interdisciplinary team members from the pool of elders (aged 65 years or older) enrolled in ECP. Enrollees had annual incomes below $10,000, seven to eight chronic medical conditions, and functional limitations in three or more Activities of Daily Living. Team members were asked to identify elders who were likely to die within 6 months, spoke English, were cognitively able to understand and respond to interview questions, and had a family member involved in their care. Once the elder completed consent procedures and agreed to participate, team members invited the identified primary family caregiver to participate in an interview with the Principal Investigator (PI; second author).

Data Collection

In-depth, semi-structured, face-to-face interviews, which ranged from 1 to 2 hours long, were conducted by the project PI, a university professor and Project on Death in America Social Work Leader. Elders and their identified family care-givers were interviewed separately at a time and place selected by the participant, most often in the participant's home. The interviews were not standardized in order to facilitate greater exploration of issues deemed most important to respondents (Padgett, 2008). Instead, each interview was structured around open-ended questions reflecting the study aims, including questions designed to explore the perceived challenges and concerns of the participants, their end-of-life preferences, and the extent to which they had discussed these issues with family members:

- What has been most difficult or challenging to you and your family members at this time?
- What are your [your family member's] concerns or worries?
- What is most important to you about the care you [your family member] receive[s] in your [their] last days?
- If you could plan it perfectly, what kind of death would you hope for [for the patient]? What would make a "good" death?

Additional questions and probes were used to explore participant preferences about the location of death, the desire for family members to be present, and the importance of family communication and saying "goodbye" during the elder's last days. In addition, the interviewer asked about the extent to which they had talked about the elders' end-of-life preferences, and their comfort or difficulty in doing so.

Data Analysis

All of the interviews were recorded on audiotape and transcribed verbatim, with participant consent. The researchers employed qualitative methods that entailed detailed readings and re-readings of each transcript, team coding, and thematic and conceptual analysis. Data analysis followed a form of *template analysis* (Crabtree & Miller, 1999) that begins with an a priori set of coding categories (i.e., a "template") based on the researchers' domains of interest (end-of-life challenges and worries or fears, care concerns, preferences, and family communication). Two researchers independently read the transcripts, identified segments that were relevant to the research domains, and used the preliminary coding template to search for and identify patterns and themes in the data. These themes were then tested within and across cases, and refined in order to generate broader and more integrated conceptual domains. Upon reaching theoretical saturation, a thematic conceptual matrix (Patton, 2002) was developed to examine the congruent (i.e., like) and incongruent (distinct) themes relevant to the domains of elder and family caregiver end-of-life challenges, concerns, and care preferences.

While no tests were conducted of inter-rater reliability, the research team employed several strategies to ensure analytic rigor. The protocol included: extended engagement, or the use of long interviews with extensive probing and clarification; independent team coding and peer debriefing; deviant case analysis in the development and testing of a final thematic schema; and careful auditing that involved documentation (including verbatim transcripts, field notes, and analytic memos) of the data collection and analytic process (Padgett, 2008).

Findings
Study Participants

Ten elders (five women and five men) and ten family caregivers (six women and four men) completed face-to-face interviews (see Table 1). The mean age of the elders was 85 years-old (range: 64-101), and family members were a mean 53 years-old (range: 47-67). Family caregivers included four daughters, three sons, one daughter-in-law, one grandson, and one wife. Nine of the dyads were non-Hispanic white, and one was African American. Elders were enrolled in the program an average of 2.6 years (range: 1.5-4), and all had multiple chronic health conditions. The most debilitating diagnoses included serious heart disease ($n = 5$), lung disease ($n = 3$), and cancer ($n = 2$). Five of the elders lived alone and five lived with their family caregivers (four with an adult child and one with a spouse).

Domains of Care

Four domains of end-of-life care framed the results of our analysis: a) the *challenges* or day-to-day difficulties related to the patient's terminal illness; b) participants' *worries* or fears about the patient's death and dying; c) *care concerns* regarding the patient's end-of-life care by formal and informal caregivers; and d) participants' hopes and preferences

Table 1 Elder and Family Caregiver Dyads

Elder	Family Caregiver
97-year-old African-American female with heart disease	47-year-old African-American grandson; single, live-in caregiver
86-year-old white female with lung disease	50-year-old white daughter; lives separately
89-year-old white male with heart disease	56-year-old white son; married, lives separately
82-year-old white female with lung cancer	52-year-old white daughter; single, lives separately
101-year-old white female with heart disease	67-year-old white son; single, live-in caregiver
84-year-old white male with heart disease	47-year-old white daughter; divorced, lives separately (in same town)
80-year-old white male with heart disease and accident-related injuries	48-year-old white daughter-in-law (married to step-son); lives separately
86-year-old white male with prostate cancer	56-year-old daughter; single, live-in caregiver
82-year-old white female with lung disease and accident-related injuries	48-year-old white son; married, lives with elder
64-year-old white male with lung disease	55-year-old white wife; live-in

Table 2 Congruence & Incongruence among Elders & Family Caregivers

Domain	Themes	Incongruent		Congruent
		Elder	**Family**	**Both**
Challenges	Experiencing decline			X
	Accepting dependence	X		
	Providing adequate care		X	
	Living with uncertainty			X
Worries	Pain & suffering			X
	Meeting elders' care needs		X	
	Becoming a burden	X		
	Anticipating the impact on survivors			X
Concerns about EOL Care	Receiving competent, consistent & responsive care			X
	Managing pain			X
	Being treated with dignity and respect			X
	Living while dying			X
A "Good Death"	Dying at home			X
	Dying quickly, without suffering			X
	Avoiding life support			X
	Being prepared	X		
	Addressing spiritual needs addressed		X	

for a *good death*. These domains reflect a range of end-of-life concerns and preferences that were expressed and elaborated on by study participants, some of which are shared or congruent, and others which are distinct to either elders or their family members (see Table 2).

Challenges

Elders and their family caregivers identified four primary illness-related challenges they struggled with on a daily basis.

Experiencing Physical and Functional Decline

Elders spoke articulately about their efforts to participate in normal daily activities in the face of decreased energy and declining physical and functional capacities, as is illustrated here:

I like to walk. I can't get out and walk. I have to have a walker so sometimes the kids take me in a wheelchair and we can walk around the campgrounds, or we'll go down by the lake. I'd like to be able to walk, too. But I can't do it. I can't go up and down the stairs so I have to stay here and let somebody else go down and do my laundry. I haven't been down the stairs in the basement for two years. (83 year-old female elder)

I can't do the things I want to do, like mow the lawn or walk down the block. It's hard to breathe . . . Yeah, feels like you're ready to die—takes your breath right away from you. (64-year-old male elder)

Family caregivers also struggled with the changes in their loved ones' functioning, often within the context of lifelong relationships:

It's just that I can't be with him like I'd like to be . . . we've been married almost 37 years so it's a long time, and, just to see him going downhill like he is. (55-year-old wife)

Accepting Increasing Dependence

Closely associated with physical and functional decline, many elders struggled to contend with the diminished autonomy and increasing dependence on others:

I miss driving . . . I have to depend on other people and I was always so independent. It bothers me when I have to ask people to haul me around and pick me up, but they don't care, they don't say anything, but I—that's one thing that bugs me but I can't change it so I'll just go on the way it is. (80-year-old male elder)

Some family caregivers were aware that decreased autonomy could be challenging for the elders, but rather than viewing dependence as a challenge they emphasized the benefits of relying on others:

He was able to take his own baths and do everything and then wham-o, here he is. He's in bed all the time and somebody has to help him bathe or whatever . . . although I tell him it's *teamwork,* that we're doing this as a team. (56-year-old daughter)

Providing Adequate Care

Family caregivers spoke at length about caring for the elders, often emphasizing the challenges and responsibilities inherent in the role of family caregiver.

Basically, I'm her number one health advocate. I've had to deal with these situations where people didn't want [her] to go to the hospital and I knew she had to, or just on and on with different things that have happened. So, I just kind of focus on her. (48-year-old son)

The challenge of providing care was often experienced as stressful by family members, given the elder's changing medical needs and the complex nature of family history and relationships:

Part of my life is on hold right now because I'm staying here to take care of her. . . . I'm married and I have a wife and we want to enjoy our life together, so as painful as it is to see your parent leave your life, it's also going to be a big transition when I finally get on with my life . . . it's really a dichotomy because you feel selfish when you think about yourself and your own situation and what your preferences are and what you'd do if you were just living in your own house with your own family versus taking care of a parent. So, it's pretty hard. (48-year-old son)

Living with Uncertainty

Both elders and family caregivers talked about the difficulties they had in coping with their uncertain futures. Although all participants were aware that the elders had limited prognoses, many struggled with not knowing how and when their terminal decline would occur:

About death? I've had pains and stuff, you know, and I had to go to the hospital and all that. I don't know if I'm gonna come home again or not. You don't know that—if you're that bad—and these blood clots can move. They can hit you just like that and you're gone. (64-year-old male elder)

For me, it's never knowing when he's going into an attack, and if I'm at work . . . I told them at work—I said there'll be days when I can't come in because he isn't good, or I'll have to leave because something's gone wrong. (55-year-old wife)

Worries or Fears about Dying

Elders and family caregivers were encouraged to talk about their concerns, worries, and fears related to dying. In response to direct questions, most of the elders initially denied any fears of death or dying. As the interviews progressed, however, elders and family caregivers raised a variety of concerns about the future. Four areas of concern or worry were expressed by a majority of the participants.

Pain and Suffering

The principal concern shared by elders and family caregivers was that the elder would experience unmanageable pain or physical discomfort as they were dying.

I'm concerned about pain and cancer, I never had anyone in my family that's had cancer, my ideas of it are strictly from novels or movies, so they give you enough pain medication to control the pain then you're going to be nauseated and sleepy and even [lose] your mind, hallucinating even, so that's not something I look forward to. (82-year-old female elder)

I guess I'm . . . afraid of the pain, if she might have a lot of pain. I don't know, it really is kind of terrifying. I don't know what it's going to be like when the, if the cancer really hits. The best thing would be if she would die from some secondary, related, symptomatic illness like pneumonia or something. (52-year-old daughter)

Meeting Elders' Increasing Needs

Family caregivers were particularly worried about their capacity to respond to the intensifying needs of the elders, and that they might lack the necessary supports and resources to continue providing care at home. Several participants feared having to place elders in long-term care institutions in the future:

I suppose my biggest concern . . . is that he will regress and have a physical deterioration that will make it virtually impossible for him to be able to continue in that apartment, making a full time placement in a nursing home type facility necessary. That's going to be hard in a lot of ways. There's the physical move and taking care of all the stuff that will need to be moved over there, and then there's just the emotional aspect for [Elder] in terms of being in a place where he just damn well doesn't want to be. (48-year-old daughter-in-law)

A related concern was that the elder might not be aware of—or might hide—signs of his or her decline.

I think probably one of my biggest concerns with my mother is whether or not she'll be totally honest and recognize when something is really wrong. And so that, that's got me some concern to the point when she did fall the last time and she was in the nursing home . . . she had fallen a couple of times earlier in the week and hadn't told anybody that she had been dizzy and that she had fallen and if she, if she had told anybody either her home nurse or us, that that was going on, then we would have intervened, so it raised questions about whether or not she could be on her own or not. (50-year-old daughter)

Family caregivers often feared a sudden decline in the elder's health, and, in particular, "something happening with no one around." Several family members expressed anxiety and guilt about going to work or returning to their own homes, and leaving the elder in the care of others.

Well, I worry every single day about her falling down and stuff like that, and what's going to be the next trigger that sends her back to the hospital for the next surgery that she can barely tolerate or not at all—that whole thing. (48-year-old son)

Becoming a Burden

A major concern of most of the elders was the fear of experiencing a long trajectory of decline, and becoming a burden on their families:

Well, I'd like to go fast. I don't want to suffer a lot and make everybody else suffer a lot. That would be important. My husband had Alzheimer's and that was

just pathetic, watching him for ten years go down-hill . . . most families now-a-days are half crazy with trying to make a living . . . they have to spend so much time with the woman working and the man working, and then to add the care of an elderly patient is just too much for them, it overburdens them so that they, the parent or the aunt or grandmother, whoever it is, begins to feel well I don't want to bother my children with this, I'll just let it go which is what I do to some extent. (82-year-old female elder)

Family caregivers did not share the concern that their elders were becoming burdens; most did not question their responsibility to provide care and support for the elders.

Anticipating Survivors' Wellbeing

Many elders worried about the needs and wellbeing of their families after their impending death. They were primarily concerned about family members' grief and ability to cope with the loss:

Just to keep my daughter as calm as possible—that's the main thing. I don't want to upset her any more than I have to. What can you do? Your parents die, that's going to happen, so . . . there is nothing to be done about it but I want to, want her to be as calm as possible. (82-year old female elder)

One elder was also specifically anxious about the spiritual wellbeing of her children and grandchildren after she died:

Well, to know that they're taken care of—their health and they're able to—their religion—stay with that. And then I hear about some of them giving up religion and they're all becoming atheists—it makes me feel kind of blue. I don't like to hear that. (101-year-old female elder)

Some elder participants worried more about practical concerns (e.g., medical bills, taxes, or loss of income) that would affect their loved ones. Many expressed regrets that they would not be around to look out for family members after death.

Well, the thing I'd be concerned about is my wife and the kids, and the house and stuff, you know? All the bills should be paid, or whatever. Well, she'd be living here by herself, you know? And if she was taken care of, or whatever she has to do—I don't think she'd ever get remarried again, but I imagine it'd be tough for her to keep on rolling, keeping the house maybe. The taxes ain't cheap. (64-year-old male elder)

I just hope that the kids will get along fine, and the grandkids, that's it. And hope the world straightens out a little bit better. All this terrorism and stuff, I don't like that but that's way beyond my help. (80-year-old male elder)

Family caregivers echoed these concerns with their own worries about life after the elder's death. Some concerns were about their anticipation of grief and loss, but several caregivers worried about pragmatic matters such as arranging funeral plans and paying bills.

> [My fears are] stupid. [Laughs], My worries are about her funeral, okay? That it will come at a really bad time, like when I'm in the middle of three hundred and forty report cards and my house is a mess, you know, and that kind of stuff that, that I won't know what to do. That there will be a division, and fighting like over the paintings and things like that [Laughs]. I want her to write people's names on the backs of the paintings so I won't have to deal with it. (50-year-old daughter)

Concerns about End-of-Life Care

In addition to their worries about dying, elders and family caregivers articulated their concerns and care preferences regarding the care the elders would receive from healthcare team members in their last days. Specifically, they reported four major preferences.

Receiving Competent, Consistent and Responsive Care

Elders and family caregivers felt that quality care required the involvement of skilled healthcare professionals who were competent, "consistent and responsive" to the elders' needs. For elders, it was of critical importance to feel they could depend on reliable caregivers that met their basic needs:

> Well [hospice] volunteers means that no one person would come every week, instead you would probably get a stream of people coming in, none of whom you knew and I don't like that idea at all. . . . Just that whoever takes care of me shows me respect . . . taking good care of me. You know, keeping me clean and fed and whatever. If I can't eat—well that's another thing but . . . I just think to take good care of me, see that my needs were taken care of. (82-year-old female elder)

For family members, these concerns seemed to be associated with their anxieties about meeting the elders' escalating needs as death approached (see above). Their descriptions of adequate care often emphasized the medical and concrete aspects of care (e.g., keeping the elder safe and clean, and ensuring their adherence to medication regimens):

> I think hygiene is way up on the scale as for as her, granny's is. Her body is so fragile and her skin is so, you know, tender, so I mean for them making sure she's gets the proper hygiene. And medical, um, well granny won't take a lot of medical, but I mean, but they're there for any medical needs. But, I think, just trying to make her comfortable as possible. (48-year-old grandson)

Managing Pain

Elders and family caregivers were concerned that the elders receive good pain control and prompt alleviation of physical discomfort at the end of their lives. For several participants, this was a primary reason for choosing hospice or palliative care services:

> Well that, the hospitals, they never used to give you enough painkiller to make enough difference because they said you were going to become addicted. Well what difference does it make at that point? And so I would want someone managing that and I . . . I think I would want to go to hospice and let them handle it. (86-year-old female elder)

> I happen to be a big proponent of hospice-type transitions from life to death. And, I'm a big believer in you make the person comfortable. At that point, I don't care if he gets hooked on a particular drug. It's irrelevant. But if he could have his needs tended to, the pain alleviated, and the transition as smooth as possible, I'd rather see that—except to go quickly. (48-year-old daughter-in-law)

Being Treated with Dignity and Respect

Elders and family caregivers also agreed that respectful treatment was of paramount concern in end-of-life care. For elders, this meant appreciating their need for autonomy and control, and being cared for in a courteous, compassionate manner. Family members also articulated the importance of having providers who treated the elders with dignity and valued each patient as a unique, "whole person":

> Just that, that whole, you know, just having respect and beauty and concern around. . . . But a nursing home staff in all fairness is totally overloaded, I mean so it's not like totally all their fault. It's our system's fault, it's like, we don't value that so much. (50-year-old daughter)

> To try to meet the person on their own level. In my mother's case, in other words, to try and find out what is important to that person and take an interest in those things with them. Share with them those things. If someone thinks clipping coupons is important, than the social worker who's coming says look at all these coupons I found, we can go get such and such at so and so or if the person is a musician and the social worker would come and say well I have a new recording of so and so's orchestra doing such and such. (52-year-old daughter)

Living While Dying

Many of the elders thought it was important to continue living as they had their entire lives. "Focusing on living" instead of dying included eating the foods they loved, participating in activities they enjoyed (e.g., walking, sewing, card-playing, and socializing) with friends and family.

Just comradeship. . . . [Having] people that are around that I will talk with, or will talk with me, and you would miss them if you don't see them at least once a week, or more than that. (84-year-old male elder)

This concern was associated with the desire to be treated with dignity and respect, and to die at home in the context of intimate surroundings, people, and routines! Elders emphasized the critical importance of having a measure of control over their lives and choice in their care during the dying process.

Well, if I could eat—to get some decent food—and they wouldn't cut me off my martinis or beer. That's about all. (80-year-old male elder)

Although not often a primary concern, most family caregivers expressed an understanding of how important it was for the elder to continue "living while dying," and sought to provide them with opportunities to enjoy their cherished activities.

Well, I think she wants to maintain a sense of normalcy, that things are still the way they used to be as much as possible. So even if life is slipping away, she still can enjoy it. She can still feel at home. So little things, like being able to watch her favorite television shows. . . . Being able to get out—she likes to get out and drive around. You know, just anything that would make her feel normal. So eating the types of things that she's enjoyed in the past, being able to go to a movie with us, go for a drive with the relatives. All the types of things like that. (48-year-old son)

A "Good Death"

In response to a being asked to describe a good death, participants expressed their fundamental end-of-life preferences for the elders' final days.

Dying at Home

Almost all participants expressed a preference for the elder to die at home. Dying at home was viewed as a more "natural death," where elders could more easily be surrounded by friends and family, and their final wishes could be best met. Several family caregivers worried that the patient's needs might outstrip the supports and resources necessary to keep the elder at home until death, but preferred that the death take place at home if at all possible.

Dying Quickly, Without Suffering

For elders and family members, the ideal death was seen as one where the elder dies swiftly, "peacefully, and without pain." One patient summed this perspective up memorably:

Just let me die. Quickly. Fast. And painlessly. . . . Stand out there and have lightening strike me, or anything that would do me in like that! (84-year-old male elder)

Many imagined a "natural" death, spending their last moments comfortably ensconced in a favorite chair or sitting in a garden surrounded by natural beauty. Some hoped they would simply be able to "go to sleep and not wake up":

Good death would be able to roll out in a wheelchair onto a garden patio and be surrounded by beautiful flowers, you know, I mean that would be all right. Just that . . . having respect and beauty and concern around you. (50-year-old daughter)

He would sit down in his chair and he wouldn't wake up. That would be ideal. (48-year-old daughter-in-law)

Avoiding High-tech Life Support

For most elders, the desire to die naturally meant not having to accept unwanted intervention, and not taking advantage of feeding or breathing "tubes," or other medical technologies meant to prolong their lives.

Well, I don't want this—I don't want to be resuscitated. If I'm going I want to go, and that's supposed to prevent them from putting me on any machines. I don't want to wake up a lunatic or something, you know, be alive—breathing but not knowing what's going on. I don't want that. . . . I want to go—no life saving treatments for me. It might be a terrible thing to say. . . . It's my life. (80-year-old male elder)

For the most part, family caregivers reported that they respected these concerns and believed it important to follow their elders' preferences, even if they did not share them:

Um yes, we, we talked, we talked about it and she just basically wants to be at home, not hooked up to any machines um, you know, just to die naturally, you know, just go. She don't want to go to a revival or resuscitory thing, you know, she dies, she just wants to die, you know. (47-year-old grandson)

Being Prepared

The elders expressed a preference to be made aware of their impending death so that they could "get things in order." Many worked to develop a sense of completion in their lives, had arranged their financial and other affairs, and felt to some extent prepared to die. Those who did not feel a sense of completion or closure reported that having time for preparation was quite important to them.

Well, I wouldn't want to go in my sleep. I'd want to prepare better. I'd want some doctor to say "[Name], you only have two days, three days, six days," whatever and then I can prepare myself better—get things straightened out with the kids, get my will set, and just have a priest with me and that's all. I don't want to die in my sleep. (80-year-old male elder)

Family caregivers were not aware of and did not share the elders' desire to be prepared for death, although some shared regrets that they had not talked enough or spent enough time with elders when they were still "able to do things."

Addressing Spiritual Needs

Many family members hoped their loved ones would achieve "peace of mind" at the end of their lives, and felt this was an important component of a good death. This sense of peace was most often expressed in spiritual or religious terms; several family members hoped that elders would achieve "spiritual closure" through faith and prayer, and wanted them to have access to clergy to talk with about their spiritual concerns.

> I guess it's um, being taken care of spiritually . . . contacting the people at the church. And have somebody come talk to him, and um, give him a peace of mind. (56-year-old son)

Although we asked questions about faith, spirituality, and religion, there was a great deal of variability in the extent to which faith was important to the elders. Most denied that having their spiritual or faith needs addressed were essential to a "good death" in the way they were to family caregivers.

Communication about End-of-Life Care Preferences

As part of our analysis, the researchers examined the ways in which families talked about death and dying, and how family communication influenced the congruence between participants in expressed challenges, concerns, and preferences. When asked about the extent to which they had discussed dying or their care preferences with family members, the majority of elders and family members—six of the ten dyads—indicated they had not done so. Three elders believed the lack of communication was due to their own lack of desire to talk about dying or end-of-life care with family members. Two others reported that it was difficult to talk about these subjects with family, either due to their own or their family members' discomfort.

> It doesn't make me feel uncomfortable but I can't think of anything that I could, that I can add to it that I haven't already thought about. . . . No, I think I'd like to talk to them about that. They don't seem to want to talk about it—'cause it's an unpleasant thing and they don't always go for it—kind of push it back. But I want to talk a little more about this. (82-year-old male elder)

Four families indicated that they had talked about dying and discussed the elders' care preferences. Even though she had talked with her husband, one caregiver indicated that she found these conversations about dying and his care preferences extremely uncomfortable.

In order to examine the relationship, if any, between participants' communication patterns and congruence in end-of-life care preferences, we compared the responses of families who reported communication constraints with those who reported open communication. As illustrated in Table 3, the level of congruence was much higher among families reporting open communication regarding dying and end-of-life care. None of the four families with open communication and half of the six families with communication constraints shared end-of-life concerns or preferences that were not congruent. Examples of the latter include: the 84-year-old male elder who stated a preference to be alone at the time of death, and his 47-year-old daughter who reported he wished to be surrounded by family; the 101-year-old female elder who expressed a strong desire to be kept informed of her evolving health status whose 67-year-old son preferred her not to be informed of these changes; and the 64-year-old male elder who expressed a strong desire to die at home without the use of life-sustaining machines, contrasting his 55-year-old wife's preference for him to die at the hospital, with full access to medical and technological resources.

Discussion

The findings of this study were generally consistent with the empirical literature on congruence between patients and surrogate decision-makers, which suggests that agreement about dying and end-of-life care ranges from poor to moderate (Engelberg et al., 2005; Moorman & Carr, 2008; Mularski et al., 2004). Elder participants acknowledged their need for support and care as their illnesses progressed, but—in contrast to family caregivers—most strongly valued their independence, and wanted to maintain control over their lives and continue to participate in activities they enjoyed. This parallels the finding that family members often underestimate the patient's need for autonomy and control over their own care (Farber et al., 2003; McSkimming et al., 1999; Singer, et al., 1999; Vig & Pearlman, 2004). Elders were greatly concerned about becoming a burden on their families, echoing another well-documented finding, particularly with older patients (McPherson et al., 2007; Vig & Pearlman, 2004).

Table 3 Communication Patterns and Congruence in End-of-Life Care Preferences

Communication Pattern	Congruence	Incongruence
Communication Constraints	3	3
Open Communication	4	0

The lack of apparent spiritual or religious needs on the part of the elders may be due, in part, to the lack of minority elder participants; a wealth of prior research suggests spirituality is of primary importance to African Americans and Latinos at the end of life (Born, Greiner, Sylvia, & Ahluwalia, 2004; Waters, 2001). One African-American elder shared that she spent all of her waking hours in prayer, but she too denied a desire to talk with others about her faith. This may reflect a perception that spiritual needs are felt to be intrinsic, and not as something that requires intervention from others.

Family caregivers felt most challenged by the responsibilities of managing and providing adequate care, and were concerned about their capacity to meet their loved ones' physical and spiritual needs as the illness progressed. The preeminence of these concerns is consistent with the literature (Terry et al., 2006) and reflects the high level of cognitive, emotional, and physical investment made by family caregivers at the end of life (Waldrop et al., 2005). Although other researchers have found strong congruence around the importance of preparation and a sense of completion in determining a good death (Engelberg et al., 2005; Steinhauser et al., 2000), in this study only elder participants identified this as a significant preference. Unlike the elders, family caregivers were concerned about elders' spiritual wellbeing, and felt that achieving "peace of mind" was essential to experiencing a good death.

Despite these differences, elders and family caregivers reported many congruent concerns and preferences. Consistent with the literature on quality of life at the end of life, most elders and family caregivers preferred that the elder die at home (Tang & McCorkle, 2003; Steinhauser et al., 2000), and for death to come swiftly, without pain or suffering (Heyland et al., 2006; Vig & Pearlman, 2004). Experiencing loss related to the elders' physical, functional, and cognitive decline, and managing advanced illness in the face of an uncertain and unpredictable future were among the most difficult challenges reported by the elders and their care-givers. Accepting the inherent uncertainty and ambiguity of the dying process may indeed be one of the more significant challenges for terminally ill patients and their families (Bern-Klug, 2004; Gardner, 2008; McKechnie, Macleod & Keeling, 2007). Elders and family caregivers also shared concerns about the wellbeing of survivors following the patient's eventual death.

There was particularly consistent agreement regarding end-of-life care preferences, specifically around the importance of reliable, high-quality care, and the avoidance of life-sustaining treatment. Another shared concern was that elders be treated with dignity and respect by formal caregivers, and would be allowed to continue living until death, a finding echoed in the literature (Chochinov et al., 2002). A finding not compatible with prior literature was the shared preference of elders and family caregivers to avoid using life-sustaining treatment. Many studies suggest that family members are less likely than older patients to prefer life-support, and that surrogates often underestimate elders' preference for aggressive measures at the end of life (Hamel, Lynn, Teno, Covinsky, Wu, Galanos et al., 2000; Pruchno, Lemay, Field, & Levinsky, 2005). The present finding may be another artifact of a sample that includes few minority elders, who are more likely than white patients to prefer life-sustaining medical treatment (Phipps, True, Harris, Chong, Tester, Chavin et al., 2003; Steinhauser et al., 2000). Nonetheless, the findings suggest the need for further exploration of patients and family preferences for life-sustaining treatment.

Replicating findings from prior research (Parker, Clayton, Hancock, Walder, Butow, Carrick et al., 2007; Teno, Lynn, Wenger, Phillips, Murphy, Connors et al., 1997), a minority of families had communicated with each other about end-of-life concerns and preferences. Despite the advantages of open family communication (Metzger & Gray, 2008), the literature on advance care planning and family communication suggests that less than 20% actually talk about dying and their preferences for care (Bradley & Rizzo, 1999; Rosnick & Reynolds, 2003; Teno et al., 1997). Lack of communication can contribute to family conflict between the elder and family surrogates, difficulties in decision-making and advance care planning, and ultimately to poorer quality end-of-life care (Kramer, Boelk, & Auer, 2006). This corroborates our finding that a lack of communication was associated with greater incongruence, and suggests the importance of future research on the impact of family conflict on end-of-life experiences and outcomes.

Conclusions & Implications

While many of these findings were consistent with the literature on congruence in patient and caregiver perceptions, the current study is unusual in that it compared the subjective experiences of older chronically and terminally ill patients with those of their matched family caregivers. This study confirms that end-of-life concerns and care preferences found with broader populations also apply to frail elders and their caregivers. The findings further suggest that there may be more family congruence around preferences for end-of-life care than around challenges, concerns, and wishes related to dying. Open family communication was associated with greater congruence in patient and family preferences, which supports prior findings that open communication is associated with better adjustment in family caregivers after the death of their loved ones (Kramer, 1997; Metzger & Gray, 2008). These results have important implications for intervention and research, as they highlight potential sources of unmet needs and conflict among dying elders and their family members.

Although there were more areas of congruence than incongruence among family members, the findings of this study suggest that healthcare professionals providing end-of-life care would be prudent to view family reports as imperfect proxies for elder's concerns, challenges, and preferences. Principle domains of incongruence included the elders' difficulties in accepting dependence, their fears of becoming a burden, and desire to be prepared for death. Unlike the elders, family caregivers were primarily concerned with providing adequate care to meet the elders' physical and spiritual care needs. The study highlights the need for more focused and comprehensive assessment of terminally ill elders and their family caregivers, and for sensitivity to potential differences in preferences and concerns.

It is perhaps not surprising that elders and family caregivers viewed the end-of-life experience somewhat differently, given their different ages, roles, and perspectives. Incongruence presents difficulties only when patients and caregivers with different views are unable to communicate openly and resolve differences with each other (de Haes & Teunissen, 2005). Family conflict and communication constraints can present significant barriers to the provision of quality care, the completion of advance directives, and the attainment of a "good death" (Covinsky, Fuller, Yaffe, Johnston, Hamel, Lynn et al., 2000; Kramer et al., 2006). Terminally ill elders and their families may therefore derive particular benefit from interventions that address congruent and incongruent experiences, and teach communication and family problem-solving skills around the end-of-life and end-of-life care. Working to enhance families' efforts to talk about and resolve differences, and to make informed decisions about care is fundamental to facilitating advance care planning, and reducing inappropriate procedures and hospitalizations.

There were some limitations to this study, which involved a small, non-representative sample of primarily white, low-income elders, recruited purposely from a unique comprehensive health and long-term care program in the Midwest. Casual generalizations should not, therefore, be made to other populations of terminally ill elders and family caregivers. The sample lacked heterogeneity in terms of race/ethnicity, and cultural factors have been shown to be important variables in end-of-life preferences (Phipps et al., 2003). There was also a good deal of variability in medical diagnosis, elders' living situations, and family caregivers' relationships to the elder, all of which may have influenced the findings.

Despite these limitations, this qualitative study identifies subjective concerns and care preferences of terminally ill elders and their family caregivers at the end of life. The findings highlight the need for more focused and comprehensive assessment of terminally ill elders and their family caregivers, and attention to potential differences in patient and family preferences and concerns. Further research into this population's unique needs and perceptions, including the dynamics of family communication and decision making at the end of life, is necessary to further healthcare efforts to better meet elders' psychosocial needs, enhance their well-being, and facilitate a "good death." Understanding elders'

experiences and preferences, identifying areas of congruence and incongruence, and improving communication in families are essential to providing quality end-of-life care to all dying patients and their families.

References

Bern-Klug, M. (2004). The Ambiguous Dying Syndrome. *Health and Social Work, 29*(1), 55–65.

Born, W., Greiner, K., Sylvia, E., & Ahluwalia, J. (2004). Knowledge, attitudes, and beliefs about end-of-life care among inner-city African Americans and Latinos. *Journal of Palliative Medicine, 7*(2), 247–256.

Bradley, E., & Rizzo, J. (1999). Public information and private search: Evaluating the Patient Self-Determination Act. *Journal of Health Politics, Policy and Law, 24*(2), 239–273.

Chochinov, H., Hack, T., Hassard, L., Kristjianson, S., McClement, S., & Harlos, M. (2002). Dignity in the terminally ill: A cross-sectional, cohort study. *The Lancet, 360*(9350), 2026–2030.

Cohen, S. R., & Leis, A. (2002). What determines the quality of life of terminally ill cancer patients form their own perspective? *Journal of Palliative Care, 18*(1), 48–58.

Covinsky, K., Fuller, J., Yaffe, K., Johnston, C., Hamel, M., Lynn, J., et al. (2000). Communication and decision-making in seriously ill patients: Findings of the SUPPORT project. *Journal of the American Geriatrics Society, 48*(5), S187–S193.

Crabtree, B., & Miller, W. (1999). Using codes and code manuals: A template organizing style of interpretation. In B. F. Crabtree & W.L. Miller (Eds.), *Doing qualitative research* (2nd ed., pp. 163–178). Thousand Oaks, CA: Sage.

de Haes, H., & Teunissen, S. (2005). Communication in palliative care: A review of recent literature. *Current Opinion in Oncology, 17*(4), 345–350.

Desbiens, N., & Mueller-Rizner, N. (2000). How well do surrogates assess the pain of seriously ill patients? *Critical Care Medicine, 28*, 1347–1352.

Emanuel, L., von Gunten, C., & Ferris, F. (2000). Gaps in end-of-life care. *Archives of Family Medicine, 9,* 1176–1180.

Engelberg, R., Patrick, D., & Curtis, J. (2005). Correspondence between patients' preferences and surrogates' understandings for dying and death. *Journal of Pain and Symptom Management, 30*(6), 498–509.

Farber, S., Egnew, T., Herman-Bertsch, J., Taylor, T., & Guldin, G. (2003). Issues in end-of-life care: Patient, caregiver, and clinician perceptions. *Journal of Palliative Medicine, 6*(1), 19–31.

Field, M. J., & Cassel, C. K. (Eds.). (1997). *Approaching death: Improving care at the end of Life.* Institute of Medicine. Washington, DC: National Academy Press.

Gallo, W., Baker, M., & Bradley, E. (2001). Factors associated with home versus institutional death among cancer patients in Connecticut. *Journal of the American Geriatrics Society, 49,* 771–777.

Gardner, D. (2008). Cancer in a dyadic context: Older couples' negotiation of ambiguity and meaning in end-of-life. *Journal of Social Work in End-of-life and Palliative Care, 4*(2), 1–25.

Hamel, M., Lynn, J., Teno, J., Covinsky, K., Wu, A., Galanos, A., et al. (2000). Age-related differences in care preferences, treatment decisions, and clinical outcomes of seriously ill, hospitalized adults: Lessons from SUPPORT. *Journal of the American Geriatrics Society, 48*(5/Supplement), S176–S182.

Heyland, D., Dodek, P., Rocker, G., Groll, D., Garni, A., Pichora, D., et al. (2006). What matters most in end-of-life care: perceptions of seriously ill patients and their family members. *Canadian Medical Association Journal, 174*(5), 627–633.

Higginson, I., & Sen-Gupta, G. (2000). Place of care in advanced cancer: a qualitative systematic literature review of patient preferences. *Journal of Palliative Medicine, 3*(3), 287–300.

Kramer, B. J., & Auer, C. (2005). Challenges to providing end-of-life care to low-income elders with advanced chronic disease: Lessons learned from a model program. *The Gerontologist, 45,* 651–660.

Kramer, B. J., Boelk, A., & Auer, C. (2006). Family conflict at the end of life: Lessons learned in a model program for vulnerable older adults. *Journal of Palliative Care 9*(3), 791–801.

Kramer, B. J., Christ, G., Bern-Klug, M., & Francoeur, R. (2005). A national agenda for social work research in palliative and end-of-life care. *Journal of Palliative Medicine 8,* 418–431.

Kramer, D. (1997). How women relate to terminally ill husbands and their subsequent adjustment to bereavement. *Omega: Journal of Death and Dying, 34*(2), 93–106.

Laakkonen, M., Pitkala, K., & Strandberg, T. (2004). Terminally ill elderly patients' experiences, attitudes, and needs: A qualitative study. *Omega: Journal of Death and Dying, 49*(2), 117–129.

McCormick, T., & Conley, B. (1995). Patients' perspectives on dying and on the care of dying patients. *Western Journal of Medicine, 163*(3), 236–243.

McKechnie, R., Macleod, R., & Keeling, S. (2007). Facing uncertainty: The lived experience of palliative care. *Palliative and Supportive Care, 5,* 367–376.

McPherson, C., & Addington-Hall, (2003). Judging the quality of care at the end of life: Can proxies provide reliable information? *Social Science and Medicine, 56,* 95–109.

McPherson, C., Wilson, K., & Murray, M. (2007). Feeling like a burden: Exploring the perspectives of patients at the end of life. *Social Science & Medicine, 64*(2), 417–427.

McPherson, C., Wilson, K., Lobchuk, M., & Brajtman, S. (2008). Family caregivers' assessment of symptoms in patients with advanced cancer: Concordance with patients and factors affecting accuracy. *Journal of Pain Symptom Management, 35*(1), 70–82.

McSkimming, S., Hodges, M., Super, A., Driever, M., Schoessler, M., Franey, S. G., et al. (1999). The experience of life-threatening illness: Patients' and their loved ones' perspectives. *Journal of Palliative Medicine, 2*(2), 173–184.

Metzger, P., & Gray, M. (2008). End-of-life communication and adjustment: Pre-loss communication as a predictor of bereavement-related outcomes. *Death Studies, 32*(4), 301–325.

Moorman, S., & Carr, D. (2008). Spouses' effectiveness as end-of-life surrogates: Accuracy, uncertainty, and errors of overtreatment or undertreatment. *Gerontologist, 48*(6), 811–819.

Morrison, S. (2005). Health care system factors affecting end-of-life care. *Journal of Palliative Medicine, 8*(Supplement 1), S79–S87.

Mularski, R., Curtis, R., Osborne, M., Engelberg, R., & Ganzini, L. (2004). Agreement among family members and their assessment of the quality of dying and death. *Journal of Pain and Symptom Management, 28*(4), 306–315.

National Consensus Project (2004). *Clinical practice guidelines for quality palliative care.* Brooklyn, NY.

National Institutes of Health (NIH). (2004). *State-of-the-science conference on improving end-of-life care: Conference statement.* Bethesda, MD: National Institutes of Health.

Padgett, D. K. (2008). *Qualitative methods in social work research: Challenges and rewards* (2nd ed.). Thousands Oaks, CA: Sage Publications, Inc.

Parker, S., Clayton, J., Hancock, K., Walder, S., Butow, P., & Carrick, S. et al. (2007). A systematic review of prognostic/end-of-life communication with adults in the advanced stages of a life-limiting illness: Patient/care-giver preferences for the content, style, and timing of information. *Journal of Pain and Symptom Management, 34*(1), 81–93.

Patton, M. (2002). *Qualitative research and evaluation methods* (3rd ed.). Thousands Oaks, CA: Sage Publications, Inc.

Phipps, E., True, G., Harris, D., Chong, U., Tester, W., Chavin, S., et al. (2003). Approaching the end of life: Attitudes, preferences, and behaviors of African-American and white patients and their family caregivers. *Journal of Clinical Oncology, 21*(3), 549–554.

Pritchard, R., Fisher, E., Teno, J., Sharp, S. Reding, D., Knaus, W., et al. (1998). Influence of patient preferences and local health system characteristics on the place of death. (SUPPORT Investigators: Study to Understand Prognoses and Preferences for Risks and Outcomes of Treatment). *Journal of the American Geriatrics Society, 46*(10), 1242–1250.

Pruchno, R., Lemay, E., Field, L., & Levinsky, N. (2005). Spouse as health care proxy for dialysis patients: Whose preferences matter? *Gerontologist, 45*(6), 812–819.

Rosnick, C., & Reynolds, S. (2003). Thinking ahead: Factors associated with executing advance directives. *Journal of Aging & Health, 15*(2), 409–429.

Scholz, R. and Tietje, R. (2002). *Embedded case study methods: Integrating quantitative and qualitative knowledge.* Thousand Oaks, CA: Sage Publications.

Shalowitz, D., Garrett-Meyer, E., & Wendler, D. (2006). The accuracy of surrogate decision makers: A systematic review. *Archives of Internal Medicine, 166,* 493–497.

Singer P., Martin D., & Kellner M. (1999). Quality end-of-life care: patients' perspectives. *Journal of the American Medical Association, 281,* 163–168.

Sneeuw, K., Sprangers, M., & Aaronson, N. (2002). The role of health care providers and significant others in evaluating the quality of life of patients with chronic disease. *Journal of Clinical Epidemiology, 55*(11), 1130–1143.

Steinhauser A., Christakis N., Clipp E., McNeilly M., McIntyre L., & Tulsky J. (2000). Factors considered important at the end of life by patients, family, physicians, and other care providers. *Journal of the American Medical Association, 284*(19), 2476–2482.

Sulmasy, D., Terry, P., Weisman, C., Miller, D., Stallings, R., Vettese, M., et al. (1998). The accuracy of substituted judgments in patients with terminal disease. *Annals of Internal Medicine, 128*(8), 621–629.

SUPPORT Principal Investigators (1995). A controlled trial to improve care for seriously ill hospitalized patients: The study to understand prognosis and preferences for outcomes and risks for treatments (SUPPORT). *Journal of the American Medical Association, 274*(20), 1591–1598.

Tang, S., & McCorkle, R. (2003). Determinants of congruence between the preferred and actual place of death for terminally ill cancer patients. *Journal of Palliative Care 19*(4), 230–237.

Teno, J., Clarridge, B., Casey, V., Welch, L., Wetle, T., Shield, R., et al. (2004). Family perspectives on end-of-life care at the last place of care. *Journal of the American Medical Association, 291*(1), 88–93.

Teno, J., Lynn, J., Wenger, N., Phillips, R., Murphy, D., Connors, A., et al. (1997). Advance directives for seriously ill hospitalized patients: Effectiveness with the patient self-determination act and the SUPPORT intervention. SUPPORT Investigators. *Journal of the American Geriatric Society, 45*(4), 500–507.

Terry, W., Olson, L., Wilss, L., & Boulton-Lewis, G. (2006). Experience of dying: Concerns of dying patients and of carers. *Internal Medicine Journal, 36*(6), 338–346.

Thomas, C., Morris, S., & Clark, D. (2004). Place of death: Preferences among cancer patients and their carers. *Social Science & Medicine, 58*, 2431–2444.

Vig, E., Davenport, N., & Pearlman, R. (2002). Good deaths, bad deaths, and preferences for the end of life: A qualitative study of geriatric outpatients. *Journal of the American Geriatric Society, 50*(9), 1541–1548.

Waldrop, D., Kramer, B.J., Skretny, J., Milch, R., & Finn, W. (2005). Final transitions: Family caregiving at the end of life. *Journal of Palliative Medicine, 8*(3), 623–638.

Waters, C. (2001). Understanding and supporting African Americans' perspectives of end-of-life care planning and decision making. *Qualitative Health Research, 11*, 385–398.

Vig, E., & Pearlman, R. (2004). Good and bad dying from the perspective of terminally ill men. *Archives of Internal Medicine, 164*(9), 977–981.

Yin, R. (2003). *Case study research: Design and methods* (3rd ed.). Thousand Oaks, CA: Sage Publications.

Zettel-Watson, L., Ditto, P., Danks, J., & Smucker, W. (2008). Actual and perceived gender differences in the accuracy of surrogate decisions about life-sustaining medical treatment among older spouses. *Death Studies, 32*(3), 273–290.

Critical Thinking

1. What are the barriers to quality end-of-life care?

2. What were the major worries and fears about dying expressed by the elders and their family caregivers?

3. What were the end-of-life preferences for the elders in their final days?

Acknowledgements—The authors' extend their appreciation to Elder Care Partnerships staff and administration, and to End-of-Life committee members who provided ongoing support and consultation. Special thanks to the elders and their family members who offered their valuable insights.

The Myriad Strategies for Seeking Control in the Dying Process

Tracy A. Schroepfer, Hyunjin Noh, and Melinda Kavanaugh

Research on end-of-life care has produced evidence that achieving a sense of control is viewed by terminally ill individuals (Singer, Martin, & Kelner, 1999; Volker, Kahn, & Penticuff, 2004b; Wilson et al., 2007) and those who care for them (Teno, Casey, Welch, & Edgman-Levitan, 2001) as playing an important role in the quality of their dying process. Terminally ill individuals have been found to consider the ability to exercise control as a desirable psychosocial outcome (Singer et al.) and a psychological comfort (Ganzini, Johnston, McFarland, Tolle, & Lee, 1998). Furthermore, the inability to achieve a sense of control has been associated with moderate to extreme suffering for some terminally ill individuals (Wilson et al., 2007) and a desire to hasten death for others (Back, Wallace, Starks, & Pearlman, 1996; Chin, Hedberg, Higginson, & Fleming, 1999; Coyle & Sculco, 2004; Oregon Department of Human Services [ODHS], 2000). Although sense of control evidently plays a key role in the psychological wellbeing of terminally ill individuals, less clear are the aspects of the dying process over which terminally ill individuals want to exercise control and the strategies they use for doing so.

In this article, we seek to advance our understanding of the role control plays in the dying process of terminally ill elders by investigating the aspects of the dying process over which terminally ill elders seek to exercise control, the strategies they use to do so, and whether they desire to exercise more control. By gaining a deeper understanding of the role control plays in the dying process of elders, health care and service providers and informal caregivers can work toward ensuring that elders exercise control in their dying process, thereby working toward the goal of improving the quality of end-of-life care.

Current Knowledge of Control's Role in the Dying Process

The literature on the role of control in the dying process is continually expanding. Some information is available regarding the aspects of the dying process over which individuals,

not necessarily elders, desire to exercise control, as well as the way in which they want to do so.

Aspects to Control

The factors motivating the consideration of a hastened death have been studied both retrospectively and prospectively. In retrospective studies, health care professionals or survivors of the deceased are asked to write case studies or respond to surveys concerning the factors cited by now deceased patients, who had considered or requested a hastened death. In prospective studies, individuals with a terminal illness (an illness likely to result in death), or who have been defined as terminally ill (less than 6 months to live), are directly asked about their consideration to hasten death and their reasons for doing so. Both retrospective and prospective studies provide insight into aspects of the dying process over which terminally ill individuals would like to exercise control.

Retrospective studies have found that loss of control over bodily functions (Back et al., 1996; Chin et al., 1999; ODHS, 2007) and physical symptoms (Volker, 2001) have served as factors motivating the consideration of a hastened death. A desire for control over the manner of death was found in both retrospective (Back et al.; Ganzini et al., 2002; ODHS, 2000; Volker) and prospective studies. In prospective studies, respondents who feared dying might become intolerable felt that having control over the manner of their death provided them with a sense of control (Ganzini et al., 1998; Schroepfer, 2006), as it did for those who feared a loss of control more generally (Chapple, Ziebland, McPherson, & Herxheimer, 2006). Respondents also noted that exercising control over the manner of death served to enhance their feelings of control over the disease itself (Albert et al., 2005), provided psychological comfort (Ganzini et al., 1998), and afforded a way to exercise control in an "untenable situation" (Coyle & Sculco, 2004, p. 703).

Other studies have sought to gain understanding about the aspects of dying over which terminally ill elders seek control by posing the question directly to bereaved caregivers, terminally ill individuals, and individuals living with a terminal illness. In one retrospective study, bereaved family members included in their definition of quality end-of-life care the ability for their deceased loved ones to have exercised control over their own health care decisions and daily routine (Teno et al., 2001). In another retrospective study (Volker, Kahn, & Penticuff, 2004a), advance practice nurses reported that patients sought control over decisions related to treatment, transitioning to dying, and end-of-life care, as well as over their comfort and dignity. In prospective studies, terminally ill individuals reported seeking to exercise control in end-of-life decisions (Singer et al., 1999; Volker et al., 2004b), over their dignity and physical comfort, the place of their death, and in preparing family for their pending death (Volker et al., 2004b). Although not all of the respondents in the aforementioned studies were elders, the information provides insight into aspects of the dying process over which terminally ill elders may desire to exercise control. To determine the control strategies used for doing so, an understanding must first be gained regarding the conceptualization of control.

Perceived Control Theories and Evidence

Numerous studies have been conducted on sense of control or, as it is often referred to in the literature, perceived control, which has to do with the *expectation* or *perception* of "engaging in actions" either to attain desirable outcomes or to evade those seen as undesirable (Rodin, 1986, p. 141). Perceived control is often presented as a "one-process construct," but Rothbaum, Weisz, and Snyder (1982) have advanced the argument that it may actually be a "two-process construct" consisting of primary and secondary control (p. 8). These researchers define primary control as the perception that the individual has the ability to *directly* influence a desired outcome or avoid an undesirable one. Such beliefs develop when individuals endeavor to change *directly* the external environment to fit their own needs and are successful. Secondary control, in contrast, is the perception that the individual has the ability to influence more *indirectly* a desired outcome (Rothbaum et al.). This perception is formed when individuals endeavor to *fit* into their external environment and are able to do so. Thus, primary control attempts are focused on the external world and secondary control attempts on the individual's internal self.

The life-span model of successful aging proposed by Schulz and Heckhausen (1996), which incorporates their life-span theory of control (Heckhausen & Schulz, 1995), builds on the notion of a two-process construct and argues that humans seek to exert control over the environment throughout their life span to attain goals. They propose three control strategies for doing so: selective primary control, compensatory primary control, and compensatory secondary control. Selective primary control involves individuals' "investment of resources" such as their time, abilities, or efforts to attain a particular goal (Schulz & Heckhausen,

1996, p. 710). When individuals' own resources are no longer sufficient to attain a particular goal, then compensatory primary control strategies become necessary, which require the assistance of others. Finally, compensatory secondary control involves the use of cognitive strategies on the part of individuals, which can include comparing their situation to someone whose situation is worse, disengaging from prior goals, augmenting the value of a new goal, or diminishing the value of an old goal (Heckhausen & Schulz). The use of compensatory secondary control strategies can work to maintain or lessen the losses that an individual is experiencing in his or her life.

Control Strategies Used

We are unaware of any research that has focused on control strategies used by elders in their dying process; however, evidence is available regarding the use of primary and secondary control strategies by elders with acute and chronic health conditions. In general, elders with chronic conditions have been found to use primary and secondary control strategies (Wrosch & Schulz, 2008). Due to age-related declines in late life, however, the tendency has been for elders to move toward using more compensatory secondary control strategies (Heckhausen, 1997). For elders experiencing a high number of health problems, Wrosch, Heckhausen, and Lachman (2000) found that the secondary control strategies of positive reappraisal and lowered aspirations were more strongly associated with their subjective well-being compared with elders who persisted in using primary control strategies.

Whether the findings regarding the control strategies used by elders with acute and chronic conditions hold true for terminally ill elders remains unclear at this time, as do the aspects over which terminally ill elders desire to exercise control. This study seeks to provide such insight by interviewing terminally ill elders about the aspects of their dying process over which they exercise control, the ways in which they exercise such control, and whether they would want more control.

Design and Methods
Participants

A purposive sample of 102 respondents was obtained at hospices throughout southern Wisconsin. Eligible respondents had to be at least 50 years of age, been told by a physician that they had 6 months or less to live, and deemed mentally competent by their nurse or social worker. Although age 50 would not normally be considered the lower age limit for elders, prior research experience with hospice populations (Schroepfer, 2006, 2007, 2008) has shown that to have enough male respondents, the age of inclusion needs to be lowered.

Procedure

A single-session face-to-face interview was conducted with each of 102 elders utilizing a mixed-method survey instrument. Interviews were audiotaped so that the qualitative portion could be captured verbatim, and the quantitative portion checked against what the interviewer recorded in the survey booklet. Interviews ranged in length from 23 to 178 min, with a mean of 63 min. Of the 102 respondents who completed the interview process, 18 respondents were dropped from the analysis because they declined to answer the control questions of interest. We have no way of knowing whether declining to answer these questions was systematically related to the level of control they exercised in their dying process. We do know, however, that a comparison between these 18 respondents and the 84 who completed the control questions revealed no differences in regard to age, gender, marital status, education, primary hospice diagnosis, or quality of life. Therefore, the final sample size used for analysis was 84.

Data Collection

Respondents were asked a series of questions regarding the control they were experiencing in their lives to determine the type of control strategies they were using. To learn about the aspects of the dying process over which they exercised control, respondents were asked if there were parts of their life over which they *felt* they had control. If respondents answered yes, they were asked to specify the parts. To determine the type of control strategy they used, they were next asked a series of questions regarding each part of their life over which they felt they had control. First, respondents were asked if *they* did things to directly control or be in charge of that part of their life. If they said yes, they were asked to talk about what they did and how satisfied they were with it. Next, respondents were asked if there were other people whom they believed helped them control that part of their life. If yes, they were asked to talk about how these individuals helped them exert control. Finally, all respondents were asked if there were other parts of their life over which they would like to exercise control. If they said yes, they were asked to specify the parts and what they felt prevented them from having control. If they said no, they were asked why they did not want more control.

Quantitative data were gathered on respondents' demographic information to explore whether the control strategies utilized by respondents differed based on their age, education, gender, marital status, or primary hospice diagnosis. Age was coded as a continuous variable, as was education, which was based on the number of years of schooling that respondents had completed. The respondents' gender was coded as a dummy variable (0 = female and 1 = male), as was their marital status (0 = not married and 1 = married/partner). Respondents' primary hospice diagnosis was grouped into four categories: cancer and, respiratory, heart, and muscular diseases.

To determine whether the use of control strategies was associated with respondents' quality of life, quantitative data were gathered via a quality-of-life measure. Based on

a previous study (Schroepfer, 2006) that sought to determine the factors that led terminally ill elders to consider or not consider a hastened death, nine factors were reported by elders as important to experiencing a quality dying process. These factors included having a reason for living, being able to maintain dignity, not feeling like a burden, living a life full of meaning and full of enjoyment, and feeling a sense of purpose, independent, useful, and hopeful. A thorough review of related literature produced several surveys containing one or more of the items but none that encompassed all nine items or that were designed for elders.

To address this problem, we used items from three survey instruments. The first is the Functional Assessment of Chronic Illness Therapy (FACIT)—spiritual well-being, a 12-item scale that has been designed to measure the spiritual domain of quality of life. Three items were borrowed from the eight-item subscale: a reason for living, a sense of purpose, and life has meaning. Tested in cancer populations (Peterman, Fitchett, Brady, Hernandez, & Cella, 2002), this survey has been found to have internal consistency, high test–retest correlations, concurrent validity, discriminant validity, and a positive association with measures of quality of life. Four items were borrowed from the FACIT—palliative care: burden, dependence, usefulness, and hope. This scale is newer and currently undergoing psychometric testing. The third survey, the Structured Interview for Symptoms and Concerns (SISC), is a 13-item instrument designed specifically for patients receiving palliative care for advanced cancer. This instrument has been found to have high interrater reliability, good test–retest correlations, and concurrent validity. The two items taken from this survey measuring dignity and enjoyment of life were reworded, as was the response set. The reason for rewording the items is that they are worded as questions in the SISC, a format that does not fit with the statement format of the other items. Rewording of the response set occurred because it appears complicated and could prove burdensome to terminally ill elders. These items were measured on a 5-point ordinal scale ranging from 0 = *not at all* to 4 = *very much*. All nine items were summed, resulting in a possible score range of 0–36 wherein a higher score represented a higher quality of life.

Quantitative Analytic Approach

Bivariate analyses were conducted to determine if the control strategies used by respondents differed based on age, education, gender, marital status, and primary hospice diagnosis, as well as respondents' quality-of-life scores. One-way analysis of variance (ANOVA) statistics were run to test the association between the control strategies used by respondents and their age, education, and quality-of-life scores. Cross-tabulations using the Pearson chi-square association test were conducted to test differences based on gender, marital status, and primary hospice diagnosis.

Qualitative Analytic Approaches

Using Schulz and Heckhausen's (1996) theoretical framework, we conducted a directed content analysis (Hsieh & Shannon, 2005) of the information concerning what respondents or others did to control the various parts of their dying process over which they felt they exercised control. Directed content analysis uses theory to predetermine the categories that will be used in exploring the qualitative data. For this study, the first author read each interview transcript multiple times and grouped responses into the following control strategy categories: selective primary control, compensatory primary control, and compensatory secondary control. Responses coded into selective primary control were those in which respondents described externally investing their efforts alone into attaining a particular goal. Respondents' descriptions of exercising control externally with assistance from others were coded into compensatory primary control. Finally, responses that described the use of cognitive strategies to exercise control internally were coded into one of three types of compensatory secondary control strategies: adjustment of goals by lowering aspirations, self-protective positive reappraisal (Wrosch et al., 2000), and self-protective social comparisons (Chipperfield & Perry, 2006). As a reliability check, two members of the research team independently coded the responses based on the strategies identified. Initially, the team members were 76 % in agreement and, after a discussion of the differing categorizations, arrived at a consensus on the remaining 24 %.

Once the directed content analysis of the control strategies had been concluded, the two team members independently coded (a) the aspects of the dying process over which elders reported exercising control and (b) the aspects over which they desired to exercise control. This analysis did not employ a theoretical framework and so the team members utilized conventional content analysis (Hsieh & Shannon, 2005). Using an inductive method, themes were identified from repeated readings of the transcripts (Patton, 1990) and preliminary codes generated to represent the themes. Separately, the team members repeatedly read through and categorized the responses to the question regarding the parts of life over which respondents felt they had control. This same approach was used with responses to the questions regarding whether respondents felt there were other parts of their life they would like to control. If respondents answered yes, then team members categorized the parts that respondents wanted to control and what they felt prevented them from exercising that control. If respondents answered no, then responses regarding why they did not want more control were categorized. As with the directed content analysis, a reliability check was conducted between the two members of the research team, with an 82 % initial agreement and full consensus reached upon discussion.

Results

The demographic characteristics of the 84 respondents were varied. Respondents ranged in age from 51 to 96 years, with a mean age of 76 years. The vast majority of respondents ($n = 82$; 98 %) were White and 2 (2 %) Black. Regarding gender and marital status, a little over half were female (55 %; $n = 46$) and 42 % ($n = 35$) married/partnered, 33 % ($n = 28$) widowed, and 25 % ($n = 21$) single/separated/divorced. Respondents were fairly well educated, with a range of 7–25 years of school completed and a mean of 13 years. The vast majority of respondents had some form of cancer (88 %; $n = 74$), and others were diagnosed with respiratory (5 %; $n = 4$), heart (4 %; $n = 3$), neurological (2 %; $n = 2$), and renal (1 %; $n = 1$) diseases.

Control Strategies Exercised

All 84 respondents described the way in which they exercised control (see Table 1). Of these respondents, 83 reported using a primary control strategy in combination with another primary or compensatory secondary control strategy; only one reported exercising a single primary control strategy. This 84-year-old never-married woman described using selective primary control. Although she had cancer, her focus was not on the illness itself but on the goal of strengthening her legs so she could be more mobile. When asked if other people helped her exercise control, she said no. Thus, although it was likely that others were assisting because her mobility was limited, she did not feel their doing so helped in her exercise of control.

Nineteen (23 %) of the 84 respondents reported they could no longer completely rely on their own resources to attain their goals and so asked for assistance (compensatory primary control). Respondents viewed asking others for assistance in a positive light noting that the assistance enabled them to maintain some control:

> I feel like I'm probably . . . see, I'm not a quitter and I may have to ask for help but I do . . . and that way I can stay on a schedule and maintain a life that I feel that I'm still contributing something to my family. (62-year-old married woman)

Awareness of the need for assistance to exercise control did not necessarily mean that respondents would not like to exercise control on their own (selective primary control). For example, a 62-year-old married woman was used to having full control of her own home and stated, "Oh yeah, I would definitely like to go back to the way it was before all of this happened and be able to maintain my complete house and not have to ask for help in anything."

Forty-two (50 %) of the 84 respondents used a combination of selective and compensatory primary control. These respondents were able to use their own personal skills and resources to attain some goals but required assistance to attain others. For example, one 70-year-old divorced man

Table 1 Qualitative Themes Regarding Control Exercised in the Dying Process (*N* = 84)

Theme	n (%)
Control strategies exercised	
Selective primary control	1 (1)
Compensatory primary control	19 (23)
Selective and compensatory primary control	42 (50)
Compensatory primary and secondary control	8 (9)
Selective primary control, and compensatory	14 (17)
Primary and secondary control	
Aspects of life over which control was exercised	
Decision making	50 (59)
Independence	18 (21)
Mental attitude	18 (21)
Instrumental activities of daily living	18 (21)
Activities of daily living	14 (17)
Personal relationships	9 (11)
Desire for more control	
Yes (*n* = 43; 51 %)	
Independence	14 (33)
Body functioning	13 (30)
Illness	10 (23)
Generativity	6 (14)
No (*n* = 41; 49 %)	
Satisfied with current level of control	31 (76)
Physical condition prevents exercising more control	7 (17)
God's in control	1 (2)
No explanation provided by respondent	2 (5)

exercised selective primary control in regard to attaining his goal of setting a daily schedule for eating, bedtime, and leisure activities; however, to attain his goal of bathing himself, he required assistance (compensatory primary control).

Compensatory secondary control was used in combination with compensatory primary control by 8 (9 %) respondents and in combination with selective and compensatory primary control by 14 (17 %) respondents. For respondents who exercised compensatory secondary control, at least one of the following three strategies was used: lowering aspirations, positive reappraisal, and social comparison. The eight respondents, who used a combination of compensatory primary and secondary control, used one of each type of control strategies. The 14 respondents who used a combination of selective primary control, and compensatory primary and secondary control, each reported one selective and one compensatory primary control strategy and one or two secondary control strategies. For those using compensatory secondary control, lowering aspirations was the most common strategy used: 16 (73 %) of the 22 respondents spoke about adjusting their goals (lowering their aspirations) concerning exercising control. For example, an 88-year-old divorced woman sought to reframe her own inability to write checks any longer such that it was something her daughter needed to experience: "I think she [daughter] just offered [to write her checks] and I said sure . . . I said that's fine. I felt it would be a good experience for her."

Quantitative analyses were conducted to determine whether respondents' demographic characteristics differed by these control strategy groups (CPC; SPC and CPC; CPC and CSC; and SPC, CPC, and CSC; Table 2). By necessity, the sole respondent who reported using only selective primary control was dropped from these analyses given the absence of variation. One-way ANOVA and chi-square tests revealed no significant differences in respondents' age, gender, marital status, education, or primary hospice diagnosis by the control strategy grouping reported (see Table 2).

A one-way ANOVA test was also conducted on the control strategy groups and respondents' quality-of-life score (see Table 2). The overall mean for quality of life was 22.6, with a range of 6–35: higher scores represent higher quality of life. Based on the finding of a significant *F* ratio, $F(3, 79) = 5.15$; $p < .01$, Tukey's honestly significant difference post hoc test was run to determine, through pairwise multiple comparisons, the control strategies that did and did not differ in regard to quality of life. The post hoc tests results revealed that respondents who used a combination of selective and compensatory primary control ($p < .05$) or a combination of selective primary control, compensatory primary control, and compensatory secondary control ($p < .05$) reported a significantly higher quality of life than respondents who used only compensatory primary control. No significant difference was found between respondents who used compensatory primary and compensatory secondary control and those who used only compensatory primary control. Although this group does not significantly differ, the result is likely due to the small sample size ($n = 8$). Thus, the overall finding from these tests suggests that exercising more than one control strategy was associated with higher quality of life than exercising only one control strategy.

Aspects of Life Over Which Control Was Exercised

Respondents were asked to name and discuss the parts of their lives over which they exercised control, and they named anywhere from one (*n* = 27; 32 %), to two (*n* = 34; 40 %),

Table 2 Demographics and Quality of Life of Elders Adopting Control Strategies (N = 84)

Demographic	SPC (1 %; n = 1)	CPC (23 %; n = 19)	SPC & CPC (50 %; n = 42)	CPC & CSC (9 %; n = 8)	SPC, CPC, & CSC (17 %; n = 14)
Age (in years), M	80.0	77.5	76.1	74.8	72.8
Education (in years), M	15.0	12.8	13.2	12.8	15.1
Gender, %					
Female (n = 46)	100.0	63.2	54.8	37.5	50.0
Male (n = 38)	0.0	36.8	45.2	62.5	50.0
Marital status, %					
Not married (n = 49)	100.0	57.9	64.3	50.0	42.9
Married (n = 35)	0.0	42.1	35.7	50.0	57.1
Primary diagnosis, %					
Cancer (n = 74)	100.0	84.2	95.2	75.0	78.6
Respiratory (n = 4)	0.0	5.3	2.4	12.5	7.1
Heart disease (n = 3)	0.0	5.3	0.0	12.5	7.1
Neurological (n = 2)	0.0	5.3	0.0	0.0	7.1
Renal failure (n = 1)	0.0	0.0	2.4	0.0	0.0
Quality of life, M		18.5 [a]	23.2 [b]	24.1 [a,b]	24.7 [b,*]

Notes: The levels of significance for continuous variables are based on one-way analysis of variance tests. Means in the same row that have different superscripts differ at $p \leq .05$. SPC = selective primary control; CPC = compensatory primary control; CSC = compensatory secondary control.

*$p < .05$.

to three (n = 14; 17 %) to four parts (n = 9; 11 %). Content analysis of these discussions revealed six thematic areas regarding the parts of their lives over which respondents felt they exercised control: decision making, independence, mental attitude, instrumental activities of daily living (IADLs), activities of daily living (ADLs), and personal relationships.

Decision Making

Exercising control through decision making was reported by 50 (59 %) of the 84 respondents, one of whom exercised control by herself and the others who did so with assistance. These respondents talked about making decisions or participating in the decision-making process with others regarding where to live, their finances, plans for death, how people provided their care, treatments they chose to receive, and their daily schedule and activities. Respondents noted that making a decision and having it supported by others provided them with a sense of control. A 72-year-old married woman stated, "I could tell her [daughter] this is what I want to do and we do it together. I feel like I'm a little bit more in control." Several respondents noted that it was not the size of the decision or what was being decided; rather, it was having a decision to make that made them feel more in control. An 86-year-old widower made this point when he said, "It's really small things like the choice of where you want to eat. It's nice if somebody gives you a choice."

Independence

Eighteen (21 %) of the 84 respondents reported that being independent was a part of their life over which they exercised control. Independence was expressed by respondents as the ability to "go where I want and do what I want," "live my own life," and "don't have to ask for help from others." These 18 respondents spoke in adamant tones when talking about having control over their independence, as illustrated by a 73-year-old married man's, "I can do what I damn well please!" and a 79-year-old widow's, "I don't *have* to ask for help from others." Control over independence was clearly very important.

Mental Attitude

Exercising control internally over their own mental attitude was discussed by 18 (21 %) of the 84 respondents. Using this compensatory secondary control strategy, a 77-year-old married man noted, "Well, I have control over my feelings; I have control over my mind." . . . An 81-year-old married man reported, "Well, I can control my mental attitude toward the disease, knowing that its terminal and I can't do much about that." . . . This ability to exercise control internally was viewed in a positive light, as expressed by one 72-year-old divorced woman who said, "Well, my viewpoint . . . is you cannot always control certain things you find yourself in but you (can) always choose your attitude."

Instrumental Activities of Daily Living

The ability to exercise control over one's IADLs was reported by 18 (21 %) respondents. Respondents spoke about being able to control their finances, order groceries over the telephone, and perform basic household chores. For example, a 67-year-old divorced woman reported exercising control over household chores: "Yesterday, my grandsons were here and they came to do the lawn and stuff like that, so I can still direct them and take care of the outdoors without being outdoors."

Activities of Daily Living

Fourteen (17 %) respondents reported exercising control over ADLs. The importance of doing so is evident in the following statement by a 73-year-old married man:

> . . . I uh, you know, I wash myself up every morning and uh, brush my teeth and all of those little tasks—don't need any help other than my wife will—we usually do it in this room and she'll bring in the equipment, you know. But if I had to, I could go into that bathroom next door and take care of it. It's just a little simpler this way so, but I could do it, and I know I could.

Although still needing assistance with her bath, a 76-year-old divorced woman made a point to let the interviewer know that she still exercises some control over her bath: "Yeah, they [hospice certified nursing assistant] insist I should be helped with a bath, but I can still lift myself up out of the tub." Concerning ADLs, the 14 respondents were all quick to point out that they exercised control, even if they were receiving assistance.

Personal Relationships

Nine (11 %) of 84 respondents talked about having control over how they relate with their family and friends. They talked about the value those relationships held for them and how they felt they had control over making sure they were positive relationships. An 81-year-old married man talked about how concerned he was by the impact his illness had on his loved ones and how he wanted to make certain the impact was positive.

> I try to influence my family's feelings toward my situation. I get the impression that . . . I'm concerned that they are also concerned about my situation—that it's affecting them now. They're calling everyday, they try to come everyday. So I'm sure it's had a direct effect on their lives.

In addition to making sure their impact on loved ones was positive, respondents also talked about ensuring that those relationships were as normal as possible. One 86-year-old widower talked about how he made sure that he and his girlfriend "date just like anybody else."

Desire for More Control

Although all 84 respondents reported experiencing a sense of control in their dying process, the question remained whether they felt it was enough. All 84 respondents were asked whether there were other parts of their life that they would like to control and 43 (51 %) answered yes. When asked to identify those parts, four thematic areas surfaced: independence, body functioning, illness, and generativity. Having identified the part of their life they wanted to control, they were then asked to talk about what prevented them from doing so.

Fourteen (33 %) respondents noted that they would like to exercise more control over their ability to be independent such as being able to stay in their house alone sometimes or being able to get in their car and drive wherever they wanted by themselves. It is interesting to note that when describing how they would exercise control in regard to their independence, all 14 respondents discussed the importance of being alone sometimes, a desire that may have resulted from the constant presence of caregivers. One 76-year-old divorced woman stated, "I would like to be independent again. . . . do what I want and go where I want . . . navigate by myself." When asked what prevented them from exercising such control, all 14 noted that it was their illness, which left them fatigued, nauseous, dizzy, or in pain.

Exercising control over their own bodies was the desire of 13 (30 %) of the 43 respondents. The functions that respondents wanted more control over were incontinence, sexual performance, muscle and leg movement, appetite, physical strength, and memory. Lacking control over functions that people normally can control was very upsetting, as evidenced by one 90-year-old married man who was struggling with incontinence: "Well, accidents happen without any warning a lot of times." Again, when asked what prevented their exercising control, all 13 people stated that it was their illness.

The third most common theme to emerge was the desire to control their illness: 10 (23 %) respondents spoke about wanting to control the impact their illness had on their ability to function physically in their daily lives. They also spoke of wanting to control their illness such that it would not be terminal. A 76-year-old divorced woman who was terminally ill with lung cancer said wistfully, "Just maybe—the only thing, oh, that's more or less a desire . . . that they x-ray me once, and see that the spots are gone . . . controlling these spots on my lungs." Although the desire was strong to exercise such control and fight their illness, respondents stated that what prevented them from doing so was that it was "not realistic."

The fourth theme that arose was the desire expressed by six respondents (14 %) to exercise control now and after their death on behalf of the next generation, a stage of development referred to by Erik Erikson as generativity

(Erikson, Erikson, & Kivnick, 1986). Erikson's seventh stage of his developmental theory, generativity versus stagnation, proposes that as part of their own development, adults assist the younger generation in leading meaningful lives. Although Erikson proposes this as a midlife stage of development, terminally ill elders who reported seeking to be instrumental in their children and grandchildren's future lives ranged in age from 62 to 84 years. For example, a 62-year-old divorced woman longed to assist financially loved ones in difficult circumstances. A 73-year-old married man talked about his need for ensuring his grandchildren's future education, and an 81-year-old married man who had lung cancer wanted to talk with young people about the dangers of smoking. Perhaps knowing that time was limited, these respondents felt the need to make a lasting impact on the next generation. When asked what prevented them from doing so, they talked about their children's resentment and need for independence. One 71-year-old widow stated:

> He's a 21 year old man . . . I guess I would like him to have ways of being helped physically, medically, healthcare-wise. I can't do any of that. . . . [I]f I were healthy, I couldn't do those things. People have to do for themselves what they have to do. I'd like to make his life easier because there are things that I've seen because I'm older.

For the 41 (49 %) respondents who answered no to the question regarding whether there were other parts of their life that they would like to control, all but 2 (5 %) provided an explanation. The vast majority (76 %; $n = 31$) reported they were satisfied with their current level of control. Some of these individuals reported their satisfaction was due to their still exercising the same amount of control as before their illness: "I'm still kind of fully in charge of what I've done before." Others spoke of feeling happy or peaceful with life in its current state: "I'm satisfied—life is where it should be." The other eight respondents provided different explanations. Seven (17 %) respondents stated that their physical condition left them unable to control other parts of their lives. An 84-year-old widow noted, "I'm not capable of doing the thing I would want to control." The eighth respondent, a 55-year-old divorced woman, remarked she did not want control because "God's in control."

Discussion

The results from this study offer an understanding of the role control plays in the dying process of terminally ill elders and the potential association it has with quality of life in the dying process. The 84 elders interviewed provided information about the strategies they used to exercise control in their dying process, the aspects over which they exercised control, and whether they desired to exercise more control.

Control Strategies

Either on their own (selective primary control) or with the assistance of another (compensatory primary control), all 84 elders were exercising a form of primary control to attain a particular goal. The fact that these elders sought to exercise primary control, although they were very ill and their time was limited, is evidence of its importance.

Another important finding concerned the mix of control strategies that terminally ill elders used to exercise control. Although about a fifth of respondents exercised only one primary control strategy, the majority used two to four primary and secondary control strategies. Respondents had goals they wanted to attain and appeared to choose a control strategy that fit with the abilities they possessed related to that goal. It is also significant that although the exercise of primary control is visible to others, the exercise of secondary control may not be; yet, changing the internal self to fit with the external world did provide these respondents with a sense of control. For example, one 63-year-old married woman, who was chair bound during the day, spent her days alone. A hospice worker came by each day and the woman always asked the worker to turn on the radio before she left. She loved to listen to the radio and felt that by asking the worker, she had control over being able to do so. One day, however, she forgot to have the worker turn on the radio. Unable to do so herself (selective primary control) or ask others to do it for her (compensatory secondary control), she turned to a compensatory secondary control strategy: "I didn't have any of them to turn on my radio. My God, I thought, well all right, no sound but I could (still) hear the birds." The use of multiple strategies is not only evidence of these elders' desire to exercise control but their adaptability in doing so.

Findings from the study also reveal that the use of multiple strategies appears to be associated with quality of life in the dying process. Although the sole use of selective primary control could not be tested due to only one elder reporting its use, comparisons were made between the use of only compensatory primary control and the use of other combinations of control strategies. The one-way ANOVA test revealed that exercising more than one control strategy (compensatory primary control) was associated with a higher reported quality of life in the dying process, which has important implications for practitioners.

Aspects Controlled

The aspects respondents reported exercising control over provided insight into the world of terminally ill elders, which, due to being home or facility bound for the most part, was a smaller world than when they were healthy. As their world grew smaller, the areas in which they could exercise control became more limited. The six thematic areas that respondents spoke of concerning the exercise of control were decision making, independence, mental attitude,

IADLs, ADLs, and personal relationships. Being able to make decisions that influenced their world and future death, to come and go and be alone, to choose their attitude, to perform IADLs or ADLs, and to ensure their relationships were positive, were the key aspects of the dying process over which respondents sought to exercise control. Realizing at some level that their world and often their ability to exercise control were constrained in ways they had not been before, respondents appeared to adapt by focusing on areas inside their world, being flexible in how they exercised control, as well as how much control they exercised.

More Control?

Study results revealed that over half of the respondents wanted to exercise more control in their dying process. Just as independence was an aspect of the dying process that many respondents reported exercising control over, 14 respondents who were not currently exercising such control desired to do so. The severity of their illness prevented exercising this control, just as it did in two other areas: their illness and bodily functions. Although they desired control in these areas, terminally ill elders were realistic regarding their inability to do so.

Perhaps the most surprising finding was that respondents wanted to exercise more control over the future success of their children and grandchildren. Erickson proposed generativity as a stage of development that takes place at midlife. Although these elders were not in midlife, perhaps in the final stage of life, the need to ensure the success of the next generation presented itself yet again. An alternative explanation may simply be that in providing for the next generation, these elders were able to leave behind a legacy of love.

Study Limitations and Future Implications

Although this qualitative study employed a large sample size, and new understandings were gained on the role of control in the dying process of terminally ill elders, limitations were present. First, 98 % of the sample were Caucasian elders. Future research should be conducted with other racial/ethnic elders to determine the extent to which culture influences the role of control in an elder's dying process. The role of the individual and the exercise of control tend to be Western values and so not all groups may view control in the same manner as the current study participants. Second, the lives of terminally ill elders are not stagnant; rather, they can shift very quickly due to advancing illness. The 84 respondents who volunteered to participate in the study may have done so because they were less ill than others who were not recruited. They may still have been at a point in their illness where they could exercise primary control more readily and rely less on secondary control strategies. The current study was cross-sectional in nature and so the results are based on one time point in

the respondents' dying process. A longitudinal study following elders throughout their dying process would provide greater insight into whether they continue to be adaptive in the use of control strategies and what they seek to control changes. Third, the respondents participating in the current study were all receiving hospice care either at home or in a hospice inpatient facility. Future studies should look at elders who are dying in other environments and not receiving hospice care, such as a hospital or nursing home. It is not clear from the current study whether the environment itself and the type of end-of-life care being provided influenced respondents' control strategies or the aspects of the dying process over which they desired control. Fourth, the respondents in this sample were terminally ill (less than 6 months to live), but it is feasible that elders with terminal or chronic conditions may experience similar physical limitations that impact their exercise of control. Certainly, the findings for this study's terminally ill respondents bear similarities to the research findings discussed in the literature review on elders with chronic conditions in that they, too, have been shown to use a mix of primary and secondary control strategies (Wrosch & Schulz, 2008) and to use compensatory secondary control strategies, including positive reappraisal and lowering aspirations (Heckhausen, 1997). Future research should look more closely at the exercise of control for elders with acute, chronic, and terminal conditions to determine the similarities and differences in regard to how control is exercised and its relationship to quality of life. Fifth, in order for terminally ill elders to exercise control in their dying process, particularly when the control strategy is compensatory and necessitates the assistance of others, family members must be supportive of their doing so. A recent study (Schroepfer, 2008) found that the relational content of social relationships defined as the "functional nature or quality of social relationships" (House, Umberson, & Landis, 1988, p. 302) was related to the consideration of a hastened death. Quantitatively, poor or conflictual support was found to be a highly significant predictor of the consideration to hasten death, and, qualitatively, if an elder felt his or her own suffering or the suffering his or her care placed on loved ones was burdensome, he or she was likely to consider a hastened death. The current study did not include measures of the relational content of those who indirectly or directly supported the elders in their exercise of control in the dying process, or the impact of relational content on their quality of life. Future studies on exercising control in the dying process should quantitatively include relational content measures and qualitatively include questions on not only how others assist an elder in the exercise of control but also the elder's experience with their doing so. Sixth, the finding regarding the association of control strategies with quality of life was limited to a bivariate analysis. Future research on this finding should employ the use of multivariate analyses to control for relevant control and predictor variables.

Practice Implications

The knowledge gained from these interviews has important implications for practitioners and family members providing care to elders during their dying process. Being cognizant of the life an elder had prior to his or her dying process and how that life has changed since the illness is important knowledge for family members to remember and practitioners to garner. As the health that once allowed an elder to be very much a part of the world outside his or her home or facility declines, so does the size of his or her world. Understanding this, family members and practitioner can seek to support the elder's exercise of control within that smaller world, as well as the strategies he or she chooses to use. If family members and the practitioner are assisting the elder with a task, then supporting the elder's need to exercise control as much as possible is key for the elder in exercising compensatory primary control. If an elder is physically limited to such a point that exercising primary control alone or with the assistance of another is not practical, then it is important that family members and the practitioner be aware that the elder may seek to exercise control internally over his or her mental attitude. Based on the expression of an elder's attitude, it may appear that he or she is giving up; however, it may actually be that he or she is taking a realistic approach to the situation and using the compensatory secondary control strategy of lowering his or her aspirations. Based on the elder's situation, the family and the practitioner must then determine whether the elder is lowering his or her aspirations unnecessarily or simply being realistic. Family members or the practitioner can then work with the elder to either reframe his or her situation in a way that allows for raising aspirations or, in the case of a realistic viewpoint, support the elder's use of the control strategy. Because the exercise of more than one control strategy appears to be associated with a reportedly higher quality of life in an elder's dying process, then family members and practitioners can work to ensure that elders have the opportunity to do so whenever possible.

Decision-making, independence, mental attitude, IADLs, ADLs, and relationships were aspects of the dying process over which the respondents sought to exercise control. Providing the support and the opportunities for such control to be possible is an important role for family and the practitioner. For example, elders who talk about the importance of their always having been independent may necessitate their family members and practitioners locating such opportunities. The elders in the current study tended to equate independence with time alone; thus, family members and the practitioner can work to ensure that the elder has a period of privacy each day. Another example is the role decision making plays in the dying process. The study's respondents were not focused on the size of a decision or the need to make one alone: They primarily wanted to be a part of the process and have the support of others in doing so. These interventions and others based on familial knowledge and a thorough assessment of an elder's pre- and post-terminal illness life will assist family members and practitioners in ensuring that elders' control preferences are supported in their final stage of life.

Funding

Support for this study was provided by the John A. Hartford Foundation Faculty Scholars Program in Geriatric Social Work.

References

Albert, S. M., Rabkin, J. G., Del Bene, M. L., Tider, T., O' Sullivan, I., Rowland, L. P., et al. (2005). Wish to die in end-stage ALS. *Neurology, 65,* 68–74.

Back, A., Wallace, J., Starks, H., & Pearlman, R. (1996). Physician-assisted suicide and euthanasia in Washington state: Patient requests and physician responses. *Journal of the American Medical Association, 275,* 919–925.

Chapple, A., Ziebland, S., McPherson, A., & Herxheimer, A. (2006). What people close to death say about euthanasia and assisted suicide: A qualitative study. *Journal of Medical Ethics, 32,* 706–710.

Chin, A., Hedberg, K., Higginson, G., & Fleming, D. (1999). Legalized physician-assisted suicide in Oregon—The first year's experience. *New England Journal of Medicine, 340,* 577–583.

Chipperfield, J. G., & Perry, R. P. (2006). Primary- and secondary-control strategies in later life: Predicting hospital outcomes in men and women. *Health Psychology, 25,* 226–236.

Coyle, N., & Sculco, L. (2004). Expressed desire for hastened death in seven patients living with advanced cancer: A phenomenologic inquire. *Oncology Nursing Forum, 31,* 699–706.

Erikson, E. H., Erikson, J. M., & Kivnick, H. Q. (1986). *Vital involvement in old age.* New York: W. W. Norton.

Ganzini, L., Harvath, T., Jackson, A., Goy, E., Miller, L., & Delorit, M. (2002). Experiences of Oregon nurses and social workers with hospice patients who requested assistance with suicide. *New England Journal of Medicine, 347,* 582–588.

Ganzini, L., Johnston, W. S., McFarland, B. H., Tolle, S. W., & Lee, M. A. (1998). Attitudes of patients with amyotrophic lateral sclerosis and their care givers toward assisted suicide. *New England Journal of Medicine, 339,* 967–973.

Heckhausen, J. (1997). Developmental regulation across adulthood: Primary and secondary control of age-related challenges. *Developmental Psychology, 33,* 176–187.

Heckhausen, J., & Schulz, R. (1995). A life-span theory of control. *Psychological Review, 102,* 284–304.

House, J. S., Umberson, D., & Landis, K. R. (1988). Structures and processes of social support. *Annual Review of Sociology, 14,* 293–318.

Hsieh, H., & Shannon, S. E. (2005). Three approaches to qualitative content analysis. *Qualitative Health Research, 15,* 1277–1288.

Oregon Department of Human Services. (2000). *Oregon's Death with Dignity Act: The second year's experience.* Portland: Oregon Health Division.

Oregon Department of Human Services. (2007). *Ninth annual report on Oregon's Death with Dignity Act.* Portland: Oregon Health Division.

Patton, M. (1990). *Qualitative evaluation and research methods* (2nd ed.). Newbury Park, CA: Sage.

Peterman, R. H., Fitchett, G., Brady, M., Hernandez, L., & Cella, D. (2002). Measuring spiritual well-being in people with cancer: The Functional Assessment of Chronic Illness Therapy–Spiritual Well-Being Scale (FACIT–Sp). *Annals of Behavioral Medicine, 24,* 49–58.

Rodin, J. (1986). Health, control and aging. In M. M. Baltes & P. B. Baltes (Eds.), *The psychology of control and aging* (pp. 139–165). Hillsdale, NJ: Lawrence Erlbaum.

Rothbaum, F., Weisz, J. R., & Snyder, S. S. (1982). Changing the world and changing the self: A two-process model of perceived control. *Journal of Personality and Social Psychology, 42,* 5–37.

Schroepfer, T. A. (2006). Mind frames towards dying and factors motivating their adoption by terminally ill elders. *Journal of Gerontology: Social Sciences, 61,* S129–S139.

Schroepfer, T. A. (2007). Critical events in the dying process: The potential for physical and psychosocial suffering. *Journal of Palliative Medicine, 10,* 136–147.

Schroepfer, T. A. (2008). Social relationships and their role in the consideration to hasten death. *The Gerontologist, 48,* 612–621.

Schulz, R., & Heckhausen, J. (1996). A life span model of successful aging. *American Psychologist, 31,* 702–714.

Singer, P. A., Martin, D. K., & Kelner, M. (1999). Quality end-of-life care: Patients' perspectives. *Journal of the American Medical Association, 281,* 163–168.

Teno, J. M., Casey, V. A., Welch, L. C., & Edgman-Levitan, S. (2001). Patient-focused, family-centered end-of-life medical care: Views of the guidelines and bereaved family members. *Journal of Pain and Symptom Management, 22,* 738–751.

Volker, D. (2001). Oncology nurses' experiences with requests for assisted dying from terminally ill patients with cancer. *Oncology Nursing Forum, 28,* 39–49.

Volker, D. L., Kahn, D., & Penticuff, J. H. (2004a). Patient control and end-of-life care. Part I: The advanced practice nurse perspective. *Oncology Nursing Forum, 31,* 945–953.

Volker, D. L., Kahn, D., & Penticuff, J. H. (2004b). Patient control and end-of-life care. Part II: The patient perspective. *Oncology Nursing Forum, 31,* 954–960.

Wilson, K. G., Chochinov, H. M., McPherson, C. J., LeMay, K., Allard, P., Chary, S., et al. (2007). Suffering with advanced cancer. *Journal of Clinical Oncology, 25,* 1691–1697.

Wrosch, D., Heckhausen, J., & Lachman, M. W. (2000). Primary and secondary control strategies for managing health and financial stress across adulthood. *Psychology and Aging, 15,* 387–399.

Wrosch, C., & Schulz, R. (2008). Health-engagement control strategies and 2-year changes in older adults' physical health. *Psychological Science, 19,* 537–541.

Critical Thinking

1. What were given as examples of the person's control over the "instrumental activities of daily living"?

2. What were given as examples of the person's control over the "activities of daily living"?

3. What were given as examples of the elderly person's control over decision making?

UNIT 7

Living Environment in Later Life

Unit Selections

Learning Outcomes

After reading this Unit, you will be able to:

- Tell what the first three steps are that Nathan Bowman-Johnston of the Philadelphia Nursing Home Transition program reports must be done to get a resident out of a nursing home and back to independent living.

- List the questions experts ask nursing home residents to determine if they are able to live independently and if the move is possible and desirable for them.

- Describe the variety of niche communities that exist for older adults today.

- Identify the fastest growing niche communities in the country at the present time.

- List the advantages for elderly persons that Michael Hunt found in the Hilldale apartments in Madison, Wisconsin.

- Identify what changes can turn residential areas into "naturally occurring retirement communities," as most seniors would prefer to age in place.

- Discuss the various services people living in a village can receive from their fellow village members or as part of their village services provided routinely and paid for by their service fees.

- Explain how Keystone's health services are better able to coordinate the services for their village patients.

Student Website

www.mhhe.com/cls

Internet References

American Association of Homes and Services for the Aging
 www.aahsa.org
Center for Demographic Studies
 http://cds.duke.edu
Guide to Retirement Living Online
 www.retirement-living.com
The United States Department of Housing and Urban Development
 www.hud.gov

Unit 4 noted that old age is often a period of shrinking life space. This concept is crucial to an understanding of the living environments of older Americans. When older people retire, they may find that they travel less frequently and over shorter distances because they no longer work and most neighborhoods have stores, gas stations, and churches in close proximity. As the retirement years roll by, older people may feel less in control of their environment due to a decline in their hearing and vision as well as due to other health problems. As the aging process continues, the elderly are likely to restrict their mobility to the areas where they feel most secure. This usually means that an increasing amount of time is spent at home. Estimates show that individuals aged 65 and above spend 80 to 90 percent of their lives in their home environments. Of all the other age groups, only small children are as house- and neighborhood-bound. The house, neighborhood, and community environments are, therefore, more crucial to the elderly than to any other adult age group. The interaction with others that they experience within their homes and neighborhoods can either be stimulating or foreboding, pleasant or threatening. Across the country, older Americans find themselves living in a variety of circumstances, ranging from desirable to undesirable.

Approximately 70 percent of the elderly live in a family setting, usually a husband-wife household; 20 percent live alone or with nonrelatives; and the remaining number live in institutions such as nursing homes. Although only about 5 percent of the elderly will be living in nursing homes at any one time, 25 percent of people aged 65 and above will spend some time in a nursing home setting. The longer one lives, the more likely he or she is to end up in a total-care institution. Because most older Americans would prefer to live independently in their own homes for as long as possible, their relocation—to other houses, apartments, or nursing homes—is often accompanied by a considerable amount of trauma and unrest. The fact that the aged tend to be less mobile and more neighborhood-bound than any other

© Keith Thomas Productions/Brand X Pictures/PictureQuest

age group makes their living environment crucial to their sense of well-being. Articles in this section focus on some of the alternatives available to the aged, from family care, to assisted living to nursing homes. In "The Great Escape," Peter Jaret points out the critical issues and problems a person must confront before deciding to move out of a nursing home and back into the community. In "Happy Together," the author points out that as the baby boomers age, they do not want to move into assisted living or nursing home facilities. The various types of neighborhoods and communities that are emerging for senior residents are discussed. In "Seniors and the City," John Buntin observes that most baby boomers hope to age in place. He raises the question of what role the government should play in making this happen. In "The Real Social Network," the author describes the advantage for seniors of moving to one of the emerging neighborhood concepts which are called villages.

The Great Escape

PETER JARET

Her new life isn't perfect. Last winter she argued with the landlord to turn up the heat in the Philadelphia building where she now lives. Once, she missed a doctor's appointment because the doorbell downstairs was broken and she didn't hear the shuttle driver buzz her. And sometimes her little apartment gets lonely.

But Arlene Johnson, 67, wouldn't dream of trading her new life for her old one. "Not in a million years," she says.

After languishing for two years in a nursing home, Johnson is living on her own. She's one of many long-term institution residents regaining independence, their numbers projected to soon swell into the thousands. This growth is happening in large part because more federal and state programs are designed to help them do it. Between 2001 and 2007, Medicaid spending on nursing home care rose a modest 9.8 percent, according to the National Center for Assisted Living. Its spending for home- and community-based care, in contrast, soared by 81.5 percent. And a federal program that encourages states to use Medicaid dollars to help nursing home residents transition back to independence received a five-year, $2 billion extension in the new health care reform bill.

But longtime nursing home residents often face big hurdles to life on their own. Determining whether they're capable can be a complicated task, requiring a thorough evaluation of circumstances that may seem beyond control.

Out of Control

For Johnson, life spiraled downward after she developed a serious infection following knee replacement surgery and had to have one leg amputated. Soon, her husband died; she was alone. Johnson tried to stay on in the row house where she'd raised her family, but flights of steps in front and back made it almost impossible. When she returned to the hospital for another operation, she reluctantly agreed to recuperate in a nursing home.

"I didn't need to be there; I could look after myself," Johnson says. "Another woman had lost a leg just like me, and she refused to get out of bed. All she did was eat and watch television. I didn't want to end up like that."

As the months passed, however, returning to life on her own began to seem impossible. Simply finding a place to live presented an almost insurmountable obstacle. "I had to find a place that didn't have steps," she says. Newspaper ads don't include such details. You have to go see for yourself. "How was I going to do that?"

Then, one day last year, she heard about a woman in the nursing home who was leaving to live on her own, thanks to a counselor who helps people make the transition back to the community.

"I waited for him in the corridor," Johnson remembers. "And I told him I wanted to be next on the list."

Deciding Whether to Move

When nursing home residents consider living on their own, experts ask these questions:

1. Do you want to live independently? You must be motivated enough to overcome frustration and inconvenience.
2. Are you able to live independently? People with limited mobility can often manage.
3. Can you afford to live independently? Government programs offer a variety of financial help.
4. Is in-home care available? Together, a doctor and a transition coordinator can help compile a list of needed services.
5. Is appropriate housing available? Requirements vary with health and mobility, and include access, safety features, security, and kitchen and dining facilities.
6. Does the home have everything you need? This includes a telephone, emergency contacts, kitchen equipment and personal care items.
7. Does the community offer necessary medical services? It's crucial to identify and perhaps contact in advance doctors, pharmacies, hospitals and emergency clinics in the community.
8. Do you have the necessary skills? These may include shopping, showering or bathing, preparing meals, budgeting and paying bills.
9. Is transportation available? Many areas have senior transportation programs.
10. Is social support available? Options include senior housing activities, religious programs, senior daycare and family visits.

Reality Check

The counselor's name is Nathan Bowman-Johnston. He works for the Philadelphia Corporation for Aging, and its Nursing Home Transition program finds resources for people who are older or have disabilities but want to live independently. Many people taken to a nursing home "may not even have a wallet or an ID," Bowman-Johnston says. "If they end up staying more than a month or two, they may lose their home when they stop paying rent. We often have to start from scratch, getting a birth certificate or some sort of identification, setting up a bank account, finding a place for them to live."

Arlene Johnson had it relatively easy. Her finances were in good order. Her Social Security checks were still being deposited into her own bank account. Because she qualified for Medicaid, some of the money that would have gone to the nursing home could be used to help pay for the services she would need—home health aides, delivered meals, a personal emergency-response medical system.

First, she needed an apartment with wheelchair access. Bowman-Johnston located a vacant one-bedroom unit in a large senior complex with an elevator. He helped Johnson fill out the application, but after it was accepted, plenty of complications remained. Her son-in-law, a contractor, widened the bathroom door to accommodate her wheelchair. The carpeting was replaced with hardwood to make it easier to wheel herself around. Grab bars were installed in the bathroom.

While Johnson was in the nursing home, thieves stripped her old row house of many possessions. "Basically I had to start over," she says. Bowman-Johnston helped round up furniture and kitchen supplies and arranged for delivery. A nurse at the nursing home bought Johnson a microwave.

Bowman-Johnston arranged for a home aide to help Johnson with chores. He also set up weekly visits from a nurse. Johnson was lucky enough to find a doctor who made house calls, although she would have to travel to her surgeon's office for checkups. Medicaid would pay for all medically related travel. For other transportation, public service was available on demand for a small fee.

While making the arrangements, Bowman-Johnston stayed in close contact with Johnson. "We have to manage expectations," he says. "What will you do in this situation—your aide doesn't show up and there's no food in the refrigerator? We have to make sure people are really motivated to do it."

When Arlene Johnson finally unlocked the door of her new apartment, she remembers, "I felt like I was getting my life back again."

Even after six months on her own, Johnson struggles sometimes. Using public transportation, especially if she has to shop at several stores, is difficult. She often asks her daughter to drive her to get groceries. "That's not easy for me, being dependent on other people." Standing on one leg when she has to cook for herself isn't easy either.

And there have been unexpected crises. One morning the fire alarm in the building went off—a false alarm, as it happened. But for a panicked moment she wasn't sure if the fire was real and whether she could get out on her own.

"You do get frustrated at times. You pray a lot," she says. "You have to be patient. But you also have to be very, very determined."

Critical Thinking

1. When moving from a nursing home to an apartment, what was the one thing that the apartment she chose had to have available?
2. When she moved to an apartment, what would Medicaid pay for in her new living environment?
3. What physical changes had to be made in the apartment that she rented to make it accommodate her and her wheel-chair?
4. What supplies did she need to live independently in her apartment?

PETER JARET lives in Petaluma, Calif.

Happy Together

Villages: Helping People Age in Place.

SALLY ABRAHMS

For years, boomers have denied they are going to get old. Now, with knees that need scoping and birthday cakes with way too many candles, the defiant generation is finally thinking about the future—especially where and how to live.

Visits to their parents in sterile, regimented assisted living or nursing homes are leaving boomers dismayed. They want better choices for Mom—and for themselves. While they may be a decade or more away from needing care, they're overhauling or honing traditional models and inventing new ones.

In choosing how they want to age, and where, boomers are helping shape the future of housing. "They have changed expectations every decade they've gone through; I don't think it will stop now," says John McIlwain, senior fellow for housing at the Urban Land Institute. Down the road, he says, "there won't be one single trend. People will be doing a lot of different things." They already are. The common denominator in existing and still-to-be-created models, say experts, is the desire to be part of a community that shares common interests, values or resources. People want to live where neighbors know and care about one another and will help one another as they age. That doesn't mean they'll become primary caretakers; if it gets to that point, outside professionals may need to help.

They also won't necessarily retire from their jobs if they live in a "retirement" community. Today's housing options reflect the attitude of older Americans: Stay active, keep learning, develop relationships and have fun for as long as possible.

Niche Communities

The concept: Live with others who share similar lifestyles, backgrounds or interests.

The numbers: Around 100 across the country. **The price:** Depends on community type.

Prices can range from $800 a month for a rental at an RV park or $1,700 at an artists' community, up to several hundred thousand dollars to buy a unit at a university community, with monthly addons of $2,000 or more that include some meals, housekeeping, social activities and medical care.

"With 78 million baby boomers, housing options are virtually unlimited," says Andrew Carle, founding director of the Program in Assisted Living/Senior Housing Administration at George Mason University in Virginia. In the next 20 years, he says, name an interest group and there'll be a community for it. "Will there be assisted living for vegetarians or a community for Grateful Dead fans? Residential cruise ships with long-term care? Absolutely."

Today's niche communities are already varied. They're geared to healthy adults but often have an assisted care component. They include places like Rainbow's End RV Park in Livingston, Texas, which offers assisted living, Alzheimer's day care, respite for caregivers and short-term care for the sick or frail. The Charter House in Rochester, Minn., provides a home for former Mayo Clinic staffers, among others. The Burbank Senior Arts Colony in Los Angeles attracts retired or aspiring artists, musicians, actors and writers. Aegis Gardens in Fremont, Calif., caters to older Asians.

The swanky Rainbow Vision in Santa Fe, N.M., is primarily—but not exclusively—for gay, lesbian, bisexual and transgender (GLBT) clients. While it has assisted living, there's also a cabaret, an award-winning restaurant and a top-notch spa. With 3 million GLBT older Americans—a figure projected to nearly double by 2030—and typically no adult children to care for them, such communities are expected to multiply.

Hands down, the fastest-growing niche community sector is university-based retirement communities (UBRCs). So far there are 50 or more on or near such college campuses as Dartmouth, Cornell, Penn State and Denison University. While residents are usually in their 70s, 80s and up—besides independent living, there is assisted living and nursing care—UBRCs will appeal to boomers, the most highly educated demographic, when they grow older, says Carle. Residents can take classes and attend athletic or cultural events at the nearby college campus, professors lecture at the UBRC, and young students can complete internships.

Five years ago, Harvey Culbert, 75, a former medical physicist from Chicago, and his wife moved to Kendal at Oberlin, which is affiliated with the Ohio college. He has audited, for free, a course in neuroscience, sings in a college group, and is taking voice lessons from a retired Kendal music teacher. "I'm always interested in improving what I do," he says.

Cohousing

The concept: A group, usually composed of strangers at the start, creates a communal-type housing arrangement that is intergenerational or all older people, with separate units but some shared common space. The group may buy the property, help design it, make all rules by consensus and manage it independently. Residents eat some dinners together and often form deep relationships. **The numbers:** 112 intergenerational cohousing communities, with another 40 to 50 planned; four elder cohousing projects, with 20 or so in the works. More than half are in California. **The price:** $100,000 to $750,000, monthly fees $100 to $300; 10 percent of projects offer rentals for $600 to $2,000 a month.

Intergenerational cohousing is geared to families with younger children but also draws boomer couples and singles. The youngest elder cohousing residents are in their 60s. Members live in separate, fully equipped attached or clustered units, and share outdoor space and a common house where communal meals take place. The common house also contains a living room and guest (or caretaker's) quarters. What's in the rest of the space depends on the members; it could be a media or crafts room, or a studio for exercise and meditation.

"I think cohousing is a marvelous way to live," says Bernice Turoff, an 85-year-old widow and member of the intergenerational Nevada City Co-housing community in California. "It's a close community where people really care about one another. If you get sick, 14 people say, 'How can I help you?'"

Charles Durrett, her neighbor and an architect who, along with his wife, Kathryn McCamant, brought the concept of cohousing to the United States from Denmark in the 1980s, says older members act as surrogate grandparents. Last year, when one of the older residents was dying, all ages pitched in to help or visit.

Today, older boomers live in both intergenerational and elder cohousing. "I'd be surprised if cohousing doesn't double every couple of years in the next 20 years," says Durrett. Getting popular: cohousing in cities.

Green House

The concept: A new style of nursing home created by gerontologist William Thomas that looks, feels and operates more like a cozy house than an institution. Ten or so residents live together and get ultra-individualized care from nursing staff that knows them well and cooks their meals in an open country-style kitchen. **The numbers:** 87 Green House projects serving 1,000 residents; 120 projects in development. **The price:** The same Medicaid and Medicare coverage ofered to traditional nursing homes; the minority paying out of pocket are charged the going rate in the area for a more conventional nursing home.

Residents' private bedrooms and bathrooms surround a living and dining room that looks like it could be in a single-family home; a screened-in porch or a backyard offers outdoor access. As much as possible, residents make their own decisions, such as when they'll wake up.

Proponents point to studies showing a Green House can improve an older person's quality of life, provide at least comparable, if not better, care than a traditional nursing home, and reduce staff turnover. "The good news and the bad news is that you get to spend the rest of your life with 10 people," says Victor Regnier, a professor of architecture and gerontology at the University of Southern California.

Stanley Radzyminski, 90, might not be able to communicate with a few dementia residents in his Green House at Eddy Village Green in Cohoes, N.Y., but says, "I really like it here. I have my own room and privacy, and if I need help, the staff is outstanding. We all want to think we can take care of ourselves, but it's not always possible."

The Village Model

The concept: Live in your own home or apartment and receive discounted, vetted services and social engagement opportunities. **The numbers:** 56, with 17 in the Washington, D.C., area alone, and 120 in development around the country.

The price: $100- to $1,000-a-year membership fee, with an average of $500 for a single member, $650 or so for a household.

Growing quickly in popularity, this model will become even more popular in the coming years, say housing experts. That's because studies show most older people want to age in place. The first village was established in 2002 at Beacon Hill Village in Boston; in the last four years alone, 90 percent of the villages have formed.

Village members call a central number for help of any kind. That might be transportation to the grocery store or the doctor, or the name of a plumber, acupuncturist, computer tutor, caregiving agency, home modifications specialist, babysitter for visiting grandkids, dog walker or home delivery company. Because the village may have up to 400 members (although new groups may have fewer than 100), vendors find it an attractive market. The group buys theater tickets in bulk, for example, or contracts with a service provider; consolidated services save everyone money.

Villages offer plenty of opportunities to socialize, whether it's taking yoga down the street with neighbors, attending outings to museums or movies, or participating in a book club, walking group or supper gathering.

Rita Kostiuk, national coordinator for the Village to Village Network, which helps communities establish and manage their own villages, has noticed something about the new people calling for information: "The majority are boomers."

On the horizon: Already, demographers are seeing more older Americans moving, or contemplating moving, into cities and suburban town centers. Rather than being saddled with a house requiring nonstop upkeep or feeling isolated in the burbs, they're within walking distance of shops, entertainment and public transportation. So their ability or desire to drive is not a big deal.

Another trend: divorced, widowed or never-married older women living together. Some who don't know one another are keeping such agencies as nonprofit Golden Girls Housing in Minneapolis busy. Golden Girls offers networking events for women who want to live together, lists requests for women looking, and steers them to services that can help. They don't match women, though; women do that themselves. Others opting for this setup are already friends.

David Levy, a gerontologist and lawyer by training, runs seven groups a week for caregivers. Inevitably, the conversation turns from the parents they care for to themselves. "These boomer women may be estranged from, or never had, kids, have diminished funds, and not a significant other on the horizon. They want to know, 'What's going to happen to me? Who will be there for me?' " he says.

It looks like they'll have choices.

Critical Thinking

1. What will the effect of the Green House concept be on nursing homes in the future?
2. What is the advantage that the villages offer to older people in terms of their preferred living choices?
3. What attracts older persons to moving to downtown cities and suburban town centers?

SALLY ABRAHMS writes about aging, boomer, health and workplace issues. She lives in Boston.

Seniors and the City

Most baby boomers hope to age in place. Should government play a role in making that happen?

JOHN BUNTIN

More than two decades ago, Michael Hunt noticed something interesting about Hilldale, a well-established neighborhood in Madison, Wisconsin. Elderly people were moving into its apartment houses in large numbers at the same time that builders and developers were struggling—and failing—to attract seniors to assisted-living communities designed for their needs. What struck Hunt, an architect and professor of urban planning at the University of Wisconsin, was that Hilldale, with apartments set close to a local library and small shopping center, was senior-friendly but not senior-segregated. Even more to the point, it was warm and welcoming to the many widowed women who moved in there. The apartment buildings were almost like dorms, with hallways that were, he says, "socially alive." Hunt had spotted something that seemed novel—what he called "a naturally occurring retirement community," or NORC.

Although the phrase was new, the phenomenon Hunt saw wasn't. Virtually every community in the country has a NORC. In some instances, it's the apartment complex people move to after their spouse dies. In others, it's a neighborhood where the children have left and residents are aging in place. According to the American Association of Retired People, more than a quarter of seniors already reside in NORCs. As the baby boom generation approaches retirement, demographers expect the growth of NORCs will accelerate dramatically.

"We need to be designing communities in which people can age in place," Hunt is convinced. "There is no way to have enough age-specific housing to take care of the elderly."

Around the same time that Hunt was noticing aging patterns in Hilldale, Fredda Vladeck was a social worker at St. Vincent's Hospital in Manhattan. Vladeck had noticed that an increasing number of older New Yorkers were showing up in the St. Vincent's emergency room with fractures or injuries suffered in falls. One housing development in particular stood out: a 2,820-unit co-op called Penn South. Established by the International Ladies Garment Workers Union in 1963, Penn South was home to a large concentration of former union members, many of them single women. But as Penn South's residents aged, their health began to deteriorate. Now, they were appearing at the hospital in disproportionately large numbers.

When Vladeck called the building's managers, they acknowledged the problem and asked if St. Vincent's could help by placing a geriatric nurse and a social worker on site. But Vladeck felt the issue was more about psychology than services. She knew that most older adults resist connecting with services until an acute crisis forces them to. And the residents of Penn South were no exception. What was needed, she felt, was a conversation changer where it's acknowledged by all that "this is an aging-in-place community, and there are things we can do in the community to make aging as normal as possible."

Vladeck had heard the term NORC. Now, she set out to turn a demographic description into a service model—one that could combine the outreach aspects of community organizing with traditional social services, such as support for home health aides. Backed by the United Jewish Communities, an umbrella group for hundreds of Jewish philanthropies, she created a model that has emerged as one of the most promising ideas for meeting the coming surge of retiring baby boomers.

In some ways, supporting NORCs is a no-brainer for state and local government officials. Demographers estimate that 90 percent of baby boomers will age in place. Making sure NORCs have amenities such as curb cuts, mass transit, libraries and other clusters of services is common-sense urban planning. The other alternatives—assisted-living facilities or nursing homes—are both associated with huge expenses, most of which are borne by state Medicaid programs, and a jarring decline in senior well-being.

But the push to expand government support for NORCs raises broader and more nettlesome issues. Up to this point, NORC services have been funded primarily by foundations and through modest fees paid by their beneficiaries. In making the argument that it's time for government to step forward, philanthropies are pursuing an old and familiar path: The nonprofit develops and pilots innovative programs, then government takes over. But given the current fiscal crisis (and the approaching retirement of millions of baby boomers), can government afford to help NORCs? Or, frankly, can it afford *not* to? It's a debate not just about how government should promote aging in place but about the role of government itself.

Vladeck's work at Penn South is a case in point. Soon after her efforts got underway, her program caught the attention of the United Jewish Association Federation of New York. The reason was demographically driven. About 25 percent of the Jewish population is 65 and over, roughly twice the national average. "The Jewish community's older adult population, as a percent of community, is where rest of the country will be in 20 years," says Rob Goldberg, senior director for legislative affairs at the United Jewish Communities. "So we are already dealing with the challenges of long-term care."

The UJA Federation set out to replicate Vladeck's NORC model in other high-rise apartment complexes where half or more of the residents were seniors. In 1999, the city of New York funded an effort to extend the model to the Deepdale Gardens apartment complex in the borough of Queens. Vladeck and the UJA decided to take the concept even further. They created a prototype "horizontal" NORC in next-door Floral Park, a neighborhood of modest single-family homes, many of them occupied by older residents.

The effort was challenging. A typical "vertical" NORC in the city was funded in part by a $1-per-month fee that was added to participating residents' rents. There was no automatic way to levy a similar fee on residents of Floral Park. Instead, UJA turned to community organizers to canvas the neighborhood, surveying residents about their priorities, organizing residents into a group that could define its own priorities and helping them connect with services. Local politicians, block associations, local businesses—everyone was brought in.

By 2005, the Floral Park NORC had taken root. Other New York state and local politicians quickly scrambled to get programs of their own. In 2006, the state passed legislation that created a neighborhood NORC model. New York now contributes $4.4 million to 17 horizontal or "neighborhood" NORCs and another 40 "vertical" NORCs statewide. New York Citys budget provides another $5.5 million, plus $1 million more in earmarks. As a result, some 67,000 New Yorkers live in officially supported aging-in-place communities based on the NORC model.

NORCs are going nationwide. In recent years, United Jewish Communities has helped underwrite more than 50 NORCs in communities around the country. As the idea has expanded, state and local governments are becoming increasingly important partners. In early 2003, the Atlanta Regional Commission (which coordinates regional planning and serves as the Area Agency on Aging for the 10-county greater Atlanta area) conducted a survey of 1,200 seniors. It found that respondents were less interested in traditional services such as Meals on Wheels than they were in fostering a strong sense of community. At the same time, the Fulton County Office on Aging was trying to figure out how to better utilize its Bowden senior center in East Point, a lower-middle class, African-American community that is located near Atlanta's international airport. With help from the Jewish Federation for Greater Atlanta, the ARC reached out to politicians, nonprofits and community groups in East Point. A local advocacy group spent six weeks canvassing NORC neighborhoods, assessing needs and mapping neighborhood resources. Public safety, transportation and home repair emerged as priorities.

The responses to these perceived needs were creative. Working with a neighborhood advisory council, for instance, the Atlanta Regional Commission (which served as the lead agency) organized a "fashion show" in which police, firefighters, water and electricity meter readers and even FedEx delivery drivers walked down a catwalk in the senior center in order to show seniors the types of people who might legitimately come onto their properties. A total of six NORCs are now up and running around Georgia.

An even more ambitious statewide effort is taking place in Indiana. In June 2007, Steve Smith, then the state director of aging, hired the University of Indianapolis Center for Aging and Community to develop a request for proposals for several NORC pilot programs.

The Indiana initiative was born of the recognition that as Indianans aged, a growing number needed help to stay in their homes. The state's CHOICE home health care program was underfunded and had long waiting lists. As a result, many seniors who, with appropriate support, might have been able to maintain their independence, were being forced into institutional facilities. The pyramid of services the state offered its seniors was, in effect, upside down. The state reoriented its dollars away from institutional care and toward community-based services, but that wasn't enough.

In tackling its RFP assignment, the University of Indianapolis did something unusual. It sought to develop a picture of the overall needs of state seniors by fielding the AdvantAge Initiative telephone survey, which assesses seniors' well-being by asking questions about their health status (have they had a flu shot? when was their last mammogram?) as well as their access to local services. The results of the statewide survey were eye-opening. A lot of respondents weren't sure where to go for services. The prevalence of illnesses such as diabetes were very high compared to the nation as a whole.

Ultimately, five NORC pilot programs were selected, with locations ranging from urban Gary to suburban Indianapolis to rural Linton. Each NORC chose its "banner issue" to target. In Linton, for instance, the focus has been on mobility. The NORC has modified homes to remove hazards, created a walking program and continues to provide transportation vouchers (and volunteer drivers).

Indiana's five NORCs are currently in their second year of operation. State officials are waiting for an evaluation before seeking to expand further.

Despite their rapid spread in recent years, NORCs as a program struggle with the fundamental question of sustainability. "We can't do it without government," says UJC's Goldberg of the effort to build a national NORC infrastructure. And yet not everyone agrees that the future of NORCs is as a governmental program. Madison's NORC, Supporting Active and Independent Lives, or SAIL, has taken a different approach. Although it was started with seed money from a federal demonstration grant, it has sought to organize itself as a fee-supported membership organization. The goal, says Michael Hunt, is "that over time it will become financially independent so we don't have to rely on city and state subsidies."

But it's more than philosophy that drives Hunt to his conclusion. He also stresses numerical reality. "We can't count on government to support this population," he says. "There's not enough money and too many people."

Nonetheless, SAIL's approach has been controversial in the NORC world. "If you charge by membership, you are encouraging people not to participate," warns Vladeck. Although SAIL has a lower-cost membership rate for low-income seniors, Vladeck and other program-oriented NORC supporters worry that SAIL's approach is too close to what is sometimes called a "concierge model."

The best-known example of that is Boston's Beacon Hill Village. Established in 2003, it provides a range of programs to seniors throughout central Boston—from weekly grocery shopping to house cleaning to help getting on the Internet. Although subsidized memberships are available for low-income seniors, most members pay an annual membership fee of $850 per household. That segregation of services by income worries Vladeck and other NORC advocates. They want to weave the

programs and culture that support aging in place into the core of existing communities. That's a goal both Vladeck and Hunt support. They just differ on the most realistic way to get there.

"From a public policy viewpoint," Vladeck says, "it's clear we need to figure out what to do to make these communities good places to grow old."

Critical Thinking

1. What are the advantages of creating "naturally occurring retirement communities" over the alternatives of assisted living facilities and nursing homes?

2. In apartment complexes in New York City, what were the costs of making the building into a "naturally occurring retirement community"?

3. In the Floral Park area of New York, which was a neighborhood of modest single family homes, there was no way to add a monthly fee, since the residents owned the homes, to create a "naturally occurring retirement community" (NORC). How was the money for this raised?

From *Governing*, June 2009. Copyright © 2009 by e.Republic Inc. Reprinted by permission via Wright's Media. contract #74389-2ycw.

The Real Social Network

Villages: Helping People Age in Place.

More than a neighborhood, a village gives older people a better chance to stay in their own home longer.

Martha Thomas

On a bitterly cold morning a few years ago, Eleanor McQueen awoke to what sounded like artillery fire: the ice-covered branches of trees cracking in the wind. A winter storm had knocked out the power in the rural New Hampshire home that Eleanor shared with her husband, Jim. "No heat, no water. Nada," Eleanor recalls.

The outage lasted for nine days; the couple, both 82 at the time, weathered the ordeal in isolation with the help of a camp stove. Their three grown kids were spread out in three different states, and the McQueens weren't very close to their immediate neighbors. "We needed someone to see if we were dead or alive," Eleanor says.

But the McQueens were alone, and it scared them. Maybe, they admitted, it was time to think about leaving their home of 40 years.

Luckily, last year the McQueens found a way to stay. They joined Monadnock at Home, a membership organization for older residents of several small towns near Mount Monadnock, New Hampshire. The group is part of the so-called village movement, which links neighbors together to help one another remain in the homes they love as they grow older.

The concept began in Boston's Beacon Hill neighborhood in 2001, when a group of residents founded a non-profit called Beacon Hill Village to ease access to the services that often force older Americans to give up their homes and move to a retirement community. More than 56 villages now exist in the United States, with another 120 or so in development, according to the Village to Village (VtV) Network, a group launched in 2010 that provides assistance to new villages and tracks their growth nationwide.

It works like this: Members pay an annual fee (the average is about $600) in return for services such as transportation, yard work, and bookkeeping. The village itself usually has only one or two paid employees, and most do not provide services directly. Instead, the village serves as a liaison—some even use the word concierge. The help comes from other able-bodied village members, younger neighbors, or youth groups doing community service. Villages also provide lists of approved home-maintenance contractors, many of whom offer discounts to members. By relying on this mix of paid and volunteer help, members hope to cobble together a menu of assistance similar to what they would receive at a retirement community, but without uprooting their household.

The earliest villages, like Beacon Hill, were founded in relatively affluent urban areas, though new villages are now sprouting in suburbs and smaller rural communities, and organizers are adapting Beacon Hill's model to fit economically and ethnically diverse communities. Each is united by a common goal: a determination to age in place. A recent AARP survey found 86 percent of respondents 45 and older plan to stay in their current residence as long as possible. "And as people get older, that percentage increases," says Elinor Ginzler, AARP expert on livable communities.

In its own quiet way, the village movement represents a radical rejection of the postwar American ideal of aging, in which retirees discard homes and careers for lives of leisure amid people their own age. That's the life Eleanor and Jim McQueen turned their backs on when they joined Monadnock at Home.

What a Village Takes

Want to organize a village of your own? The Village to Village (VtV) Network offers information on helping villages get started. Membership benefits include tools and resources developed by other villages, a peer-to-peer mentoring program, and monthly webinars and discussion forums.

- To find out if a village exists in your region, the VtV website has a searchable online map of all U.S. villages now open or in development.
- The creators of Boston's Beacon Hill Village have written a book on starting a village: *The Village Concept: A Founders' Manual* is a how-to guide that provides tips on fund-raising, marketing, and organizational strategies.
- Existing resources can make your neighborhood more "villagelike," says Candace Baldwin, codirector of the VtV Network. The best place to start is your local agency on aging. The U.S. Department of Health and Human Services offers a searchable index of these services.—M.T.

"To dump 40 years of building a home to move into a condominium doesn't appeal to me at all," Jim says. "The idea of Monadnock at Home is, I won't have to."

You could call it the lightbulb moment—literally: A bulb burns out in that hard-to-reach spot at the top of the stairs, and that's when you realize you're dependent on others for the simplest of household chores. "It's horrible," says Candace Baldwin, codirector of the VtV Network. "I've heard so many stories from people who say they can't get on a ladder and change a lightbulb, so they have to move to a nursing home. A lightbulb can be a disaster."

Especially when the homeowner won't ask for help. Joining a village can ease the resistance, says Christabel Cheung, director of the San Francisco Village. Many members are drawn by the opportunity to give aid as well as receive it. "A lot of people initially get involved because they're active and want to do something," she says. "Then they feel better about asking for help when they need it."

Last winter Blanche and Rudy Hirsch needed that help. The couple, 80 and 82, live in a three-story brick town house in Washington, D.C.; they pay $800 per year

in dues to Capitol Hill Village (CHV). During the blizzard-filled February of 2010, Rudy was in the hospital for hip surgery and Blanche stayed with nearby friends as the snow piled up. On the day Rudy came home, Blanche recalls, the driver warned that if their walkways weren't clear "he'd turn around and go back to the hospital." She called CHV executive director Gail Kohn, who summoned the village's volunteer snow brigade. A pair of young architects who lived nearby were quickly dispatched with shovels.

The Hirsches have discussed moving; they've postponed the decision by installing lifts so Rudy can get up and down the stairs. Remembering her visits to a family member who lived in a retirement home, Blanche shudders: "Everyone was so old. It's depressing."

Avoiding "old-age ghettos," says Kohn, is a major draw for villagers. She touts the intergenerational quality of Capitol Hill, full of "people in their 20s and people in their 80s," and CHV organizes a handful of events geared toward people of different ages. One program brings high school freshmen and village members together in the neighborhood's public library, where the kids offer informal computer tutoring to the older folks.

Such social-network building is a natural outgrowth of village life. Indeed, Beacon Hill Village was founded on the idea of forging stronger bonds among members. "There was a program committee in existence before the village even opened its doors," says Stephen Roop, president of the Beacon Hill Village board. "Most of my friends on Beacon Hill I know through the village."

One fall evening in Chicago, Lincoln Park Village members gathered at a neighborhood church for a potluck supper. A group of about 80—village members and college students who volunteer as community service—nibbled sushi and sipped Malbec wine as they chatted with Robert Falls, artistic director of Chicago's Goodman Theatre.

Lincoln Park Village's executive director, Dianne Campbell, 61, doesn't have a background in social work or gerontology; her experience is in fund-raising for charter schools and museums, and she lives in Lincoln Park. To village member Warner Saunders, 76, that's a big plus. "She doesn't see us as elderly clients who need her help," says Saunders, a longtime news anchor for Chicago's NBC affiliate, WMAQ-TV. "I see Dianne as a friend. If she were a social worker, and I viewed my relationship with her as that of a patient, I would probably resent that."

For Saunders, Lincoln Park Village makes his quality of life a lot better. He recently had knee and hip surgeries, and his family—he lives with his wife and sister-in-law—relies on the village for transportation and help in finding contractors. "I'd call the village the best bargain in town," he says.

Others, however, might balk at annual dues that can approach $1,000 for services that might not be needed yet. To expand membership, many villages offer discounts for low-income households.

At 93, Elvina Moen is Lincoln Park Village's oldest, as well as its first "member-plus," or subsidized, resident. She lives in a one-room apartment in an 11-story Chicago Housing Authority building within Lincoln Park. The handful of member-plus residents pay annual dues of $100 and in return receive $200 in credit each year for discounted services from the village's list of vetted providers. Since joining, Moen has enlisted the village to help paint her apartment and install ceiling fans.

But beyond home improvements, Moen doesn't ask a lot from the village yet—she's already created her own village, of a sort. When she cracked her pelvis three years ago, members of her church brought her meals until she got back on her feet; she pays a neighbor to help clean her apartment. Her community-aided self-reliance proves that intergenerational ties and strong social networks help everyone, not just the privileged, age with dignity.

Social scientists call this social capital, and many argue that we don't have enough of it. What the village movement offers is a new way to engineer an old-fashioned kind of connection. "As recently as 100 years ago most everyone lived in a village setting," says Jay Walljasper, author of *All That We Share: A Field Guide to the Commons*, a book about how cooperative movements foster a more livable society. "If you take a few steps back and ask what a village is, you'll realize it's a place where you have face-to-face encounters." He compares the village movement to the local-food movement, which also started with affluent urbanites. Think of a village as a kind of "artisanal retirement," a modern reinterpretation of an older, more enlightened way of life. And just as there's nothing quite like homegrown tomatoes, "there's no replacement for the direct connection with people who live near you," Walljasper says.

Strong, intergenerational communities—just like healthy meals—are good for everyone. Bernice Hutchinson is director of Dupont Circle Village in Washington, D.C., which serves a diverse neighborhood. Many members are well-off; some are getting by on Medicaid. "But at the end of the day," says Hutchinson, "what everyone wants is connectedness."

Connectedness alone, of course, can't ensure healthy aging. What happens next—when villagers' needs grow beyond help with grocery shopping or the name of a reliable plumber?

To meet the growing health demands of members, villages boast a range of wellness services, and many have affiliations with health care institutions. Capitol Hill Village, for example, has a partnership with Washington Hospital Center's Medical House Call Program, which provides at-home primary care visits for elderly patients.

A new village—Pennsylvania's Crozer-Keystone Village—flips the grassroots Beacon Hill model: It's the first village to originate in a health care institution. Barbara Alexis Looby, who oversees the village, works for Keystone, which has five hospitals in the southeastern part of the state. A monthly fee gives members access to a "village navigator," who schedules medical appointments and day-to-day logistics like errands. Members also get discounts on Keystone's health services. Because the village and the hospital system are aligned, says Looby, "the boundaries are flexible. You care for people when they come to the hospital, and you are in a position to coordinate their care when they leave." Keystone hopes this integration will lead to fewer ER visits and hospital readmissions.

How long can a village keep you safe at home? It depends. But Candace Baldwin, of VtV, says that the trust factor between members and the village can help family members and caregivers make choices and find services.

Michal Brown lives about 30 miles outside Chicago, where her 89-year-old mother, Mary Haughey, has lived in a Lincoln Park apartment for more than 20 years. She worries about her mom, who has symptoms of dementia. Brown saw a flyer about Lincoln Park Village in a pharmacy and immediately signed her mother up. Through the village, Brown enrolled her mom in tai chi classes and asked a village member to accompany her as a buddy.

Just before Christmas, Haughey became dizzy at her tai chi class. With her buddy's help, she made it to the hospital, where doctors discovered a blood clot in her lung. Without the village, Brown is convinced, her mother might not have survived.

Through the village, Brown has also learned about counseling services at a local hospital to help plan her mother's next steps. "We can add services bit by bit, whether it's medication management or home health care. The village knows how to get those services."

Nobody knows what Mary Haughey's future holds, but the village has given her options. And it has given her daughter hope that she can delay moving her mother to a nursing home. For now, it helps knowing that her mother is safe, and still in her own apartment, in her own neighborhood.

Critical Thinking

1. In terms of services needed by older persons, what are the advantages of joining and living in a village neighborhood?

2. How does the village movement hope to provide residents a menu of assistance similar to what they would receive in a retirement community?

3. What is the common goal of each village community?

MARTHA THOMAS is a Baltimore-based freelance writer.

Reprinted from *AARP The Magazine*, May/June 2011. Copyright © 2011 by Martha Thomas. Reprinted by permission of Martha Thomas.

UNIT 8

Social Policies, Programs, and Services for Older Americans

Unit Selections

Learning Outcomes

After reading this Unit, you will be able to:

- Explain why Japan has few concerns about the solvency of its retirement program while it has the most rapidly aging population in the developed world.

- Describe how most government-run retirement programs around the world are financed.

- Describe the three myths that the author believes exist regarding the future of the Social Security program.

- Identify one of those myths that you think has the greatest credibility and tell why you think that is so.

- Identify what the author believes is the biggest change the United States will have to confront and deal with in the 21st century.

- List the four areas on which the demographic shift in the population is going to have the greatest impact.

- Identify the major benefits that the author believes will result for the nation's new health care law.

- Enumerate the different groups that support keeping rather than repealing the Affordable Care Act.

- Explain the different positions of the Republicans and Democrats regarding how to utilize future savings in the Medicare program.

- Identify the proposals that have been suggested for reducing the growth and costs of Medicare.

- Identify the major advantage of a government-run health insurance plan.

- Cite how expanding and improving health care in the country could be paid for so that it would not increase the national debt.

- Identify the different groups of people who depend on Social Security to provide a large part of their income.

- Explain why, at age 65 and older, Social Security provides a larger share of woman's income than it does for a man.

- Identify the problems created for the federal budget by an aging and longer-living older population, lower fertility rates, and a smaller younger population.

- Describe the effect on the U.S. economy of low fertility rates.

Student Website

www.mhhe.com/cls

It is a political reality that older Americans will be able to obtain needed assistance from governmental programs only if they are perceived as politically powerful. Political involvement can range from holding and expressing political opinions, voting in elections, participating in voluntary associations to help elect a candidate or party, and holding political office.

Research indicates that older people are just as likely as any other age group to hold political opinions, are more likely than younger people to vote in an election, are about equally divided between Democrats and Republicans, and are more likely than young people to hold political office. Older people, however, have shown little inclination to vote as a bloc on issues affecting their welfare despite encouragement by senior activists, such as Maggie Kuhn and the leaders of the Gray Panthers, to do so. Gerontologists have observed that a major factor contributing to the increased push for government services for the elderly has been the publicity about their plight generated by such groups as the National Council of Senior Citizens and the American Association of Retired Persons (AARP). The desire of adult children to shift the financial burden of aged parents from themselves onto the government has further contributed to the demand for services for the elderly. The resulting widespread support for such programs has almost guaranteed their passage in Congress.

Now, for the first time, there are groups emerging that oppose increases in spending for services for older Americans. Requesting generational equity, some politically active groups argue that the federal government is spending so much on older Americans that it is depriving younger age groups of needed services.

The articles in this section raise a number of problems and issues that result from an ever-larger number and percentage of the population living to age 65 and older. In "Dignified Retirement: Lessons from Abroad," the author discusses how the retirement age of people in different countries affects their economic stability and growth. In "Social Security: Fears vs. Facts: What Social Security Critics Keep Getting Wrong," the author attempts to dispel many of the fears that exist in the minds of the American public regarding the future of the Social Security

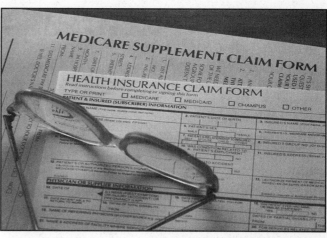

© Kent Knudson/PhotoLink/Getty Images

program. In "Beyond Wisdom: Business Dimensions of an Aging America," Yash Gupta maintains that from a business perspective we must face questions being raised by an aging workforce and population.

In "Keep the Health Care Act," the author outlines what he believes are the major benefits for keeping the recently passed Health Care Act. In "Medicare May Soon Take New Shape," the author points out the different views of Republicans and Democrats that are presented regarding what is the best way to continue Medicare services and cut costs. In "7 Critical Maneuvers," James Toedtman outlines the areas of concern that must be addressed and resolved by the U.S. House and Senate before a national health care bill can be approved. In "Protect Social Security," the author points out the current solvency of the Social Security program and what principles should be followed to guarantee its future financial stability. In "Population Aging, Entitlement Growth, and the Economy," the *AARP Public Policy Institute* observes what would have to be done with the current social service programs and federal taxation to keep the government deficit no worse in 2050 than it is today.

Internet References

Administration on Aging
www.aoa.dhhs.gov
American Federation for Aging Research
www.afar.org
American Geriatrics Society
www.americangeriatrics.org
Community Transportation Association of America
www.ctaa.org
Community Reports State Inspection Surveys
www.ConsumerReports.org

Medicare Consumer Information from the Health Care Finance Association
http://cms.hhs.gov/default.asp?fromhcfadotgov_true
National Institutes of Health
www.nih.gov
The United States Senate: Special Committee on Aging
www.senate.gov/~aging

Dignified Retirement

Lessons from Abroad

Sylvester J. Schieber

There aren't many mysteries about the financial challenges posed by the aging of America's population. While little consensus exists on how to shore up Social Security, there is widespread understanding that the system will be in deficit within a decade of the first baby boomers' retirements, which start in 2008. The Medicare financing outlook is even bleaker; the federal health-insurance program for the elderly is already in the red even as a costly new prescription drug benefit is being implemented. Front-page stories about corporate pension plans that go belly up or are cut back, at the same time that retiree health-benefit programs are curtailed, add to the general anxiety.

But perhaps the biggest concern Americans should have about their retirement system is the sheer inertia that has prevented the nation from addressing its problems. For more than two decades, we have known about the demographic challenges facing Social Security. We knew before prescription drug benefits were added to Medicare coverage that the system was in trouble. It makes for a sad spectacle indeed that we enjoy the rare advantage of being able to see the future with clarity yet are unwilling to act.

Meanwhile, other countries have started to address some of the same challenges, and they have done so with greater inventiveness and determination than the United States has shown. The list of pioneers ranges from the familiar example of Chile to the less noted examples of Sweden, Germany, and Canada. All offer lessons from which America can learn.

By some measures, America's aging problem is relatively minor compared with what other developed countries face. For every retired person in America, there are currently about four working people. (Australia, Canada, and the United Kingdom have similar ratios.) In Japan, the ratio is closer to three workers per retired person; in Italy, it's down close to two, and Germany is not much better off than that.

The demographic future also looks at least as favorable for the United States as for any other developed country. The retirement burden on American workers is not expected to be any greater in 2030 than it already is today in Germany or Italy. By that year, Germany's burden is expected to be twice and Italy's 2.5 times America's. Italy will have only one active worker per retiree. Other developed countries, such as Switzerland and the Netherlands, will be in better positions than that but will still face bigger burdens than the United States.

Perhaps the most important lesson to be learned from abroad comes from countries that are less reliant on pensions to provide income security to older people. They do not rely as much on pensions for the simple reason that many older people in these countries are still working. Japan presents an especially interesting case. It has the most rapidly aging population in the developed world, but its retirement burden in 2030 is expected to be attenuated because older people in Japan tend to work later into life than their counterparts in most other developed countries. The average retirement age for Japanese men is nearly 67.

The undeniable fact is that many people, especially in the world's developed economies, are retiring at ages when they could still be highly productive. An astonishing 38 percent of Italians in the 50-to-54-year-old bracket are already out of the labor force, and hardly anyone in Italy between 60 and 64 still works. Granted, Italy is an extreme case; even in Sweden, workers are less likely to retire early. But the trend toward early retirement is widespread.

The most significant influence on when the majority of people leave work behind is the structure of the retirement system: An earlier "normal" retirement age or more generous benefits for early retirement lead, predictably, to more retirements. In Iceland, 81 percent of the population between the ages of 60 and 64 is still in the labor force, largely because of incentives in the retirement system that encourage people in that age bracket to continue working. Even in the United States, 47 percent are still economically active during those years. In Europe, the comparable numbers range from 22 percent in Germany to only 14.5 percent in France.

In Iceland, the average man works until age 67. In France, his counterpart retires at 59. Such variations help explain the range of costs associated with different retirement systems. In France, the average remaining life expectancy for a male at the typical retirement age is 20.5 years. It is 13.7 years in Iceland. All else being equal, a male retiree in France will cost about 60 percent more in retirement benefits than one in Iceland simply because of the longer duration of retirement.

Slowing Economic Growth

Pension payouts are not the only cost of retirement. By withdrawing their labor from the economy, retirees also slow economic growth, making it harder to underwrite retirement costs. If a country has a growing elderly population that does not contribute to national output and workers have an incentive to retire in their fifties, the particular method of financing retirement—pay-as-you-go, like Social Security, or fully funded retirement accounts—doesn't matter a great deal. There will, in any case, be trouble down the road.

Most government-run retirement systems around the world operate similarly to the U.S. Social Security system: Benefits paid to current retirees are financed on a pay-as-you-go basis, out of revenues from current workers. There's little or no "money in the bank." Beneath this level of general similarity, however, there are some significant differences in how public pension systems are structured, how large a role private pension plans play, and, most important for our purposes, how willing policymakers have been to make the hard choices needed to ensure the survival of these systems.

One little-appreciated difference between the American system and most others has to do with its basic architecture. Most other countries have two-tier publicly financed retirement systems. The United States has a single tier.

In most of those other countries, virtually every citizen is entitled to a basic first-tier benefit upon reaching retirement age. In some cases, this benefit comes in the form of a universal "demogrant"; in others, recipients face income or assets tests that may reduce the size of the benefit or, in some cases, eliminate it.

On top of this basic benefit, these countries provide a separate, second tier of retirement benefit that is proportional to a worker's preretirement earnings. The second-tier benefit usually accounts for the largest share of the total retirement pension.

What's important is that the first tier is explicitly funded by general tax revenues, not by earmarked employer and employee contributions. As a result, the first-tier basic benefit seems to voters less like "their" own money, less like something they are entitled to. And that makes it politically easier for policymakers to adjust this part of the retirement system.

In the United States, the whole Social Security benefit is based on earnings, but it includes elements of the first- and second-tier benefits provided in other countries. Low-wage workers receive larger benefits relative to their earnings than those with high earnings, an arrangement that hides the character of the implicit basic benefit in our system. Yet workers with higher levels of covered earnings receive larger absolute benefits, which links payouts to covered earnings levels, albeit indirectly. Virtually all benefits are financed through payroll tax contributions. The structure of the U.S. system has led people to believe that they have "paid for" their benefits even though the benefits are highly subsidized.

Such perceptions matter a great deal. In Canada, for example, legislators were able several years ago to impose a means test on the basic pension through the income tax system, reducing benefits for higher-income retirees. Australia, too, has cut back its basic benefit, though with a twist. All Australians are still entitled to a relatively generous basic benefit, set at roughly 25 percent of the average worker's earnings, but it is subject to a means test that reduces recipients' benefits as their earnings and assets increase. In the past, Australians nearing retirement age did everything they could to avoid losing out under the means test—going on shopping sprees, taking round-the-world voyages, or doing whatever else it took to jettison some of their wealth. As a result, Australia in the early 1990s implemented a mandatory retirement savings program designed literally to force workers to save so much that many would fail the asset and income tests.

There has been a lot more innovation around the world in the second tier of public pensions. These pay-as-you-go programs are usually financed by contributions from both employers and employees, and they have traditionally promised workers a future "defined benefit" linked to their earnings during their working years. Social Security is such a system. Americans of working age are reminded of this every year when they receive a statement in the mail from the Social Security Administration showing, based on their contributions so far, how big a Social Security check they can expect in retirement. Such defined-benefit programs are in the deepest trouble, and reforms are under way from Canada to Japan and Sweden.

Some countries have shifted their retirement programs to a more fully funded basis—meaning they are now putting "money in the bank" to pay for future benefits. In the late 1990s, for example, Canada raised the contribution levels of employers and employees and created a separate, non-government board to invest the the money in stocks and bonds, seeking higher returns. The United States has been reluctant to pursue similar policies because of political concerns over how the government might manage what could become the largest pool of investment capital in the world.

Defined-Contribution Places Burden on Individual

Traditional defined-benefit programs guarantee people a certain fixed payout in the future. But several countries have moved toward a bigger role for "defined-contribution" plans. In such systems, the ultimate payout is not fixed in advance but is determined by the level of return on the invested money. In some countries, employers select the defined-contribution plan provider. In others, individuals choose from a series of authorized private-fund managers. The investment risk in both cases is largely borne by the individual account holder, although some systems provide a guaranteed minimum return of some sort. The theory here is that at retirement, workers will simply receive benefits in accordance with what they have contributed.

Since the 1980s, a number of countries have even adopted defined-contribution plans as the primary element of their second tier. The example that has received the most attention is Chile, which radically reformed its pension system in 1981. In essence, the Chileans transformed their severely dysfunctional pay-as-you-go system into private individual retirement accounts. The accounts are mandatory, fully funded, fully vested, and portable. Workers must contribute 10 percent of their annual earnings to their retirement accounts and choose where to invest their savings from funds offered by highly regulated, specialized, private-fund management companies. Workers also must purchase term life insurance and disability insurance from their pension managers. All told, the package comes to about 13 percent of gross pay. At retirement, participants have a retirement nest egg whose size will vary depending on how the investments have performed.

Two main criticisms have been leveled against the Chilean system: The fund management companies have extracted very high fees, and large numbers of Chileans are not covered because they are self-employed or too poor, or for other reasons. However, the system has been reasonably successful, with many workers enjoying more secure retirement prospects than they did under the old system. A number of other Latin American countries have followed the Chilean example.

Roughly a decade after Chile acted, Australia embarked on an equally radical reform. Beginning in 1992, employers were obliged to contribute a share of workers' pay (now nine percent) to privately operated retirement funds. As a result, most workers will accumulate enough assets so that they will not qualify for Australia's meanstested first-tier basic pension until much later in their retirement (as they exhaust their savings) than under prior policy. Australian voters accepted this change because there would not be significant reductions in basic pensions for many years and because those affected would have a bigger pot of personal savings at retirement.

Sweden created supplemental private accounts without much fuss during the mid-1990s as part of a larger reform of its pension system; it now requires that workers contribute 2.5 percent of covered pay to individual accounts invested through government-approved investment managers. At the same time, Sweden made a revolutionary change in the traditional pay-as-you-go system that still provides the main pension benefit for Swedes. Under the new setup, workers continue to pay contributions to the system, and they amass retirement accounts—even though in reality their contributions are quickly paid out to current retirees. But as the change is phased in, workers' accounts will be treated as what they really are: virtual or "notional" accounts, with no assets backing them. The accounts are bookkeeping devices. As a result, there is no defined benefit. Benefits are not determined until a worker reaches age 61, when they will be set in a two-step process.

In the first stage, a basic benefit will be determined on the basis of the group's remaining life expectancy. As life expectancy increases in the future, monthly pensions will decrease to keep the total lifetime value of pensions relatively constant. In the second step, the benefit will also be adjusted so that each age group's expected lifetime benefits will be covered by what is anticipated in worker contributions during the course of its retirement period. This latter demographic adjustment will keep the system in balance as the number of retirees grows relative to workers. The result will almost certainly be a reduction in benefits, as well as much less strain on the Swedish economy.

The individual accounts Sweden mandated in the 1990s were not hugely controversial. Political leaders educated the public about the need for reform, and the accounts were part of a larger overhaul. The system's alterations were to be implemented in the future on a gradual basis. It is remarkable that attempts in the United States to shift toward such supplemental personal accounts in our Social Security system, most recently by the Bush administration, have proved so controversial, denounced as somehow being an abrogation of the "social" character of the U.S. system. The accounts that most American supporters have talked about range from 2 percent to 4 percent of earnings, not much different from the 2.5 percent Sweden has legislated.

Policymakers in Germany and Japan took a long, hard look at the Swedish example several years ago when they grappled with their own painful reforms. Neither was willing to move to Swedish-style notional accounts, but in both cases they adopted provisions for their defined-benefit systems that mimic the demographic adjustment the Swedes will use in determining future benefits. German and Japanese leaders took that route, most observers agree, in part because they thought it would be easier to get people to accept reforms if it were not so clear what the implications of the changes would be.

Americans are now experiencing—unwittingly, for the most part—the effects of just such a delayed reform undertaken in 1983, during Ronald Reagan's presidency. Congress raised the age at which Social Security benefits would be paid, but it deferred implementation until 2000. As a result of the reforms, people retiring this year will need to wait until eight months after their 65th birthday to stop working if they want to receive full benefits; people who are now 46 or younger will need to wait until their 67th birthday. There is a lesson in the fact that this delayed reform provoked virtually no protest in 1983 or when it began phasing in 17 years later.

Private versus Public Pensions

Private pensions are the other big element involved in thinking about how to pay for retirement. Such pensions loom larger in the retirement landscape of some countries, such as the United States, than others, but it seems clear that their role is likely to grow everywhere. As a rule, where public pensions are rich, private pensions tend to be spare, and where public plans are small, private pensions tend to be more substantial. In the past, it made little sense for a German employer to provide a generous pension, for example, since the country's public pension already allowed workers to retire at virtually the same standard of living they enjoyed while working.

But the remorseless logic of demographic change has led even the Germans to try to strike a new balance between public and private pensions. As part of a controversial package of public-pension tax increases and benefit cutbacks in 2000, the Social Democratic government of Chancellor Gerhard Schröder created tax incentives designed to encourage employers to establish voluntary supplemental retirement savings plans for workers and thus to take some of the pressure off the public system. Schröder's successor, Angela Merkel, recently declared that private pensions must be increased and that it will be necessary for Germany to push the normal retirement age up to 67.

Because Americans as a whole are not as dependent on the national pension, the United States enjoys some advantages in addressing the challenge of an aging society. Shoring up Social Security should be a much more manageable task than it has been in countries such as Germany and Sweden, where retirees are heavily dependent on public pensions. And mandating private pensions or savings programs, as many countries have already done, should not be as disruptive or expensive as it might be in countries where employers and workers do not already have a lot of experience with voluntary private plans. Requiring that all workers have supplemental accounts to boister the national pension, as Sweden has done, would seem to play to the generally successful American experience with 401(k) plans.

What remains an obstacle is the fear that such accounts will unduly expose workers to the risks of the stock and bond markets. There are risks in financial markets, and anyone who argues otherwise is misleading us about the choices we face. At the same time, many Americans have forgotten the painful 1977 Social Security reforms that reduced benefits for the "notch babies" (people born between 1917 and 1922) by as much as 20 percent relative to prior law. If U.S. workers aren't required to save some added amount of their pay in individual accounts, the Social Security benefit reductions that loom in the future probably will be far more widespread. If America doesn't address this problem soon, the eventual cutbacks will likely have to include some people on the verge of retirement, if not those already retired. Every path has risks, but the risks are greater in doing nothing until the onset of a crisis.

If the United States does not take to heart the lessons that some other countries have learned, it will be forced to repeat the unpleasant experiences of those that refused to act until there was no alternative. The Germans discovered that they had no choice but to reduce pension benefits, not just for future retirees but for existing ones. The Japanese learned that legislators confronted with such a crisis may come to blows on the floor of parliament. The future that looms before the United States is neither a blur nor a mystery. Its outlines can be seen with all the clarity of an actuarial table, and so can the choices.

Critical Thinking

1. In countries with a two-tier retirement benefit program, how is the first tier funded?

2. In "defined contribution" retirement plans, how is the ultimate payout to the retiree determined?

3. What would be the advantage to American workers to be required to save some amount of their pay into individual retirement accounts?

MR. SCHIEBER is vice president of U.S. Benefits Consulting at Watson Wyatt & Company. From "Paying for It," by Sylvester J. Schieber, Wilson Quarterly, Spring 2006, pages 62–69.

Social Security: Fears vs. Facts

What Social Security Critics Keep Getting Wrong

LIZ WESTON

I've been writing about Social Security for nearly two decades. But even I still have trouble wrapping my brain around some of the system's complexities—from how benefits are calculated to how the trust fund works. So it's not surprising that myths about Social Security persist, often fed by the program's critics. With the debate about Social Security's future once again heating up, these three myths need to be put to rest—so we can focus on the real issues.

Myth #1: By the Time I Retire, Social Security Will Be Broke

If you believe this, you are not alone. More and more Americans have become convinced that the Social Security system won't be there when they need it. In an AARP survey released last year, only 35 percent of adults said they were very or somewhat confident about Social Security's future.

It's true that Social Security's finances need work, because over the long term there will not be enough money to fully cover promised benefits. But radical changes aren't needed. In 2010 a number of different proposals were put forward that, taken in combination, would put the program back on firm financial ground for the future, including changes such as raising the amount of wages subject to the payroll tax (now capped at $106,800) and benefit changes based on longer life expectancy.

Myth #2: The Social Security Trust Fund Assets Are Worthless

Any surplus payroll taxes not used for current benefits are used to purchase special-issue, interest-paying Treasury bonds. In other words, the surplus in the Social Security trust fund has been loaned to the federal government for its general use—the reserve of $2.6 trillion is not a heap of cash sitting in a vault. These bonds are backed by the full faith and credit of the federal government, just as they are for other Treasury bondholders.

However, Treasury will soon need to pay back these bonds. This will put pressure on the federal budget, according to Social Security's board of trustees. Even without any changes, Social Security can continue paying full benefits through 2037. After that, the revenue from payroll taxes will still cover about 75 percent of promised benefits.

Myth #3: I Could Invest Better on My Own

Maybe you could, and maybe you couldn't. But the point of Social Security isn't to maximize the return on the payroll taxes you've contributed. Social Security is designed to be the one guaranteed part of your retirement income that can't be outlived or lost in the stock market. It's a secure base of income throughout your working life and retirement. And for many, it's a lifeline. Social Security provides the majority of income for at least half of Americans over age 65; it is 90 percent or more of income for 43 percent of singles and 22 percent of married couples. You can, and should, invest in a retirement fund like a 401(k) or an individual retirement account. Maybe you'll enjoy strong returns and avoid the market turmoil we have seen during the past decade. If not, you'll still have Social Security to fall back on.

Critical Thinking

1. Why do so many young people think Social Security will go broke before they can benefit from the program?

2. Where are Social Security's surplus funds invested to earn money for the program?

3. If the Social Security program went out of existence and people were to invest individually for their own retirement, do you think many of them would do so with adequate investments to assure they had a secure retirement income?

As AARP The Magazine's personal finance columnist, LIZ WESTON offers advice on everything from car loans to home sales.

Beyond Wisdom: Business Dimensions of an Aging America

Reconsidering our Assumptions, Prejudices and Policies about Older people.

YASH GUPTA

I magine this.

You are boarding a routine business flight. As you get on the plane you notice the pilot looks perhaps a bit . . . *grandfatherly*. In fact, he is only two years away from his FAA-mandated retirement age.

You sit and open a magazine. You know, in advertisements airline flight attendants always look like the champagne they are pouring: fresh and bubbly. But looking around the cabin at the flight crew the words that instead come to mind are *mature* and *no-nonsense*. All three flight attendants are in their 50s.

You are belted comfortably, your seat is in the upright position, and you have just felt the wheels lift off the runway from LaGuardia Airport.

Only a couple minutes into your flight there is a loud bang, followed by another loud bang. Flames shoot out from the plane's two jet engines, and then they both go silent. Less than three minutes later, the pilot makes one terse announcement: prepare for impact.

The next thing you know you're floating on the Hudson River and the flight crew is quickly and efficiently moving you on to the wings of the aircraft. They know their jobs.

Flight attendant Doreen Welsh is 58. She's been flying since 1970—almost 40 years experience. Sheila Dail is 57. She's been flying since 1980, and the other flight attendant, 51-year-old Donna Dent, has been flying since 1982.

As you watch the rescue boats approach, one thought goes through your mind: At moments like this, who needs fresh and bubbly?

The story of Flight 1549 suggests that in our society perhaps we have been too quick to praise youth, too ready to underestimate the value of age, wisdom and experience. One thing is certain: as we look forward to the middle years of the 21st century, we are going to have ample opportunity to discover if our assumptions, our prejudices, and our policies about older people are valid—or if perhaps we have some serious reconsidering to do.

Good morning.

I am so pleased to be here today. And I am honored to be asked to deliver the Elizabeth L. Rogers, MD Visiting Lecture in Geriatric Medicine. Thank you, Chris, for that very kind and generous introduction. Dr. Durso is a graduate of the Carey Business School, having received his MBA degree in 2007. We are exceptionally proud to call him an alumnus of our school.

In years past this lecture has offered insights into how scientists, clinicians and health care administrators might improve the health, well-being, and medical outcomes of aging Americans.

Today, I want to take a somewhat different approach. You may have wondered, 'What has the dean of the Carey Business School got to say about geriatric medicine?' The answer is this: about the medical science of geriatrics, very little. But regarding the *outcomes* related to our ability to enable people everywhere to live longer—a great deal. This morning I want to turn our focus from the causes of increased life spans to their effects.

Every seven seconds another American turns 65. We are a graying population. And that huge cohort of Americans known as the baby boomers is just entering their senior years. What does this mean to us as a society, as a nation, and as an economic player in a newly globalized world economy? For too long we have been focused on the freshness and bubbly effervescence of youth. What we now need to understand is the capacity, wisdom and experience of older age. What can we expect—and how can we best prepare—for this marked change in our society, when the number of Americans 65 years and older moves from about 12 percent of our population today, to a projected 20 percent in the year 2030?

When we look back at the 20th century, we see an era of unprecedented technological change and progress. It witnessed everything from the invention of radio and television to airplanes, rockets and the atom bomb. But perhaps the single greatest achievement is what happened right here-and in other academic medical centers around the world.

The biomedical revolution of the 20th century profoundly altered our world—more than television or radio, more than jet travel, more than the atomic bomb. Consider this: life expectancy at birth in the United States in 1901 was 49 years. At the end of the century it was 77 years, an increase of greater than 50 percent. Similar gains have been enjoyed throughout the world. Life expectancy in India and The People's Republic of China was around 40 years at midcentury. At century's close it had risen to around 63 years. Vaccines and antibiotics and better understanding of human health, nutrition and disease states have led to these enormous advances.

This may have been not just the crowning achievement of the 20th century, but even perhaps one of the most profound revolutions in recorded human history. And while it was just gathering steam, in 1936, a Columbia University professor by the name of Robert K. Merton published an article in the American Sociological Review titled "The Unintended Consequences of Purposive Social Action." In this article, Professor Merton postulated that when we take bold and even visionary action, even if everything goes according to plan, sometimes paradoxes and strange outcomes can arise. This was the first formulation of what is now commonly called the law of unintended consequences.

Today, as we unfold the 21st century, this law of unintended consequences has special relevance to the great increase in life spans achieved in the 20th century. One hundred years ago, in the developed world as a whole, about 3 percent of the population was over 65. Today that number is 15 percent. By 2030 it will be 25 percent. Think of it—a quarter of the population aged 65 or older! And many of them will be considerably older. By the year 2050, five percent of the American population— that's one in 20—will be age 85 or older.

The unintended consequences of this profound demographic shift will be felt around the globe. In particular, I think there are four areas in which it will have enormous importance. First: at the societal or sociological level. Second: in the economic and thus the political sphere. Third, in all matters related to health care, and in particular, how resources within this $2 trillion industry are allocated. And finally, number four, in the realm of education. In the next few minutes I'd like to consider what the demographic changes ahead mean in each of these four areas.

Aging as a Social Issue

Here in the United States, the aging of America coincides with, and amplifies, the diversifying of America. This country has a long tradition of accepting immigrants. I should know. In the second half of the 20th century that immigrant stream came increasingly from non-European countries. In general, immigrant families tend to have higher birth rates. By the turn of the millennium, whites in the U.S. had an average of 1.9 births per woman, compared with 2.0 births among Asian Americans, 2.2 births among blacks, and 3.2 births among Hispanics.

This has a two-fold effect. First, as is often reported, the country is becoming less white. In 1980, Caucasians comprised 82 percent of the American population. But by 2020, they will be just 62 percent of the population—still a majority, but considerably reduced. And the skew of that population will be especially noteworthy. More and more white Americans will also be older Americans. At the same time, more and more of the youngest generation are being born to non-whites. In 2001,

for instance, ethnic minorities in the U.S. contributed 42 percent of all births, even though they made up only 31 percent of the population.

It is not my intention here to make any sociological observations or predictions based upon purely racial or ethnic characteristics. But it is worth considering one behavioral tendency in light of this shift in color across generations. Americans tend to segregate by race where they live, and have continued to do so even after segregation laws were abolished. Now older Americans are congregating to a greater degree in certain regions because of weather, or in specific communities like the Erickson retirement communities pioneered here in Maryland. But we must ask: how will this play out? Because of the national demographic shift, those centers will become increasingly more white than the population at large. This, along with wealth and social status differentials, will perhaps make it more difficult for the people in those communities to find common cause with their neighbors and fellow citizens in the larger public sphere. Democracy however, only works when we find the means to work together.

In rural and non-mobile societies, aging is a process that occurs at home, in the embrace of an extended, multi-generational family structure. In some important sense in this situation the older people become honored and important members of the community.

This is not the case for us. Advances in medical care and reduction in disease burden among older Americans means that today's retirement communities are active and vital places. But they are increasingly forming worlds of their own. There has been little attention paid to the social consequences of older Americans self-segregating in this way. Are we in fact creating 'geriatric ghettos' that are self-contained, self-referential and in some profound way disconnected? Do we stand in danger of losing the shared commitment to the common good?

Certainly there is evidence suggesting that as the population ages, its commitment to the next generations declines. We see it when we enter a debate about shared sacrifice for the nation's future, but Social Security and Medicare are immediately exempted. We see it when any talk of tax increases to reduce a national debt that could potentially cripple future generations is rejected out-of-hand. And we see it when the news has images of Medicare recipients holding signs protesting against health care reform.

We face a challenge, therefore, as more and more Americans enter their senior years. We must find ways to prevent— as much as possible—a generational disconnect magnified by issues of race, ethnicity, social class, and living arrangements from becoming a generational chasm.

Aging as an Economic Issue

This morning I am speaking largely to the *American* experience of an aging population. However it is important to remember this occurs in a *global* context that has profound implications for our economic competitiveness and standards of living. Across the globe, the average age of national populations is advancing as countries rich and poor have fewer children.

In Britain it took 130 years—from 1800 to 1930—[or the fertility rate to fall from an average of five children per family to two, the replacement rate of fertility that leads to stable populations. In South Korea, that transition took just 20 years, from 1965 to 1985. In Iran it dropped from seven in 1994 to fewer than two by 2006—and the number for women in Tehran is just 1.5! We are witnessing an unprecedented race to stable population states, and we know that as families get smaller, they get richer too. What this also means is that many emerging economies today have vast resources of young people. In India the average age is 25. In Mexico it is 23. Compare that with Japan or Italy at 42, or the United States at about 36.

Historically, aging populations have meant slower rates of economic growth. A country with an average age of 23 or 25 is in a 'Goldilocks period' with few dependent children, few dependent grandparents, and a lot of adults in the middle who are ready and eager and willing to work. As the average age of a country moves into the 40s, an increasingly larger proportion of the population is made up of retirees. The result? The rate of economic growth falls.

These demographic changes have enormous business implications. Where will we get the workers necessary to make our economy function? In the U.S. the workforce grew by almost 30 percent in the 1970s as the baby boomers grew up and more and more women went to work. Through the 1990s and up to the present time the rate was around 12 percent. In the next few decades it will be only two or three percent. What was once a flood of new workers will decline to a trickle.

Prior to our current economic troubles, the Bureau of Labor and Statistics was projecting a shortfall of 10 million workers in the U.S. economy next year. In Western Europe the potential problem is even more severe.

If you try to foresee what cataclysmic challenges confront the business community in the decades ahead there are three that warrant special attention. On a global level, how can we build new models of environmentally sustainable businesses? On the transnational level, how will we incorporate and embrace the enormous emerging economies of India, China and other Asian countries? And on a national level, how will we adapt to older consumers and older workers? Today's mature adults control more than $7 trillion in the United States, representing 70 percent of the total wealth. As our population ages, more and more spending power will be concentrated in the hands of older and older customers. American companies will have to adjust not only what they are going to sell and the services they will provide, but also the makeup of the workforce that will perform these functions.

This new demographic reality can have surprising repercussions. Three years ago the U.S. Army raised its age limit for enlisting from 35 to 42. The Army recruits about 80,000 soldiers a year, and now about 5 percent of its incoming corps is made from this new category of older soldiers. The aging of America has profound implications for employment trends.

But where this trend is most problematic is in the area of retirement, and the expectation of most Americans that after a lifetime of work they will be able to enjoy a significant period of leisure as a sort of reward. Already this notion is beginning to meet conceptual as well as practical challenges. It is no coincidence that publications like the Harvard Business Review has begun to print articles with headings like "It's Time to Retire Retirement".

Our whole retirement system, and the expectations that have grown up around it, is a study in the law of unintended consequences.

When the Social Security system was introduced in 1935 most existing schemes used age 65 as the age of retirement, so the planners made a rough guess that this was a good age for their system too. At that time typical American workers were expected to live and collect benefits for only a year or two beyond the age of 65. Subsequent studies showed that this age produced a manageable system that could easily be made self-sustainable with only modest levels of payroll taxation. In the United States, as in most other countries, we adopted a 'pay-as-you-go' formula that depends upon the generation of current workers to pay the expenses of surviving retirees.

What wasn't anticipated is what happens when the average worker begins living 12 or more years beyond their retirement date, as they do today, with projections of even greater life spans ahead. In the OECD countries an average man in 1960 could expect to spend 46 years in the workforce and a little more than one year in retirement. By 1995, the number of years in the workforce had decreased to 37, while the number of years in retirement had jumped to 12. In Italy by the year 2000, the median retirement age had dropped below age 59, and the typical worker could look forward to a retirement duration of almost 21 years! But who is paying the bills?

On one hand this is a wonderful achievement. But more retirees living longer coupled with the slowing of the growth of the labor pool means that you will have fewer workers available to cover, through their payroll taxes, the costs of retirees. This is a problem in America, but in Europe it is very nearly a crisis, with predictions of only two workers available per retiree by mid-century. And in China, which has a two-decade history of enforcing its one child policy, the possibility exists of one day having less than one worker per retiree. This is where crisis becomes catastrophe. Can these systems even be sustained?

The evidence suggests there is a real danger here, especially when you consider the tax rates imposed to prop them up. Twenty-four countries (two-thirds of which are in Europe) now have payroll tax rates that equal or exceed 20 percent of wages.

Part of the reason for creating retirement systems like Social Security in the first place was to remove workers from the labor force to make room for younger workers just starting out. It was a humanitarian means of backfilling employment. However, this is a blade that cuts both ways.

Just as you can arbitrarily choose a retirement date in order to encourage workers to move out of the labor pool, so too you can—at least in theory—raise that age to move more workers back in. The United States, Britain and other countries have already begun moving in that direction, but of course it is not easy as a political matter to simply announce to people they now have to work more years before retiring.

Here is an area where the business community has an opportunity and an obligation to play an important leadership role. Remember there are very few industries—.., other than commercial airline pilots—. . , that have mandatory retirement ages. The challenge facing American businesses is to develop new and flexible working arrangements for older workers that will allow them to enjoy a comfortable half-way experience between full employment and full retirement. This will both address national labor needs *and* ease the strain on our payroll-based retirement system.

Aging and Health Care

I think we can all agree that it is in the realm of health care that the aging of America is drawing the most attention.

I don't need to tell a gathering of the nation's leading geriatricians that there is an underlying disconnect between our health care system as it currently exists, and the requirements of an efficient and well-managed program. Recent reports have warned of shortages of 24,000 doctors and nearly 1 million nurses in a decade's time. The number of trained geriatricians in this country is shockingly low-one estimate says there are fewer than 8,000 in practice and the number of Americans with chronic illness or degenerative conditions such as cancer, cardiovascular disease or arthritis is astonishingly high—in excess of 100 million. These are illnesses that require long-term care management, typically by teams of highly skilled caregivers.

Meanwhile, the supply of voluntary, unpaid caregivers is shrinking as smaller families, with fewer children, and more working women, reduce the number of potential candidates. It is worth noting that in the United States today, twenty percent of women ages 40 to 44 have no biologic children. Who will provide care for them when they reach advanced age? As is sometimes the case, the difficult choices facing us as we age are generally issues we choose not to discuss.

As a society we have become very good at denying our own mortality. There is a saying that Europeans know that death is *inevitable;* Americans *believe* that death is *optional.* I have always found that rather telling.

There was a fascinating column in the *New York Times* not long ago about a study conducted by the Pew Research Center. The center surveyed about 3,000 adults aged 18 and older and asked them first how old they were, and then how old they felt. They discovered that there is a gap between actual age and what we would call reported age. Not only that, the gap gets larger the older the person responding to the questions. Most adults over the age of 50 reported feeling 10 years younger than their actual age. But between 65 and 74 a sizable number reported feeling between 10 and 19 years younger, and there was a significant number of 75-year-olds who reported feeling 20 years younger than their real ages.

It is not surprising then that today's older Americans-and particularly the baby boomer generation—have driven unprecedented demand for vitamins and tonics, cosmetic surgery and knee replacements, and youth-giving therapies of all kinds.

On the Internet a website called RealAge offers a 150-question test covering lifestyle and family history. From that information assigns a 'biological age' of how young or old your habits make you. It then makes recommendations of how to get 'younger' through better living and non-medical solutions, such as sleeping more or taking multivitamins or daily exercise. To date, this online test has been taken by—are you ready for this?—more than *27 million* people. www.realage-dot-com. Don't worry, I will be happy to repeat that web site address for you at the end of my remarks if you want to make a note.

This is an important metric. It is a telling indication of the deep and abiding interest among older Americans of feeling and looking younger than their actual age.

And it suggests two trends, the first of them fairly obvious. Number one, if you have a drug, device, therapy or procedure that in some way turns back the clock—or even makes the claim to halt or reverse aging without even offering any proof—there is an enormous and ready-made market waiting out there and the potential to make huge sums of money. Consider only Viagra, popularly portrayed as a fountain of sexual youth, which has recorded U.S. sales in excess of $1 billion since it came on market 10 years ago. And that doesn't even consider its main competitor and market leader Cialis!

But there is a second trend that may be more problematic. How will an aging America choose to spend its limited health care dollars, both for current care and for research into new therapies? Health care professionals are aware that chronic disease is perhaps the primary driver of medical costs and accounts for something on the order of 80 percent of health care expenditures. If—just hypothetically speaking—we could discover a pill to prevent diabetes, the health care savings, and the reduction in human misery and premature death, would be enormous. Now the likelihood of such a pill being discovered is small. But we do know already, starting today, that if we could reverse the epidemic of obesity, particularly childhood obesity, that has engulfed this nation, we could make huge strides in reducing the subsequent incidence of diabetes.

But even in the United States medical resources are finite and limited. How are we to balance the demand for the management and treatment of the growing number of diabetics—particularly among the elderly—with the opportunity to reduce the incidence of this disease at some future date?

I would suggest that the allocation of increasingly scarce health care resources is going to be the greatest national challenge to arise from the demographic shift now underway. There will be a strong temptation to stint on future health goals in order to address the acute medical needs of the present. But I am also an optimist in this regard, because I believe the enormous pressures to make more efficient use of our health care dollars will present unique opportunities for visionary business leaders to create new models and modalities of health care delivery.

Aging, Education, and the Knowledge Base

When Captain Chesley Sullenberger glided his crippled U.S. Airways airplane to a near-miraculous landing on the Hudson River, he did so with more than 40 years and 27,000 hours of flying experience.

Since 2007, Captain Sullenberger has run his own safety consulting business which provides emergency management, safety strategies and performance monitoring to the aviation industry. He is, in other words, a world-class expert in aviation safety, and it is fair to say, the person you would most want to have at the controls of your air flight in that critical situation.

In no small way, Captain Sullenberger is emblematic of how older Americans by their many years of experience and education represent an irreplaceable national resource of skills and wisdom.

This, of course, is a particular provenance of our universities, the institutions uniquely designed to define, protect and transmit our civilization's store of knowledge. Our system of higher education will need to play a leading role in finding and educating those million nurses, 24,000 doctors, and all the other workers in health care and beyond that will be needed in coming years.

Some colleges and universities are already beginning to look at the pool of older Americans who skipped college the first time around, as perfect candidates to fill these needs. In Kentucky, the state university system wants to double the number of adults in the workforce holding college degrees in the next 12 years. To do so they have identified more than 10,000 state residents with some college credits completed, and are wooing them back to complete their degrees in an effort called Project Graduate. In Ohio there are an estimated 450,000 citizens with some credits but no degrees who are being targeted under a plan called Complete to Compete.

Currently in the U.S. about three percent of all part-time and full-time undergraduate students are age 50 or older. Looking forward, our colleges and universities—and yes, our schools of business—must help prepare for the profound changes that will accompany an older, grayer America.

In one sense, we have already arrived at an inflection point, which has been amplified by a slowdown in voluntary retirements because of the recession and losses in the value of retirement portfolio assets. Dropping retirement rates can lead to a core productivity problem as more and more people hold on to their jobs for longer and longer. These more expensive workers have the effect of raising costs and potentially putting companies at an economic disadvantage. And in seniority-based systems where the last hired is first fired—for instance union jobs—a deep and prolonged downturn can have the effect of removing younger and newer workers permanently, as they are forced eventually to find other lines of work.

Meanwhile, when a bad economy forces workers to stay long after they would like to retire, you build a pent-up demand for retirement. When the economy recovers and stock portfolios rebound, you are suddenly faced with a capacity problem when retirees leave in great numbers, taking all their knowledge and experience with them.

This is the so-called 'knowledge transfer' challenge. Although it has been much discussed in recent years, its solution remains more of an aspiration than a successful practice. Few companies have put mechanisms in place to make knowledge transfer happen. A 2003 survey by the Society for Human Resource Management suggested there is little planning underway to prepare for the effects of the coming wave of retirements. More than 70 percent of companies responding had no benefits or programs available to retain key older workers; nearly 60 percent did not directly recruit mature workers.

In America we face a special challenge. Throughout the 20th century, the United States led the world in one very important statistic. We were the nation with the highest percentage of young people aged 18 to 22 enrolled in college. This is no longer the case. Other countries are doing better at providing their young people the education they need to thrive in the knowledge economy. We often talk about how expensive elite schools like Johns Hopkins have become. This is what grabs the headlines. But it is the nonelite schools that educate the vast majority of our college students that really need our attention. In the mid-twentieth century we sent tens of thousands to college on the GI Bill. Then later as part of the Great Society we provided Pell Grants to give college opportunities to many thousands who could not otherwise afford it. And at the same time, there were many no-cost or extremely low-cost opportunities to get a college education, such as the City College system in New York, and the California state university system. This represented an investment in our future, and it gave us a huge competitive advantage. But we have retreated from these programs, and abandoned some outright.

Here again, and in the starkest terms, we see a potential conflict of the generations arise. With limited financial resources, do we focus on making sure American seniors have secure and stable retirements? Or, do we maintain our historic investment in the world's best and most open system of higher education?

The problem is compounded by the skew in fertility rates mentioned earlier. A greater percentage of children are being born to families further down the economic ladder. Consider that in the context of this stark reality: a child born to a family in America with a household income of $90,000 or more has a one-in-four chance of going to college. If the family income is $35,000 or less, that chance drops to just one-in-forty.

While American businesses must be re-examining how they can best use the skills and abilities of an aging workforce, they must also have their eyes to the future. They must be forging partnerships with colleges and universities to help prepare the future generation of business leaders. Some elite institutions have begun offering free education to the children of families making minimum wage or below. Here at Johns Hopkins, we have the Baltimore Scholars program that offers a free Hopkins undergraduate education to any qualified student who graduates from the city school system. This is a start, but much much more will be needed.

From a business perspective, we face an urgent and critical need to address the aging of America strategically. We must begin by asking, what skills do we need? What skills are we in danger of losing? And how can we find innovative new approaches to retain—and when necessary replace—these skills, recognizing that the steady and significant growth in the labor force we have come to expect may no longer be available? Business mind-sets must change, marketing strategies must change, HR policies must change, and change is never easy. But at the core, this demographic shift—and in many industries it is going to be felt more like an earthquake—is a wonderful opportunity to re-engineer, re-imagine and rejuvenate how business is done in America.

Let me conclude by thanking you for indulging me in this exploration of at least some of the societal and business implications of the global demographic transformation we are witnessing. For those of us involved in business, either academically or in practice, this is a tremendously exciting and challenging time to be grappling with these issues.

To sum up, in 2006, almost 500 million people worldwide were 65 and older. By the year 2030—just two decades from now—that total is projected to increase to 1 billion, or one out of every eight people on earth. Midway through the coming decade-and for the first time ever-people over 65 will outnumber children under the age of 5. This is a tidal wave of change, and it will have dramatic effects on social entitlement programs, labor supply, trade and savings around the globe. Socially and economically, medically and educationally, these changes present unique challenges. Many of these issues are new, and we are still coming to terms with their solutions.

For my part, I am convinced above all of one thing: it is by insuring the future of our young people that we can best provide for those who grow old.

A strange way to end a lecture dedicated to geriatric medicine you may think. But this makes perfect sense, because remember, we were all young once. Our challenge is to gain the wisdom and experience of a Captain Sullenberger, but never lose the excitement, the enthusiasm, and the optimism of our youth. As a nation we are growing older. The challenge is, how young can we remain? And yes, for those who are curious, I did pay a visit to that little quiz you can find at www-dot-realage-dot-com. My score? 25.

This is an audience that has probably thought more than any others about the aging of America. I hope I have been able to provide some fresh insight. Thank you for giving me this opportunity to offer my perspective. Now I would be delighted to take your questions and comments as we continue this discussion.

Thank you.

Critical Thinking

1. What is the danger created by older Americans moving to retirement communities?

2. What is the result for a country where the average age of the population moves into the 40s?

3. What effect has an aging population had on the work force?

4. What effect has an aging population had on government retirement programs?

YASH GUPTA, Dean, Carey Business School, Johns Hopkins University.

Address delivered at the Elizabeth L. Rogers, M.D. Visiting Lecture in Geriatric Medicine, Baltimore, MD, November 12, 2009. Copyright © 2010 by Yash Gupta. Reprinted by permission of the author.

Keep the Health Care Act

It will strengthen Medicare and help Americans afford insurance coverage.

A. BARRY RAND

Recent attacks on the nation's new health care law underscore how divided and confused Americans are by the law and the impact it will have on them individually and on the country. We recognize there are serious arguments on both sides of this debate. We have analyzed them carefully and conclude that the Affordable Care Act will help millions of Americans afford insurance coverage, will strengthen Medicare and will add new benefits and protections that will help you and your family.

That's why AARP strongly opposes efforts to repeal the Affordable Care Act.

It includes many important benefits that are already improving health care for older Americans and their families:

- It strengthens Medicare by lowering drug costs for seniors in the Medicare Part D "doughnut hole" and by adding free preventive services. It also cracks down on waste and fraud while prohibiting any cuts to your guaranteed benefits.
- It improves insurance coverage, especially for those with preexisting conditions, who can no longer be denied coverage.
- It expands coverage by allowing parents to keep their children on their policies until age 26.
- It makes insurance more affordable by providing tax breaks and establishing state "exchanges" to provide greater choice and transparency for individuals and small businesses.
- It gives Americans a new option to plan and pay for the cost of long-term services through a voluntary insurance program known as the Community Living Assistance Services and Supports (CLASS) Act.

Repealing the Affordable Care Act would eliminate these important improvements and, according to the nonpartisan Congressional Budget Office, would add to our deficit and national debt, not decrease it. AARP is not alone. The American Heart Association, American Cancer Society, American Diabetes Association, as well as many women's health organizations, patient groups and others, object to repealing the law.

We have two goals at AARP: To ensure that the new law is implemented at the federal and state levels to garner maximum benefits for all Americans, and to ensure that they understand what the law means for them and how to make the best health care decisions.

These benefits vanish if the Affordable Care Act is repealed. Instead, doughnut hole charges soar. Those with preexisting conditions lose coverage. Preventive counseling and services disappear. Millions of young adults lose coverage. Insurance companies have free rein to deny coverage and raise rates against the ill and older people. And millions of small businesses will lose tax credits that are helping them provide their employees with health care coverage for the first time.

This is what's at stake in this debate. AARP will continue to fight to make sure that we do not regress to the health insurance practices of the past that ultimately drive up costs and do more harm than good.

Critical Thinking

1. What are the two goals the AARP want to pursue in support of the new Health Care Act?
2. What are the benefits lost if the Affordable Care Act is replaced?
3. Why does AARP think it would be a serious mistake to regress to health insurance practices of the past?

Medicare May Soon Take New Shape

Challenge: How to keep program solvent while providing good care.

ROBERT PEAR

President Obama has deep disagreements with House Republicans about how to address Medicare's long-term problems. But in deciding to wade into the fight over entitlements, which he may address in a speech Wednesday afternoon, the president is signaling that he too believes Medicare must change to avert a potentially crippling fiscal crunch.

So the real issue now is not so much whether to re-engineer Medicare to deal with an aging population and rising medical costs, but how.

Even before they debate specific proposals, lawmakers across the ideological spectrum face several fundamental questions:

Will the federal government retain its dominant role in prescribing benefits and other details of the program, like how much doctors and hospitals are paid and which new treatments are covered? Will beneficiaries still have legally enforceable rights to all those services?

Will Medicare spending still increase automatically with health costs, the number of beneficiaries and the amount of care they receive? Or will the government try to limit the costs to taxpayers by paying a fixed amount each year to private health plans to subsidize coverage for older Americans and those who are disabled?

Public concern about the federal deficit and debt has revived interest in proposals to slow the growth of Medicare, including ideas from Mr. Obama's deficit reduction commission. Here are some leading proposals:

- Increase the age of eligibility for Medicare to 67, from 65.
- Charge co-payments for home health care services and laboratory tests.
- Require beneficiaries to pay higher premiums.
- Pay a lump sum to doctors and hospitals for all services in a course of treatment or an episode of care. The new health care law establishes a pilot program to test such "bundled payments," starting in 2013.
- Reduce Medicare payments to health care providers in parts of the country where spending per beneficiary is much higher than the national average. (Payments could be adjusted to reflect local prices and the "health status" of beneficiaries.)
- Require drug companies to provide additional discounts, or rebates, to Medicare for brand-name drugs bought by low-income beneficiaries.
- Reduce Medicare payments to teaching hospitals for the cost of training doctors.

In debate last year over Mr. Obama's health plan, Republicans said repeatedly that he was "raiding Medicare" to pay for a new entitlement providing insurance for people under 65. The Senate Republican leader, Mitch McConnell of Kentucky, said the Democrats were using Medicare as a piggy bank. Senator Jim Risch of Idaho said, "We are talking about a half-trillion dollars that is being stolen from Medicare." Senator Charles E. Grassley of Iowa said the cuts "threaten seniors' access to care."

Now it is Republicans, especially House Republicans, proposing to cut the growth of Medicare, with a difference.

"Any potential savings would be used to shore up Medicare, not to pay for new entitlements," said Representative Paul D. Ryan, Republican of Wisconsin and chairman of the House Budget Committee.

The House is expected to vote this week on his budget blueprint for the next 10 years.

Mr. Ryan points to Medicare's prescription drug coverage as a model. That benefit, added to Medicare under a 2003 law, is delivered entirely by private insurers competing for business, and competition has been intense. Premiums for beneficiaries and costs to the government have been much lower than projected.

Republicans rarely mention one secret to the success of Medicare's drug program. Under presidents of both parties, Medicare officials have regulated the prescription drug plans to protect consumers and to make sure the sickest patients have access to the drugs they need.

Many Democrats like Medicare as it is: an entitlement program in which three-fourths of the 47 million beneficiaries choose their doctors and other health care providers, and one-fourth have elected to enroll in managed-care plans. These Democrats acknowledge that care could be better coordinated, but say that could be done in the traditional fee-for-service Medicare program, without forcing beneficiaries into private health plans offered by insurance companies.

Marilyn Moon, a health economist and former Democratic trustee of the Medicare trust fund, said serious discussion of changes in Medicare was warranted, and she noted that the government spent more than a half-trillion dollars a year on the program. Still, Ms. Moon said, it would be preferable to shore up Medicare without "the philosophical sea change" sought by Republicans, who would give private insurers more latitude to decide what benefits are available and what services are covered.

Obama administration officials said Tuesday that Medicare could save $50 billion over 10 years by reducing medical errors, injuries, infections and complications that prolong hospital stays or require readmission of patients.

In any program as big as Medicare, which accounts for one-fifth of all health spending, even decisions about small, seemingly technical questions can have vast consequences for beneficiaries, the health care industry and the economy as a whole.

Gradually raising the eligibility age, for example, would save $125 billion over 10 years, the Congressional Budget Office says.

But it would increase costs for people who would otherwise have Medicare. Some of those 65- and 66-year-olds would obtain insurance from Medicaid or from employers, as active workers or retirees, thus increasing costs for Medicaid and for employer-sponsored health plans.

If Congress decided to make a fixed contribution to a private health plan on behalf of each Medicare beneficiary, lawmakers and lobbyists could spend years debating how to set payment rates and how to adjust them, based on increases in consumer prices or medical costs or the growth of the economy.

Those decisions would directly affect beneficiaries. Under the House Republican proposal, the Congressional Budget Office said, beneficiaries "would bear a much larger share of their health care costs," requiring them to "reduce their use of health care services, spend less on other goods and services, or save more in advance of retirement."

The history of Medicare is filled with unsuccessful efforts to rein in costs. Private health plans entered Medicare with a promise to shave 5 percent off costs, but ended up costing more than the traditional Medicare program. For two decades, Congress has tried to limit Medicare spending on doctors' services, but the limits have proved so unrealistic that Congress has repeatedly intervened to increase them.

Critical Thinking

1. How do the Republicans and Democrats differ in terms of possible new entitlements to the Medicare program?

2. How do the Republicans and Democrats differ in terms of whether the Medicare beneficiaries should be forced into private health plans offered by insurance companies?

3. Has the cost of current Medicare prescription drug coverage handled by private insurance companies been higher or lower than expected?

7 Critical Maneuvers

JAMES S. TOEDTMAN

In heavy construction, fitting the last pieces can be the most complicated part of the entire structure. So, too, with the effort to rebuild the nation's teetering health care system. Assembling the final pieces of the health care project won't be easy. The whole construct has been continually buffeted by conflicting political agendas, the soaring costs of broad-scale reforms and hundreds of special interests—forces still in play as lawmakers now try to bring it all home in one historic health care bill. To be sure, lawmakers and President Obama agree on the broad framework that expands coverage, tightens regulations on insurance firms and narrows the "doughnut hole" for prescription drugs. They also agree the cost of doing nothing is too high. But working through the details of actuarial tables, debt calculations, medical device costs, local politics and prescription drug economics has proved to be just short of overwhelming. Here, then, are some of the final stress points where Democrats, Republicans, special interests and the House and Senate all converge.

1 Should There Be a Government-run Insurance Plan?

The Problem: Reducing the cost of insurance and making coverage more affordable for millions of Americans who do not have access to employer insurance.

The Proposals: The vast majority of Americans get their health insurance through employer plans or from government plans, including Medicare, Medicaid and veterans plans. For the rest—mostly small-business employees, the self-employed and the uninsured—lawmakers would create state exchanges where Americans could choose insurance plans from among the private companies competing in their state. The House and many senators also favor creating a government-run insurance plan to compete with private plans in order to reduce the costs of insurance. The House has a single national public plan. The Senate bill gives each state exchange the choice of including the public plan as an option. Others favor state cooperatives that people could join to get better prices on their policies. This is the most contentious issue in the reform debate, even though the Congressional Budget Office estimates it affects only 2 percent of the population.

The Payoff: The public plan could help reduce insurance costs and make coverage more widely available.

2 How Do We Pay for Reforms?

The Problem: Expanding and improving health care coverage over the next 10 years will cost roughly $900 billion, and that cost must be paid for without adding to the nation's ballooning budget deficit.

The Proposals: The House bill calls for a new 5.4 percent tax on couples making over $1 million a year. But the "millionaire's tax" is a non-starter in the Senate, where lawmakers favor a tax on insurance companies that offer high-priced "Cadillac" plans with premiums higher than $8,500 for individuals or $23,000 for families. Insurance companies argue the tax will be passed along to consumers, resulting in higher premiums. The Senate also wants to increase Medicare payroll deductions for individuals making more than $200,000 and levy annual fees on medical device makers and drug companies.

The Payoff: Adequate financing expands health care coverage to more Americans without adding to the deficit. The tax on insurers could help lower systemwide costs.

3 How Can We Deal with the Doughnut Hole?

The Problem: About 26 percent of Part D Medicare enrollees find themselves in the coverage gap known as the doughnut hole, where they must pay the entire cost of their prescription drugs until their out-of-pocket expenses in 2010 reach $4,550. Only 4 percent come out the other side, where coverage resumes. Studies show people in the gap take health risks by giving up their meds or stretching, them.

The Proposals: The pharmaceutical industry has agreed to cut its brand-name drug prices in half for those people caught in the doughnut hole, for a savings of at least $30 billion over 10 years. House Democrats' proposals have gone further, narrowing the gap over time to close it completely by 2019 and authorizing the government to negotiate Medicare drug prices.

HEALTH CARE BY THE NUMBERS

Most people are currently insured ...
as of 2009

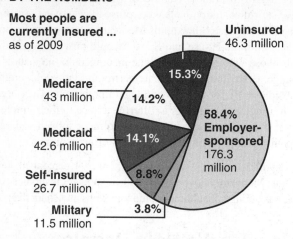

Uninsured 46.3 million — 15.3%

Medicare 43 million — 14.2%

Medicaid 42.6 million — 14.1%

Self-insured 26.7 million — 8.8%

Military 11.5 million — 3.8%

58.4% Employer-sponsored 176.3 million

... But the number of uninsured continues to rise

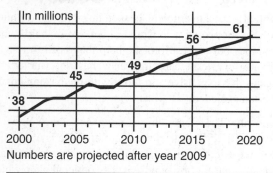

In millions

38 · 45 · 49 · 56 · 61

2000 · 2005 · 2010 · 2015 · 2020

Numbers are projected after year 2009

The Part D doughnut hole

The amount you must spend to get out of the coverage gap has risen $950, or 26%, in five years

2006	$3,600
2007	$3,850
2008	$4,050
2009	$4,350
2010	$4,550

Costs of employer-provided plans

Average health insurance premiums for family plans

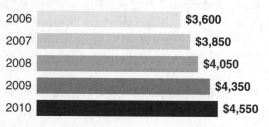

■ Worker contribution
▨ Employer contribution

1999 — $1,543 / $4,247 — **$5,790** Total per family/year

2009 — $3,515 / $9,860 — **$13,375** Total per family/year

But closing the gap is costly, and the Senate may resist that added expense.

The Payoff: The Senate bill would lower out-of-pocket expenses for those in the doughnut hole by 50 percent. But the House bill would go further and gradually close the gap entirely.

PREMIUMS vs. WAGES

Premiums continue to rise faster than earnings

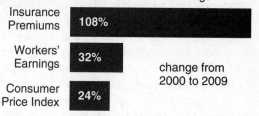

Insurance Premiums	108%
Workers' Earnings	32%
Consumer Price Index	24%

change from 2000 to 2009

HEALTH CARE COSTS: $2.3 trillion

Where the money comes from
in billions of dollars

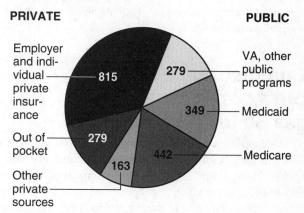

PRIVATE — PUBLIC

Employer and individual private insurance — 815

Out of pocket — 279

Other private sources — 163

VA, other public programs — 279

Medicaid — 349

Medicare — 442

And where it goes
in billions of dollars

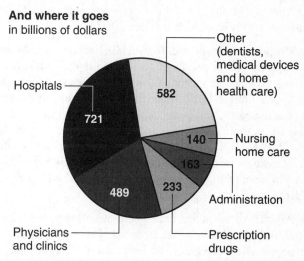

Hospitals — 721

Other (dentists, medical devices and home health care) — 582

Nursing home care — 140

Administration — 163

Physicians and clinics — 489

Prescription drugs — 233

Sources: U.S. Census; "In Search of Health Care Reform," *Washington Post,* June 9, 2009; U.S. Centers for Medicare & Medicaid Services; Commonwealth Fund; Kaiser Family Foundation.

4 How Do We Strengthen Medicare and Control Its Costs?

The Problem: Medicare costs are growing at an alarming rate and must be controlled.

The Proposals: Growth in Medicare spending for the next decade would be cut by about 3 percent. The House would trim $440 billion, the Senate $420 billion. Savings would come from reducing Medicare fraud, waste and inefficiencies and by cutting overpayments to Medicare Advantage plans, which now cost 14 percent more than traditional Medicare. Other savings are achieved through a menu of innovations—from paying doctors based on good outcomes for their patients, not just the number of procedures they perform, to helping Medicare patients with transitional care once they leave the hospital. The Senate also wants to give a Medicare commission authority to cut program costs, while the House would authorize the administration to negotiate lower drug prices for Medicare.

The Payoff: Without cutting guaranteed benefits, Senate and House bills shore up the solvency of the Medicare trust fund for five additional years. There are new incentives for primary care doctors and for nurses' education. Patients would receive free preventive screenings.

5 Can Insurance Be Made More Accessible to Adults Ages 50 to 64?

The Problem: Many older Americans who are too young for Medicare have difficulty obtaining coverage because insurance companies charge more as people age—sometimes 10 times more than they charge younger people—and often reject older applicants because they have preexisting medical conditions. An AARP study found that 7.1 million people ages 50 to 64 are uninsured, a 36 percent increase since 2000.

The Proposals: Under the House bill, insurers would be able to charge older people no more than twice as much as they charge younger customers, while the Senate proposals set a higher limit of three to one. Insurance companies argue that insuring older Americans, who tend to have more health problems, is more expensive, and they are working hard to keep a higher ratio. Both the House and Senate plans would prevent insurers from denying coverage for preexisting conditions and from charging higher premiums based on health or gender.

The Payoff: A limited age ratio would mean lower premiums for the 50-to-64 age group, and no denial of coverage for health or gender would mean greater access to affordable insurance.

6 Who Faces Mandates? Who Gets Subsidies?

The Problem: How to extend health insurance coverage to as many Americans as possible.

The Proposals: House and Senate proposals require people to buy health insurance, but those who can't afford it would receive subsidies. Individuals who refuse to get coverage would be fined. The House bill extends Medicaid to more low-income families; both the House and Senate would provide tax credits to help those who must buy private insurance on the insurance exchange. Both House and Senate permit individual tax credits or subsidies only for citizens and legal immigrants. The Senate wouldn't require employers to offer insurance to their employees, but if employees qualify for government subsidies, larger companies would be fined if they don't offer insurance.

The Payoff: Both bills would cover about 94 percent of legal residents. Mandatory coverage could lead to lower insurance premiums, as younger, healthier people join plans and share the risk.

7 How Do We Help People with Long-Term Care Costs?

The Problem: The government is spending billions on nursing home care for people who would rather live in their homes or communities but can't afford the help they need to remain there. Private long-term care insurance has not worked for many because it's expensive and those with preexisting conditions are often excluded.

The Proposals: The Community Living Assistance Services and Supports (CLASS) Act, as the insurance plan is dubbed, is included in the House and Senate bills, though some lawmakers and the insurance lobby oppose it. The optional plan, which would help with long-term care needs, would be financed by employee payroll deductions. The coverage would provide cash payments of up to $150 a day for help with essential daily activities such as bathing and dressing. The money could also be spent on assistance such as building a wheelchair ramp or respite breaks for family caregivers. The Senate bill also includes more home-and community-based services, and more legal protections for older people.

The Payoff: The bills would help families caring for older or disabled relatives; the Senate bill offers more benefits and legal protections.

Critical Thinking

1. How would the House and Senate propose making health insurance more accessible to 50–64 year old persons?

2. How could health insurance be extended to as many Americans as possible?

3. How do the House and Senate propose to help people with long-term care costs?

Protect Social Security

A. Barry Rand

In August, we celebrate the 75th anniversary of Social Security. Ever since Ida Mae Fuller received the first Social Security check in January 1940, Social Security has provided the foundation of retirement security and helped people to live their lives with independence and dignity.

At AARP, we are committed to protecting and fighting for Social Security so that people 75 years from now will still enjoy the peace of mind it provides today. We also know that Social Security needs to be strengthened for future generations, and we will work diligently toward that goal.

We understand that Social Security is much more than just a public policy. It is a guaranteed pension that, on average, replaces 40 percent of a retiree's wages. And because it is risk-free—the only part of the retirement system that is—it is the lifeline that many older Americans, their families, people with disabilities, widows and other survivors count on for their day-to-day lives.

Fighting for, protecting and strengthening Social Security won't be easy. The president's bipartisan fiscal commission—co-chaired by Alan Simpson and Erskine Bowles—and others in Washington are targeting Social Security to help close the growing federal budget deficit. More than most, we understand the importance of balanced budgets, but it's essential that the deficit not be closed by cutting benefits that today's seniors and future generations have earned over a lifetime of hard work.

If Washington wants to restore confidence in our nation's budget, lawmakers should deal with what's really caused our federal deficit. The fact is, Americans pay for Social Security, and it hasn't added one dime to the deficit. It's a sacred promise we make to seniors, our children and our grandchildren—one that must not be broken. We believe that.

As we look ahead, we are guided by some basic principles:

- Any changes to Social Security should be discussed as part of a broader conversation about how to help Americans prepare for a secure retirement, especially as other sources of retirement income—such as pensions, savings and home equity—have been crumbling over the past decade.
- If you pay into Social Security, you should receive the full benefits you've earned over a lifetime of hard work.
- Your Social Security benefits should keep up with inflation for as long as you live.

- You should continue to be covered in case you become disabled and can no longer work, and your family should continue to be protected if you die.
- We will provide educational support and advocate policies to help people save. And we will encourage better pensions and more private savings in addition to—not at the expense of—Social Security.

So as we celebrate Social Security's 75th anniversary in August, we need to protect and strengthen Social Security so future generations will continue to have a strong foundation of income they can count on in retirement for the next 75 years. You can count on AARP to lead this fight.

Critical Thinking

1. What percentage of a 65 or older person's income is provided by Social Security?

2. Why should a 65 or older person expect to be able to draw a Social Security check for the rest of their life?

2. What factor causes Social Security payments to be increased from time to time?

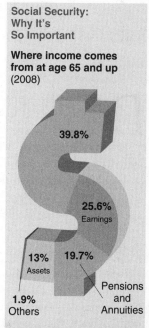

Social Security: Why It's So Important

Where income comes from at age 65 and up (2008)

- 39.8%
- 25.6% Earnings
- 13% Assets
- 19.7% Pensions and Annuities
- 1.9% Others

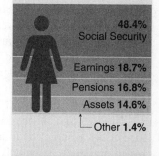

Where women's and men's income comes from at age 65 and up (2008)

- 48.4% Social Security
- Earnings 18.7%
- Pensions 16.8%
- Assets 14.6%
- Other 1.4%

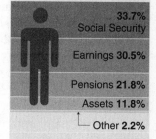

- 33.7% Social Security
- Earnings 30.5%
- Pensions 21.8%
- Assets 11.8%
- Other 2.2%

Population Aging, Entitlement Growth, and the Economy

JOHN GIST

D emographic aging—the graying of the baby boomers, increasing longevity, and low fertility rates—is changing the age structure of the United States. Many experts say these changes will have an unsustainable impact on the federal budget by causing rapid growth in federal spending for health and retirement benefits for older Americans, especially for Social Security, Medicare, and Medicaid.

Demographic aging may also negatively affect the U.S. economy and American families. Low fertility rates will slow the growth in the labor force; fewer workers will be available to support an aging population. A slower-growing labor force will slow economic growth. If left unchecked, increased deficits and government debt will choke off investment and further stifle economic growth. The slowing of economic growth will mean stagnant wages and slower family income growth as well. Health costs, which have outstripped economic growth even in prosperous times, will continue to increase faster than family incomes.

Can we afford our aging society? Is our fiscal future as bleak as many experts claim? In this report, John Gist takes a long-term perspective on these questions, examining the historical experience with "entitlements" and projecting out to the middle of this century. Looking backward, entitlement spending has actually been remarkably stable as a percentage of gross domestic product (GDP) for the past two decades, with one exception—health care. By 2016, Social Security will still consume about the same share of the economy as it did when Ronald Reagan was first elected president. Eventually, Social Security's costs will rise by two percent of GDP, but after 2030, when the last boomer has retired, Social Security will resume a gradual and manageable growth path. Other nonhealth entitlements will remain a smaller share of GDP than they were 40 years ago.

It is in health care only where entitlement growth presents serious future challenges. Rapid growth in health care costs is really nothing new, however. Overall health care costs, including Medicare and Medicaid, have risen faster than the economy for decades and are projected to do so indefinitely, with Medicare

overtaking Social Security as the largest federal program within 20 years. However, contrary to much conventional wisdom, population aging is not the chief cause of this growth. An aging population accounts for only about one-sixth of Medicare's growth since 1970.

Our long-term budgetary challenge is to maintain the integrity of the social insurance programs that provide health and income security for current and future retirees without sustaining economic ruin. Our ability to achieve that goal will depend chiefly on two factors: the growth rate of health care costs and the willingness of the populace to be taxed. A starting point for avoiding a future "train wreck" would be to maintain the same level of spending restraint in our health programs that we have already achieved in the past decade *and* refrain from enacting any additional tax cuts, allowing revenues to rise automatically. This would hold the primary deficit (revenues minus noninterest spending) to a level in 2050 no larger than it is today. Because debt would still be rising in this scenario, additional policy solutions would be needed. Reforms to the health care system, making Social Security solvent, introducing greater budget discipline, getting people to work longer and save more would allow us to provide economic and health security while achieving fiscal stability and sustaining long-term economic growth.

Critical Thinking

1. What are the two factors that will allow the United States to maintain the integrity of the federal budget in the long run?

2. What is the starting point for maintaining a reasonable federal budget and spending level?

3. If the federal budget could be stabilized by a spending restraint on health programs and no tax cuts, what would the deficit (revenues minus non-interest spending) be in 2050?

For full report, see *AARP Public Policy Institute Paper* #2007–01. In Brief prepared by John Gist, January 2007.

Test-Your-Knowledge Form

We encourage you to photocopy and use this page as a tool to assess how the articles in *Annual Editions* expand on the information in your textbook. By reflecting on the articles you will gain enhanced text information. You can also access this useful form on a product's book support website at www.mhhe.com/cls.

NAME: DATE:

TITLE AND NUMBER OF ARTICLE:

BRIEFLY STATE THE MAIN IDEA OF THIS ARTICLE:

LIST THREE IMPORTANT FACTS THAT THE AUTHOR USES TO SUPPORT THE MAIN IDEA:

WHAT INFORMATION OR IDEAS DISCUSSED IN THIS ARTICLE ARE ALSO DISCUSSED IN YOUR TEXTBOOK OR OTHER READINGS THAT YOU HAVE DONE? LIST THE TEXTBOOK CHAPTERS AND PAGE NUMBERS:

LIST ANY EXAMPLES OF BIAS OR FAULTY REASONING THAT YOU FOUND IN THE ARTICLE:

LIST ANY NEW TERMS/CONCEPTS THAT WERE DISCUSSED IN THE ARTICLE, AND WRITE A SHORT DEFINITION:

NOTES

NOTES

NOTES

NOTES

NOTES